HOTEL
AND
HOSPITALITY MANAGEMENT

HOTEL
AND
HOSPITALITY MANAGEMENT

Editor
Rajender Singh

KALPAZ PUBLICATIONS

Delhi-110052

HOTEL AND HOSPITALITY MANAGEMENT
(Management, Tourism)

ISBN: 81-7835-003-3
Price : ₹ 900

Published in 2016 in India by
Kalpaz Publications
C-30, Satyawati Nagar
Ashok Vihar Phase-III
Delhi-110052
E-Mail: kalpaz@hotmail.com

Printed at: G. Print Process, Delhi.

CONTENTS

1

Hotel Organisation

In the early 1990s, some hotels eliminated entire levels of management or combined managerial responsibilities so that the organization became flatter. In the typical functional chart the executive assistant manager may be eliminated, making division heads directly responsible to the general manager (GM). Some hotels have eliminated separate managers at the division level, with all department managers reporting directly to the GM. However this restructuring has occurred, organizations are still formed around principles such as those outlined by Stoner and Wankel. They said that the organizing process involves balancing a company's need for both stability and change. They go on to outline organizing as a multistep process, based on that proposed by Dale.

— Details all the work that must be done to attain the organization's goals.

— Provides for dividing the total work performed into a group of activities that can be performed by one person or a group of people.

— Combines the work of an organization's members in some logical and efficient manner.

— Sets up a mechanism to coordinate the work of the organization members into a unified, harmonious whole.

— Sets up a mechanism to monitor the effectiveness of how well the organization is achieving its goals.

In the modern hotel organization, even a re-engineered one, a linear line and staff structure has emerged to reflect this theoretical organizing process.

Line functions

Hotel employees in line functions have regular or semiregular contact with the organization's guests. The line operations in a hotel organization are the rooms division and food and beverage division. Obviously, some departmental functions within each line division involve more or less guest contact than others, depending on the nature of the jobs.

The underlying commonalty in these cases is that most of these employees are hands-on participants in the assembly and delivery of the hotel's services. For instance, under most circumstances security people will not have much regular guest contact; housekeeping staff may have somewhat more guest contact; in the rooms division, obviously the front office staff will have the vast majority of guest face-to-fact contact.

Staff functions

Staff functions are generally those behind the scenes sorts of activities that support the line functions and, under most circumstances, employees filling these functions have little or no guest contact, although a major component of their job is to influence the quality of a guest's stay. Engineering has been included as a staff function for those reasons The success of the engineering function heavily influences the quality of the guest's stay.

At the same time the other functions of the engineering department support the activities of almost every other department in the hotel.

For example, the engineering department maintains and repairs equipment that is crucial to all of the hotel's line functions from the food production equipment in the kitchen, to the tables and chairs in the dining room, the accounting machines, the furniture in the lobby, and the carts that the bellhops use to transport guest luggage. Viewed in this way, the engineering department can be considered a true staff department that serves and supports at any given time any or all of the other departments in the hotel.

Other typical hotel organization charts will place the engineering department in the rooms division because engineering works best there in the hotel's organization or because of tradition. This situation may also be true for other departments that in the past have been traditionally thought of as rooms division functions. Security is one example. In some organizations housekeeping has been changed to a staff function rather than one that belongs strictly in the rooms division, for housekeeping by definition keeps the entire house.

Organizational design

This section will review some of the general management principles of organizational design, including the important but often neglected topic of a hotel's meeting structure.

The elements of organizational structure

If the efforts of people in organizations are to be channelled toward productive ends, structure must be given to their activities. Aldag and Stearns list five ways by which managers give structure to organizations:

(1) work specialization,

(2) departmentalization,

(3) patterns of authority,

(4) spans of control, and

(5) methods of coordination.

Whenever a manager decides to make an organizational change, he or she will usually have to take these five elements into account.

Specialization

If there is more than one way to accomplish something, management must make a conscious decision about how to divide tasks among workers. At one extreme is the case of little or no specialization where an individual worker is responsible for all the tasks required to complete a job. An example is the chef in a small country restaurant who single-handedly prepares an entire meal for 20 guests. It's rewarding to have total control over a project and motivating to see the results of one's efforts.

The problem, however, is that as the demand for products or services increases, it becomes more difficult for individuals or small groups to increase their output without changing the way they are organized. One of management's tasks is to determine the extent to which work and jobs should be specialized. As a general rule, specialization holds out the possibility of greater worker productivity and managerial control over tasks. On the other hand, dividing complete jobs into smaller subunits tends to increase the need for coordinating the activities of numerous workers, each involved in separate, specialized tasks. Also, overspecialization can result in jobs so narrow that workers lose interest, motivation drops, error rates increase, and quality suffers.

Departmentalization

As organizations grow in size, managers are faced with the need to group certain jobs together in order to ensure efficient coordination and control of activities. Most restaurants have chosen to departmentalize with food preparation and food service as separate functional departments. This is a very logical and practical solution. There are distinctly different kinds of work performed in preparing and serving food, both in the process and the function of the two activities. Forming departments along *functional lines* is the most common method of organizing a business.

Authority

Every time managers restructure a job or move members of a group working together into different departments, they are faced with the question of how much decision-making authority to grant individual workers, managers, or departments. Organizations are never totally centralized or decentralized with regard to decision making. Rather, they tend toward one direction or the other. A number of factors must be taken into account when deciding the pattern of authority that is best for an organization. Managers must consider the experience and personality of subordinates, the environment in which they work, the business strategy to be followed, and the management style with which they feel most comfortable. Line executives are those who have responsibility over business units that provide products or services to customers and account for the revenues of the business.

The rooms and food and beverage departments account for most of a hotel's revenue. On the other hand, staff departments are set up because the principles of work specialization and departmentalization suggest efficiencies from such an organizational design. The personnel and engineering departments of a hotel are examples of staff units. Once set up, however, staff departments sometimes cause organizational problems. The basic issue is, how much authority should functional staff executives have over line executives? At one extreme, line executives could be given total authority. At the other extreme, staff executives, in their speciality areas, could be granted authority over line executives.

Two examples of positions between these extremes would be:

(1) line executives would be required to consult with staff specialists only before making a decision, and

(2) line and staff executives would be required to make joint decisions.

Whatever the situation, top executives such as hotel general managers (GMs) must arbitrate line-staff disputes when they develop.

Spans of control

Spans of control relate to the number of subordinates reporting to a supervisor. In the past, some management scholars advocated an ideal span of control of exactly seven subordinates. That simplistic view is no longer held. The ideal span of control is dependent on:

— Task similarity-the more similar the tasks of subordinates, the wider the span of control can be.

— Training and professionalism-the more trained and skilled a subordinate, the less supervision required and the greater the span of control can be.

— Task certainty-the more routine and predictable the work tasks, the greater the span of control can be.

— Frequency of interaction-if relationships require frequent interaction, the span of control must be narrow.

— Task integration-the more a supervisor must integrate and coordinate the tasks of subordinates, the narrower the span of control must be.

— Physical dispersion-the more widely dispersed subordinates are, the fewer a manager can properly supervise.

Some of these factors may work in opposite directions. For example, fast food restaurants are operationally quite similar to each other, suggesting a broad span of control. However, their physical dispersion works in the opposite direction of limiting span of control.

Coordination of activities

Problems arise when organizations do not properly coordinate their activities. In simple organizations of only a few people, coordination is usually not a major concern. Problems develop, however, as organizations grow in complexity.

Pooled interdependence refers to activities that can be performed with little interaction between individuals or groups. Suppose a hotel has three telephone operators. Each can usually perform the required duties independently (that is, without any interaction with the others), as can room maids and cashiers at food outlets. Because these workers need not interact among themselves, coordination of their activities is best accomplished by proscribing standardized rules and procedures for each to follow, by intensive individual training, and by direct supervision.

The role of coordination is to ensure that each independently performed task is carried out at the same level of efficiency and quality.

Sequential interdependence occurs when one task's

output becomes a second task's input. This is typical of production-line operations, where products are progressively assembled. A hotel example is the guest checkin process. The "output" of a front desk becomes an "input" to the accounting department in the form of a guest billing record, or folio.

Coordination also requires identification of the linkages that exist between activities. Still greater coordination is required in cases where the output of Unit A is input for Unit B, and the output of Unit B is input for Unit A. Whenever there is a high level of interaction between work units they are said to exhibit *reciprocal interdependence.*

One example is the coordination needed to host a major convention. Rooming decisions made by the front desk must be coordinated with accounting, sales, housekeeping, and reservations; function room usage requires interaction between convention services, engineering, food and beverage, and accounting. Because any one department's output and activity affect numerous other departments, mutual adjustments among each are required.

Close coordination is only possible through *direct communication* and joint decision making between the units involved. While standardized plans and procedures are helpful, they cannot possibly solve all the problems resulting from such a high degree of departmental interaction. Direct communication and group meetings become a necessity to ensure proper coordination when activities involve reciprocal interdependence.

Static principles of organizational design

Experience has accumulated for centuries about how to organize institutions such as government bureauracies, the military, religions, large commercial trading companies, and since the industrial revolution, large manufacturing concerns.

Chain of command

A hotel's organizational chart depicts the chain of command. It should be possible for any employee to trace his or her way up the organization chart's chain of command all the way to the GM. The typical pyramid shape of an organization chart is consequence of the chain of command and the span of control concept discussed previously. Chain of command is a very powerful concept. It provides structure in an organization by setting forth a system of subordinate-superior accountability for everyone.

The chain of command affects communication within organizations for both subordinates and superiors. If a GM wants to make a change in housekeeping, chain-of-command considerations would have the GM communicate through the rooms department manager, who in turn will speak to the director of housekeeping. The traditional chain-of-command structure in a hotel would have the baker responsible to the chef and the chef responsible to the food and beverage director. Accordingly, the baker should communicate with the chef and not directly with the food and beverage director. While it is important to be aware of possible chain-of-command problems, too strict an adherence to this principle can take away the spontaneity in an organization. Experienced hotel GMs often break with this principle, but in a way that is not harmful to the hotel.

The immediacy of some problems in hotels sometimes requires hotel executives to issue orders directly to subordinates two or more levels down in the organization. GMs may also want to maintain personal control over some project or aspect of the hotel and choose to bypass immediate subordinates in order to do so. This does little harm as long as everyone knows what is happening and the organizational climate is otherwise healthy and trusting.

Delegation

Delegation can range from assigning a minor task to a subordinate to granting complete responsibility for a major undertaking. It's important for both superior and subordinate to understand and agree on the level of responsibility, the freedom of action, and the amount of authority that accompanies a delegated task. There are various levels of delegation, each of which is useful in different circumstances. Here are some examples of orders that result in different degrees of delegation:

(1) gather information for my decision,

(2) set out two or three alternatives; I'll then choose,

(3) make a recommendation for my approval,

(4) make a decision but inform me of it before proceeding,

(5) take action but inform me of it before proceeding, and

(6) take action on your own; it's not necessary to communicate with me regarding this matter.

The extent to which authority is delegated depends in part on the experience of the subordinate. Young, inexperienced subordinates can expect only limited delegation until they have proven themselves. The amount of authority delegated will usually increase as trust between superior and subordinate is built. It's been said that when a person becomes a manager he or she gives up earning an honest living.

Hotel managers don't usually make beds, cook food, or provide service directly to guests. Rather, their job is to see to it that the organization they manage provides proper guest services.

Hotel functional organizational design

Individual hotels are usually organized along functional lines with departments grouped according to the particular work activity in which they are engaged. The hotel is divided along functional lines into five separate administrative departments: rooms, food and beverage, sales and marketing, personnel, and accounting. The five department heads report directly to the GM. Each department is further subdivided into smaller organizational units. These subdivisions represent additional refinements of the work performed and the knowledge and skills of the people in each subunit.

The rooms department

The rooms department performs the lodging function of a hotel. Reservations must be accepted, guests must be hospitably received and assigned clean rooms, the status of available and occupied rooms must be kept current, guests must receive mail and phone messages promptly, security must be maintained, public spaces such as lobbies must be kept clean, and guest questions must be answered. These are some of the important functions of the rooms department. The rooms department is divided into a number of subunits, each of which performs rather specialized tasks. In many instances, these subunits are also referred to as departments.

For example, the laundry department, which in a 500-room hotel is quite large, is responsible for cleaning and pressing all the hotel's linens and employee uniforms as well as guest laundry. Its function is extremely specialized. Little of the knowledge and skills required to manage a laundry operation are transferable to other areas of hotel operations. The front office is where guests are greeted when they arrive at the hotel, where they're registered, and where they're assigned to a room. Telephone operators and other guest communications functions usually fall under the front office department. The hotel's bell staff is also part of this department. Reservations takes and keeps track of a hotel's future bookings. The housekeeping department is responsible for cleaning guest rooms and public spaces. Security is responsible for guest safety.

Finally, the engineering department is responsible for the operation and maintenance of the hotel's entire physical plant, including electrical, mechanical, heating, air conditioning and ventilation, structure, and plumbing. It also performs minor repairs and renovations. A great deal of interdependence exists within the rooms department, thus calling for close coordination of activities between subunits. Linkages exist between the front office and the reservations department. Reservations must inform the front office of the number of presold rooms each day to ensure that a current inventory of rentable rooms is always available. Conversely, the front office must let reservations know whenever walk-in guests (those without reservations) are registered. Linkages also exist between the front office and housekeeping, Information regarding room status must flow both ways: When a guest checks out, the front office must inform housekeeping so the room may be cleaned. Once a room is cleaned, housekeeping must inform the front office so that it may be sold. These are both examples of reciprocal interdependence in which individual units provide each other with inputs.

Other linkages within the rooms department are illustrative of sequential interdependence, which occurs when the output of one unit becomes the input of another. An example is housekeeping's inability to properly provision a guest room if the laundry does not supply enough clean towels or bed sheets. Another less obvious example deals with the output of information from one department to another. For example, engineering cannot replace a defective light switch in a guest room if housekeeping does not report the problem. These examples illustrate the reciprocal and sequential interdependence that exist between individual units within the rooms department.

Sales and marketing

This department is quite small, thus making intradepartmental coordination much easier. Also, the department is removed from most day-to-day operational problems faced by other departments. Still, there is a division of work among sales managers based usually on the types of customers a hotel is attempting to attract. Individual sales managers often specialize in corporate accounts, conventions, or tour and travel markets. Also, sales managers are sometimes further subdivided along geographical lines such as regional or national accounts. Still, the sales staff, even for a 1,000-room hotel, usually does not exceed a dozen or so. Sales managers work more or less independently in their particular market segments. Thus, problems of intradepartmental interdependence are usually not severe.

Personnel

A hotel's personnel department is a staff organization set up to handle a specialized function. It serves no customers, books no business, and prepares no meals, yet it plays a vital role in a hotel's efficient operation. The personnel department is subdivided into three subfunctions: employee recruitment, benefits administration, and training. The personnel director is expected to be an expert on labour law and to advise managers in other departments. While these three subfunctions are related to each other, there are not many problems of interdependence. Instead, the personnel department's major challenge occurs as it attempts to interact with other hotel departments.

Accounting

The accounting department often combines both staff and line functions. Its traditional role is recording financial transactions, preparing and interpreting financial statements, and providing management with timely reports of operating results. Responsibilities also include payroll preparation, accounts receivable, and accounts payable. These functions are the responsibility of the assistant controller for finance. There is, however, another dimension to the accounting department that deals with various aspects of hotel operations, cost accounting, and cost control throughout the hotel. This aspect often results in the department being called the controller's department rather than the accounting department. Two areas that are the central concern of accounting control are rooms and food and beverage.

The accounting department's front office cashier keeps track of all charges to guest accounts. The night auditor must reconcile all guest bills with the charges from the various hotel departments. Although these employees work at the front desk and sometimes have direct guest contact, they are members of the accounting department and report to the assistant controller for operations. The food and beverage controller, along with the food and beverage cashiers working in the accounting department, keep track of the revenues and expenses of the food and beverage department.

Food and beverage cashiers report to the assistant controller for operations, and the food and beverage controller reports directly to the hotel controller. The food and beverage department may be responsible for food preparation and service, but the accounting department is responsible for collecting revenues! The food and beverage controller verifies the accuracy and reasonableness of all food and beverage revenues. The accounting department is responsible for keeping track of and preparing daily reports on the costs of the food and beverage used in the hotel. In many cases, the accounting department is also responsible for purchasing and storeroom operations.

Finally, the director of systems is responsible for designing the accounting and management information systems used throughout the hotel. This discussion demonstrates the accounting department's direct involvement in a number of day-today operational aspects of the hotel. Two final points about the accounting department.

Accounting is responsible for collecting and reporting most of a hotel's operational and financial statistics. It therefore plays an important hotelwide staff role as data provider for decision making and budget preparation. In addition, the accounting department head has a dual responsibility not only to the hotel's GM but also to the hotel chain's financial vice president or to the hotel's owner. The reason for this dual reporting relationship is to provide the hotel corporation an independent (from the GM) verification of the accuracy of the financial and operating results of the hotel. Thus, unity of command is routinely violated in the case of hotel controllers.

Strength and weaknesses of a functional organization

The reason for organizing a business along functional lines is to group together employees who perform similar tasks or have similar skills. The strength of a hotel's functional organizational design is the resulting efficiency within individual departments or subunits. Performance of common tasks allows for work specialization, which increases overall productivity.

Since functional departments perform similar tasks, workers will rapidly develop specialized skills and knowledge. Training is easier because of task similarity and the many opportunities for inexperienced workers to learn from experienced workers. This helps new employees quickly learn the skills and behavioural patterns that lead to success. A functional organization is a logical way to organize work because it fosters efficiency, teamwork, and coordination within departments. However, the functional design's most important strength is also the source of its greatest shortcoming.

All departments must keep hotelwide goals of customer service and profitability in mind rather than focus narrowly on their own concerns. A method must be found to coordinate the activities of individual departments and to set hotelwide strategies and goals. Left to themselves, it is unlikely that individual departments would be capable of doing this. Specialization at the department and subdepartment levels results in the need for leadership at the top of an organization. Someone above the departments must set the overall strategic course of the hotel, set hotelwide goals, coordinate activities between departments, and arbitrate interdepartmental disputes.

A hotel's functional organization demands strong leadership at the top. While functional departments produce specialists within a narrow skill category, they do not develop executives with broad hotel exposure. Consider the heads of a hotel's marketing and food and beverage departments. These two executives might only have superficial knowledge of each other's speciality. Their education and work experience will likely be so different that either would be at a loss if placed in the other's department. The director of sales might have a marketing or general business degree and have spent a career in sales-related work.

The food and beverage, director, on the other hand, could have a culinary diploma and a hospitality degree, extensive food production and service experience, and little or no sales experience. One often finds accountants running the controller's office; engineers in charge of engineering and maintenance; individuals with degrees in personnel administration heading the personnel department; and a variety of educational backgrounds among rooms managers. Managers educated in hotel administration are capable of filling most department head slots.

The longer managers stay in one department the more narrowly specialized they become. While a manager may perform well within one department, he or she may be unprepared.when it comes to problems that require a hotelwide knowledge and perspective. Narrow specialization can result in bias, mistrust, and friction between departments unless upper management takes steps to counter this. Individual departments may pursue their own narrow interests rather than broader overall goals and objectives. This is a particular problem for hotels because of the need for close interdepartmental cooperation in providing guest services. There are numerous possibilities for service breakdowns in hotels.

A well-thought-out set of standard operating procedures and systems can decrease the chances of many routine mistakes. Still, because of the amount of reciprocal interdependence that exists between departments, close cooperation is a must. Nowhere is this more important than at the department-head level, where differences in functional specialities are most extreme.

The vehicle often used to foster cooperation between functionally specialized departments is the Executive Operating Committee (EOC).

The executive operating committee

The EOC is made up of the GM and other hotel senior executives. There's no magic formula as to whom should be on the EOC, but usually it's those executives who report directly to the GM. Thus, the EOC consists of the most senior members of a hotel's management staff: the heads of the functional departments who report directly to the GM and are responsible for a hotel's major budgetary units. A subgroup of these executives, the GM, rooms manager, sales and marketing director, food and beverage director, and controller, usually produce the hotel's occupancy, revenue, and profit forecasts for each year. This forecast forms the basis for the hotel's overall annual budget, and meeting annual budget goals determines executive bonuses.

The exact duties of an EOC vary from hotel to hotel, and they can be spelled out in detail or left ambiguous. A hotel's EOC could be loosely or highly structured. An important question GMs need to answer is the amount of authority they wish to delegate to the EOC. Depending on the circumstances, one EOC might be structured to make certain group decisions, a second might play a strong though consultative role to the GM, and a third might have a weak or nonexistent decision-making role. Quite apart from decision making, EOCs play an important communications role within hotels.

The more participative the GM's management style, the more likely the EOC will be engaged in joint decision making. Authoritarian GMs will find little need to foster a strong EOC. The greater the need for change within a hotel, the more likely it is that frequent EOC meetings will take place. The less experienced the hotel's department heads, the more helpful frequent EOC meetings will be because they can serve as a learning and training vehicle for inexperienced managers. Under the influence of a skilled GM, the EOC can play an important role. Some of the ways it may be useful are:

— To foster group problem solving and decision making.

— To build a feeling of joint responsibility for overall hotel performance.

— To help instill common attitudes and beliefs among top executives.

— To foster top-down, bottom-up, and horizontal communication.

— To assign duties, assess progress, and control activities.

— To build interdepartmental cooperation.

Well-managed hotels address the need for coordination of activities through an elaborate structure of committees and meetings. Just like a hotel's organization chart, these committees and meetings constitute a formal part of a hotel's organizational structure. A hotel's committee and meeting structure is usually proscribed by the GM. Each group's responsibilities are spelled out (sometimes in great detail), regular meeting schedules are promulgated, and minutes are often taken and distributed to participants and to higher-level executives, including the GM.

The committee and meeting structure of a hotel should be a well-thought-out part of a hotel's formal organizational structure. The purpose of the committees and meetings in a hotel is as varied as the hotel. They address a variety of concerns, including daily operations; intradepartmental and interdepartmental issues;

hotelwide concerns; and financial, personnel, and marketing issues. It will pay dividends to review this list carefully. The meetings a hotel holds provide clues about what it takes to manage the hotel. One of the first things to note is the sheer number and diversity of meetings. Surely, one might say that if a hotel were to hold all these meetings there would be little time left over to do any work! In fact, the effective management of hotels requires frequent meetings. They are part of the work of the hotel.

As elementary as it may seem, it is very easy for a hotel to fail to keep its managers and employees adequately informed. This shortcoming can have disastrous consequences with regard to the attitudes and morale of a hotel's staff. A second complaint relates to service breakdowns that occur as a consequence of too few meetings.

Hotels are subject to frequent, usually daily, changes. Meetings must be scheduled frequently in such an environment or their effectiveness will be lost. Too few meetings result in confusion over a hotel's goals and objectives. People need to know what is important to the hotel. What does it value most? What does it stand for? What constitutes good performance? Since hotels provide many intangible services, a constant effort must be made, at all levels, to provide answers to these questions. Meetings are an effective means of accomplishing this vital management function. Hotels are businesses that require an extraordinary degree of interdepartmental cooperation in order to provide quality guest service.

The functional organizational design used in most hotels fosters efficiencies within each department of a hotel but is weak when it comes to coordination between departments. One of the organizing strategies employed to overcome this problem is a formal meeting structure that fosters interdepartmental communication and cooperation. Thus, an important part of management's organizing function is to design an effective meetings structure that compensates for and complements a hotel's functionally departmentalized organization.

Theory of interdepartmental conflict in hotels

The prevalence of interdepartmental conflict in hotels seems to be one of the distinctive features of their operation. Despite this, interdepartmental conflict is an area of research that has been somewhat neglected not only in the hospitality industry but throughout management research. Whereas conflict between employer and employee (vertical conflict) has been the subject of considerable study and analysis, that between employees operating at the same hierarchical level (horizontal conflict) has been largely ignored.

The frequency with which hotel and catering operations appear to experience inter-departmental conflicts cannot be adequately explained by concepts of interpersonal differences or merely through a greater understanding of the external environment in which the actors behave. Horizontal conflicts within hospitality seem to occur irrespective of the external environment of the unit. Hence, there would appear to be something in the nature of the operation or the social environment of the hospitality industry that causes or heightens intergroup differences within it.

Researchers have tended to explain the industry's interdepartmental conflicts within a unitary frame of reference and have placed undue emphasis on ideas of personal difference. The result is that solutions have largely revolved around the establishment of superordinate goals. The pluralistic approach is seemingly more realistic in accepting that the organization is made up of a multitude of different groupings that may well have different interests and goals.

This article outlines four possible reasons for the heightened interdepartmental conflicts in the hospitality industry, either in isolation or collectively:

(1) interdependence—the relationship that exists between departments,

(2) environment—the framework within which activities occur,

(3) rewards—the nature of the total payment package,

(4) status and stigma—the perceptions of workers within the industry about themselves and others.

Interdependence

The level of interdependence between departments in many situations is necessarily high if the customer is to receive a satisfactory service. A number of studies have indicated that where there are high perceived levels of interdependence between departments then inter-departmental conflict tends to increase.

Interdependence in hospitality situations in caused by the nature of work flows; the product or service that the customer receives is the outcome of close and often immediate cooperation between two or more departments. Coupled with this, the time requirements for coordination are very short compared with other industries. In fact, they can often be measured in minutes or seconds. The reasons why interdependence causes conflict between departments can be considered in a fourfold manner: autonomy, reciprocity, role conflict, and goal differentiation.

It has been suggested that there is a struggle for autonomy in the workplace, and that there is a fundamental conflict between the desire for independence and the necessity of interdependence. Where this struggle for autonomy is frustrated, then conflict will arise between the parties who are directly concerned. This could be the situation between the kitchen and the restaurant where the waiting staff cannot feel in control of their work because they are dependent on chefs for their raw materials.

Snow further develops this concept in relation to the hospitality industry by suggesting that staff have a desire to be in direct control of their own work, yet in positions of interdependence this is clearly not possible. Thus, they try to exert pressure on those with whom they are interdependent, resulting in conflict. Perceived reciprocity may also be a cause of conflict due to interdependence between the parties. Where it is perceived by one of the sides that the other has acted unfairly or without due concern or a favour has been done but not returned, then there appears the potential basis for a conflict situation. Where levels of interdependence are particularly high, as between the kitchen and the restaurant, then the opportunities for this type of conflict tend to increase.

One party may often have to ask "favours" of the other in order to satisfy the guest or meet the internal requirements of the situation. Goal differentiation between the parties is probably the most important reason cited in the literature to date for interdepartmental conflict in hotels. Bowey, Nailon, and Mars and Nicod all considered interdependence to be a determinant of interdepartmental conflict in restaurants and hotels, as the interdependent parties placed different demands upon the situation.

The chef's concern was primarily with quality and that of service staff primarily with speed. In other situations this might be reversed, but the different objectives of the staff seem to heighten the problems of interdepartmental conflict caused by interdependence and will vary with the nature of the situation. Mars and Nicod suggested that there are likely to be higher levels of conflict in lower classes of establishment where there is a greater differentiation between the waiter's desire for speed and the chef's aspirations for quality than in better classes of establishment, where both parties have a great concern for quality.

Environment

The social environment may also be a cause of conflict. The environment of the hospitality industry has a number of distinctive features that may add to the development of conflict situations; these include the triadic relationship that exists between management, staff, and customer; the speed of operation, causing stress and pressure for the operatives; the styles of leadership used; and the territorial perspectives of the participants. Many staff members face situations in which the demands placed upon them by the customer and those by the situation and their working colleagues conflict. This type of role conflict certainly adds to the stress inherent in the task and to the existing conflict between those departments that have direct contact with the customer and those that do not.

Staff who occupy positions at the interface between the organization and the customer (boundary roles) have been identified as adapting their attitudes and work behaviour to cope with this situation and thereby emphasizing their differences from colleagues in other departments. The perspective taken by Homans of considering groups in terms of their internal and external environments may be of assistance in understanding the effects of the triadic relationship. The external environment and the predominant features of the triadic relationship are dictated by the nature of the tasks that staff undertake.

The internal environment of the group may well be dictated by the external environment in which it operates, and this provides the answer as to why, for instance, chefs and waiters may perceive themselves to be very different types of people. Studies on waiting staff have shown them to be highly individualistic in their perspective, yet kitchen staff have the reputation of stronger collectivism. Such differences in group solidarity and the different value systems that emerge may aggravate the conflicts between the parties. Hence, the real source of the conflict may lie in the external environment that the participants face, especially their role in interacting with the customer, rather than in any form of direct relationship between the two groups.

The environment in which staff conduct their activities may be one of stress and pressure. If the working relationship presents a source of stress rather than reward or satisfaction, then this could lead to the staff looking for an outlet for this pressure, the most immediate outlet being those people from other departments with whom they come into contact for resources. Whyte noted how waiters and waitresses "let off steam" at the hot plate due to the pressure exerted upon them by guests.

Although the recipients of these outbursts were the chefs, they were not the direct cause of the problem but merely the people with whom the service staff had the most immediate contact, and they were the most obvious target for the service staff frustrations. The nature of the hospitality environment at unit level tends to require a multitude of quick decisions to cope with the large number of unplanned and unpredicted situations that arise.

Shamir suggests that the industry is characterized by a desire for rigidity in operations at the corporate level and flexibility in the units. Whereas this would appear to call for an organic form of organization, the industry has been typified by more authoritarian leadership styles and more formalized organization and communication patterns. This style of leadership and organization in a situation that appears to call for a different approach may add to the conflicts faced by the parties. Staff also develop territories for themselves and may start to perceive themselves as entities that act independently from other parts of the firm. Any intrusion directly or indirectly into their territory may be treated as an invasion and resisted as such.

The kitchen and the front desk have very clear physical barriers that divide them from other departments, and chefs have a reputation of building a strong territorial perspective about their place of work. Yet in the restaurant/kitchen relationship, waiters must come directly to the interface between the two territories, the hot plate, many times within their normal processes of work, making them resistant to the potential "intruder to their territory" and increasing the conflict between the parties. Certainly, the nature of the environment in which tasks are performed and the tasks themselves would seem a key factor in determining the reasons for interdepartmental conflict in hospitality organizations.

Rewards

Rewards may cause conflict between departments through perceived differences in individual rewards or perceived differences in the distribution of scarce resources. Feelings of deprivation with regard to rewards tend to emerge from a basis of comparison. Whenever one party believes that it is less well off than parties in other departments, a basis for conflict is established. One would expect rewards to be of primary concern to workers in the industry, which it is often viewed as one with a low pay scale. This has not always been found to be the case; Snow and Shamir both speak of the social orientations of workers within the industry. However, recent research by Kung in Hong Kong into job satisfaction and labour turnover among food service personnel in chain hotel operations suggests that there may be a cultural element that should be considered.

The presence of tips as a feature of the industry is likely to lead to distorted perceptions with regard to the earnings of other staff. In a nonservice organizational setting the reward system is directly responsible for linking the individual with the organization and its goals; in situations where a substantial proportion of the individual's income is not received through the organization, there is no mechanism to link the individual to the organization and its goals. If this is the case for only one set of dependents within a highly interdependent situation, then the basis for potential conflict is formed. The most typical conflicts occur between departments, one of which is a direct recipient of tips whereas the other is not. Waiters are recipients, chefs nonrecipients; chambermaids are recipients, receptionists nonrecipients.

The reason for this could be that tip recipients develop different attitudes from nonrecipients. For instance, recent research by Shamir found that tip recipients had a more favourable attitude toward the customers and the management than nonrecipients. Although Shamir does not indicate their relative perceptions of each other, it is clear from his work that the perceptions of their jobs by tip recipients and nonrecipients differs. Snow also noted that perks such as tips had the effect of dividing staff within the organization, with the result that common interests were not realized. Differences in perceived rewards may be further distorted by the perceived opportunity for fiddles between the various departments. Certainly, as Mars and Mars and Mitchell have pointed out, fiddles are an important part of the total reward package. When one party perceives the opportunity for fiddles as higher within another department, this may be a source of conflict between the two departments. Scarce resources are quoted by a number of authors as a reason for interdepartmental conflict. In hospitality situations, scarce resources could be considered in terms of personal rewards or departmental resources.

Where there is a struggle for scarce resources between departments and where it is perceived by one of the parties that the distribution of resources has not been equitable, then the likelihood of interdepartmental conflict increases.

If workers do perceive themselves as being employed in a low-pay industry, then perceived differences in reward may be strongly felt and add to conflict that occurs between departments. Rewards may well be seen as a major source of conflict between staff in the hospitality industry.

Status and stigma

The rigid organizational hierarchies of the hospitality industry and the traditions under which they have grown have led to a very highly differentiated and established status system. This status system develops around the job title that the individual carries.

Some positions carry a particular status within the organization, whereas others, such as that of the kitchen porter, carry a distinct stigma. This is clearly an issue of perception; how members of staff perceive themselves and others within the work situation. If they perceive their positions as being of low status or others of high status, then this may be a cause of conflict between the parties.

As Sofer points out, people behave in the workplace according to their perceptions of reality, and in industrial conflicts a crucial factor is the reality of opposed interests as perceived by the parties. The status system is established through tradition and myth and reinforced through group pressure. Where staff are grouped together around a similar task the tend to develop ideologies that emphasize their distinctive contribution to the organization and that differentiate them from other groups with whom they have contact. Hence, each group may develop its own subculture and values, which may involve negative or indifferent attitudes toward other organizational groups.

Certainly, conflict occurs in hospitality situations when there are differences in belief between the parties. Although the occupational hierarchies that develop may differ somewhat between establishments, there does seem to be some uniformity in the way in which waiters/chefs and housekeeping staff/ receptionists perceive each other. These perceptions appear to be based upon traditionally negative preconceptions and may form a basis for conflict between the departments.

Members of these groups find their range of occupational choice limited to the lowest paid, least skilled work, which would not be considered acceptable to those people who are able to work elsewhere. In many cases these workers may be reluctant entrants, who are forced into the industry through a lack of opportunity elsewhere in the labour market. They will probably enter the industry with a perceived sense of stigma, which may then be reinforced by colleagues, management, and customers. They will be particularly receptive to the opportunity for conflict with other departments, as their involvement with the organization is likely to be low.

There does appear to be a tendency among immigrant groups within the industry to work together and form very cohesive groups based upon nationality, religion, or values/beliefs. This may well be a primary source of conflict where perhaps the waiters are predominantly Spanish and the chefs West Indian.

Whyte also noted that the conflict across the hot plate was in part a sexual conflict, as chefs were male and the waitresses female, and the males tended to believe themselves superior. Service staff are in a subordinate position to the needs of the customer, and it is a part of the adjustment process to accept that role. Where this position is partially refuted, there may be a feeling of role incongruence on the part of the staff member.

Also, service staff are often required to act out two differing roles, one with the customer and one with fellow group members or with staff from other departments. It has been noted that due to this duality of the roles, service staff tend to be very sensitive to threats to their self-image, whether they come from customers or fellow workers.

Missing standards

Lack of agreement on expectations

A lack of consensus on standards generally gives rise to an ineffective corporate culture. No one agrees on what work is to be performed, let alone how well it should be done and what methods are appropriate. Each employee may do it his or her way. One supervisor will apply different standards than others do, and those standards may even change from day to day. Because top management has not set up a method for achieving consensus on what should be happening in operations and service delivery, a multitude of standards may exist for each job. As a result, the product is inconsistent, guests are confused (or displeased), and managers and employees are dissatisfied.

Inconsistent delivery of products and services. Inconsistency is probably the most frequent cause of problems in assuring service quality. When an entree is prepared differently by each cook, when one room has enough towels while the next one doesn't, when one front desk clerk is warm and the next is abrupt, the guest will be dissatisfied. The hotel or restaurant will seem like an entirely different one on each visit, depending on which set of standards the guest experiences. When guests don't know what to expect from a hotel or restaurant, they often just stay away.

Measuring and managing quality. If there is no consensus on standards, it follows that they can not be measured. Yet measuring employees' conformity to standards is a critical management task. This function typically involves coaching, discipline, team building, and documenting and evaluating performance.

In particular, many managers dismiss the idea of measuring quality by reporting the commonly shared idea that "you can't measure service because it's intangible." Service is a real social event between the employee and the guest. Its quality can be observed and documented through guest focus groups and guest feedback. Evaluation based on activity, not results. How often are employees rewarded for looking busy, regardless of what results they achieve with all their activity? In both the management suite and the front desk, performance is often evaluated in terms of "sweat on the brow," "bean counting," or simple appearance. In such cases, the quality of the work performed is not as important an evaluation criterion as the number of hours worked or the number of crises encountered.

The goal of guest service is obscured when promotions, recognition, and compensation are not the result of meeting agreed-upon standards. Instead, corporate games and a good appearance—down to the right colour tie—can be more important to getting ahead than, say, achieving a low turnover rate among employees or having high guest satisfaction.

Symptoms

The cult of ineffectiveness places great emphasis on remedies for symptoms rather than on delving for underlying problems. On superficial inspection many operational and guest service problems seem simple. If a waiter is rude, he must be told to be pleasant. This is like treating a fracture with a Band-Aid; the solution does not get at the underlying cause of the problem. In fact, the waiter's rudeness may have less to do with the individual waiter and more to do with inappropriate selection and training or poor management practices. In problem solving, symptoms must be used as clues for discovering the real problem.

Absence of teamwork

Many corporate cultures reward competition among company employees. Some businesses actually encourage conflict and one-upmanship. When employees are rewarded for taking individual action, the development of teams can be thwarted. Yet a busy front desk, a crowded dining room, and a driveup window at lunchtime demand that hotel and restaurant employees work as a team to deliver prompt and satisfactory guest service.

Trailing

Trailing is the most common means used by managers for training new staff members. In this method, a new hire trails an experienced employee to learn how the job is done. This practice transfers one of the most important managerial responsibilities to a line employee. The new hire learns the operation's policies as they are understood by the experienced employee, who may not have a clear view of the company's objectives. Any time a manager might save this way is soon lost in correcting problems created by the practice. Moreover, even when training is handled by managers, it is seldom based on clearly stated job standards or founded on basic competency. To do the job right the first time, employees must be given the skills and knowledge necessary to meet a company's performance standards.

Sink-or-swim management

Management trainees are also victimized by a form of on-the-job training—but they often don't have even the luxury of another manager to observe. Managers and supervisors are often expected to sink or swim as they are introduced to new responsibilities. Line employees particularly face this situation when their outstanding performance wins them a promotion.

Recriminations

Rather than treat a guest complaint or other product problem as an opportunity to improve the operation, complaints are often occasions for blame, defensiveness, and finger pointing. Part of the problem is that people don't like to admit direct responsibility for making a mess of a job, preferring instead to sweep problems under the rug. But management also has a duty to limit problems in the first place by establishing a complete understanding of how each job should be done. When management has laid this foundation, problems can be identified and solutions found without unnecessary recriminations.

Effectiveness

Many hospitality managers fail to recognize the difference between effectiveness and efficiency. Merely completing a job ahead of a deadline is not sufficient to ensure excellence. The work must be done on time, of course, but the effort must result in achievement of established standards. The definition of "getting the job done" should include delivering the product or service right on the first try.

An organization is more than the sum of all its operations and departments. It also includes a culture that influences much of what occurs in the business. This culture is shaped—intentionally or accidentally—by the actions of the company's top managers. This informal social organization affects all levels of the company, and it strongly influences the company's ability to deliver its products and services to the customer. Rather than allow a cult of ineffectiveness to grow, top managers should consciously promote a culture emphasizing consistency, productivity, and participation at all levels in problem solving and achieving consensus on standards.

2

MANAGEMENT AND LEADERSHIP

Human relations skills are the ones most needed and most used by any hospitality manager at any level. Whereas lower-level managers use more technical skills, and upper-level managers use more conceptual skills, all levels of management need human relations skills the most. These involve the ability to interact effectively with many different people: customers, peers, subordinates, and superiors. Poor interpersonal skills represent the single biggest reason for failure, especially in the early and middle stages of a manager's career.

Nature of management

Management jobs in hospitality vary according to many different factors, such as the size of the operation and specific job responsibilities. Management jobs, however, do have three things in common: they share demands, constraints, and choices. Demands tell them what has to be done, such as certain specific tasks; constraints, such as budgetary or physical ones, limit what they can do; choices allow managers to select exactly what work is performed and how it gets done. Managers also share certain functions or processes in which they are involved: planning, organizing, coordinating, leading, and controlling. Together, they are referred to as the *classical or traditional functions of management* and they provide a way to classify the many activities in which managers are engaged. Planning refers to determining what is to be done, such as positioning the operation within a competitive market.

Organizing is the task of establishing the organizational chart—a hierarchy of company employees—and establishing the chain of command. Coordinating is getting the units and subunits within the organization to accomplish what has been planned. Leading is the process by which managers communicate with subordinates about getting certain plans and projects done; it also refers to how managers establish the tone, or general character, of their organization.

Controlling is evaluating or comparing progress or results to objectives and standards that were decided upon earlier in the planning process, thereby linking the last step to the first step in the management cycle. Many studies support the concept that managers spend their time fulfilling the classical management functions. One group of researchers has expanded the five managerial functions to eight: planning, representing, investigating, negotiating, coordinating, evaluating, supervising, and staffing—what the group calls the *PRINCESS factors*. Their research also shows that managers in different jobs and at different levels spent varying amounts of time in each function.

Other areas of interest when examining managerial work include how managers distribute their time among the classical functions, other functions in which managers are involved, with whom managers interact, and the qualities of managerial work. In a review of the management literature, Hales summarized the known features of managerial work as shown here:

1. It combines a specialist/professional element and a general, managerial element.
2. The substantive elements involve, essentially, liaison, man-management, and responsibility for a work process, beneath which are subsumed more detailed work elements.
3. The character of work elements varies by duration, time span, recurrence, unexpectedness, and source.
4. Much time is spent in day-to-day trouble shooting and *ad hoc* problems of organization and regulation.
5. Much managerial activity consists of asking or persuading others to do things, involving the manager in face-to-face verbal communication of limited duration.
6. Patterns of communication vary in terms of what the communication is about and with whom the communication is made.
7. Little time is spent on any one particular activity and, in particular, on the conscious, systematic formulation of plans. Planning and decision making tend to take place in the course of other activity.
8. Managers spend a lot of time accounting for and explaining what they do, in informal relationships and in politicking.
9. Managerial activities are driven by contradictions, cross-pressures, and conflicts. Much managerial work involves coping with and reconciling social and technical conflict.
10. There is considerable choice in terms of what is done and how: part of managerial work is setting the boundaries of and negotiating that work itself.

Management jobs differ in terms of their level within the organizational structure. There are basically three levels: *supervisory, middle,* and *top management*. The number of people at each level will vary tremendously depending on the size of the organization and how many locations it operates. A small family-run restaurant may have a few supervisors, and the family functions in effect as both middle and top management.

A fast-food chain with a large number of company-operated stores may have unit and assistant managers, who function as supervisory management, and various middle managers—central office support staff—all the way up the top management, including the senior staff and the chief executive officer of the company. Supervisory management is a unique level. In some organizations, supervisors are not even seen as part of management; but when they are, they are the first on the managerial ladder.

Hourly employees report to them, and the supervisor in turn reports to a manager. They are in a tough position because they have to deal with the complaints, requests, and concerns of employees; pressure from management to get tasks done; and the demands of guests to meet their service needs. Managerial jobs also differ in the extent of their responsibilities. Managers who have specialized responsibilities, such as front office manager or dining room manager, are called *functional managers*. Those with broader, multifunctional responsibilities are referred to as *general managers*, such as the ones who run hotels and restaurants.

Perspectives on management

In the early twentieth century, when writings on management began to take shape, the work of Frederick Taylor and Frank and Lillian Gilbreth focused on getting tasks done as efficiently as possible. Their work was done at a time when labour was in short supply. They founded the *scientific management school*, which used such procedures as analysing through time studies how work is done, determining the most efficient way to do a task, creating performance standards, selecting and training workers to perform the task, and finally setting pay rates and incentives. Taylor and the Gilbreths realized good results: less worker exhaustion and higher productivity and earnings.

The scientific management school held that workers have a natural tendency to take it easy but are motivated by money; therefore, financial incentives and piecework—payment per item or task completed—were used to increase productivity. The next such management step was the *human relations school*, which Elton Mayo, Fritz Roethlisberger, and William Dickson dominated in the 1920s and 1930s. This theoretical school examined the emotional and social side of people at work, which the scientific management school neglected.

The *Hawthorne study*, the most well known research of the human relations school, found that when workers were given a lot of attention it improved both morale and productivity. According to this school of thought, managers need to look at the psycho logical and social needs of people at work in order to get worker cooperation and, with it, increased productivity. Workers are also motivated by more complex needs than money. This school attributed worker apathy to poor work conditions, such as management practices that were too controlling.

Mayo felt good enough about human nature to write that managers can trust employees, and that letting groups of employees make some of their own decisions will increase both morale and productivity. Because of

Mayo, focus was put more on people management skills rather than technical ones. During the early 1900s, Henri Fayol, a Frenchman, worked on identifying the functions of an organization. He broke down an organization's activities into six functions: technical (such as production), commercial (such as buying and selling), security, financial, accounting, and managerial.

Within the activities of management he identified and described the functions—planning, organizing, commanding, coordinating, and controlling—that became known as the classic or traditional functions of management. He outlined other concepts of management, many of which are still in use today, such as the following:

— *Division of work:* A worker who has to perform fewer tasks can improve performance.

— *Authority:* The right to give orders and reward or punish the person who does or doesn't carry them out correctly.

— *Unity of command:* Each employee shall have one boss.

— *Subordination of individual interests to general interest:* If managers supervise fairly and firmly and set a good example, they can get individuals to serve the organization's interests.

— *Compensation:* Remuneration should be fair in terms of reflecting economic conditions and rewarding efforts.

— *Line of authority:* The chain of command should be respected.

— *Employee initiative:* Managers should stimulate employees to carry out some plans themselves.

— *Team spirit:* Managers should build teamwork, as it helps the organization and its employees.

Fayol's greatest contribution was distinguishing managerial work from the other functions performed within the organization. Douglas McGregor elaborated on the contrasting beliefs of the scientific management and the human relations schools in his own work, published in 1960, which he called *Theory X and Theory Y*. Each theory explains basic assumptions of human nature that managers hold about the way employees view work, and also about how they can be motivated.

Theory X managers tend to be more autocratic, while Theory Y managers tend to be more participative. McGregor felt Theory Y is not the answer to all of a manager's problems, but is a basis for improved management and organizational performance. Taking off from Theory Y, William Ouchi in 1981 published a new approach, *Theory Z,* based on his study of Japanese organizations.

Theory Z basically proposes that employees who are involved are the key to increased productivity. Other Japanese-inspired Theory Z characteristics that can improve productivity and quality include fewer explicit rules and team decision making and responsibility. The validity of Theory Z has not been proved; however, it provides some stimulating ideas for managers. During the 1960s and 1970s, various models of foodservice systems were published. An organization is really a system composed of interdependent parts, some unrelated, and designed to accomplish certain objectives. Systems management involves the coordination of all parts of the organization to meet stated objectives.

A systems manager realizes that when he or she intervenes in a system of interrelated parts and processes, those actions may affect many parts or subsystems. Of current interest is the excellence model, derived in large part from *In Search of Excellence* by Thomas J. Peters and

Robert H. Waterman. In their best-selling book, the authors listed eight attributes of well-run American companies:

— Action-oriented

— Close to the customer

— Autonomous and entrepreneurial

— Productive through convincing employees that their best efforts are necessary, and rewarding them

— Organized around hands-on, value-driven managers

— Committed to the business they know best

— Structured with few administrative layers and lean upper management

— Simultaneously centralized and decentralized

Although not all the companies displayed all eight principles to the same degree, the principles were visible in all of them. Some of the authors' conclusions are especially applicable to the hospitality industry; for example, that managers have to get back to basics such as quality service to customers, innovations, and the need to create commitment in organizations.

The employee-oriented part of the excellence model is also relevant in an industry in which keeping employee morale high is difficult due to low pay, a hectic pace, and often less-than-ideal working conditions. In the sequel, *A Passion for Excellence,* Peters and coauthor Nancy Austin emphasize how organizational pride and enthusiasm are crucial for managerial success. They feel managers need to be a combination of *cheerleader*, enthusiast, coach, and facilitator. In terms of starting and maintaining exceptional business performance, the authors advocate only two approaches: give the customer superior service and quality, and constantly innovate.

None of these management theories is always the right one or the best one. Research continues to tell us that given certain characteristics of people and their work, some management practices will work better than others.

Nature of leadership

Although much research has been done on leadership, especially over the past seventy-five years, there is still no clear understanding of what distinguishes leaders from nonleaders, or effective leaders from ineffective ones. There isn't even a single definition of what leadership is; actually, hundreds have been formulated. One function of managers is to lead. In this context, leading can be defined as the process by which managers interact with subordinates to get certain plans and projects accomplished, as well as how managers determine and maintain an organization's culture.

In other words, "Leadership is what gives an organization its vision and its ability to translate that vision into reality," as Warren Bennis and Burt Nanus stated in *Leaders*. Good leadership may result in some of the following:

— High productivity

— More customer satisfaction and quality of service

— Enthusiastic employees

— Committed employees

— Higher trust levels

— Greater creativity

This list does not include all the potential benefits of good leadership to an organization. Depending on the situation, there are probably many more.

Perspectives on leadership

Several theories try to explain the key to effective

leadership. The first school of thought on this compared various personal characteristics, or traits, such as intelligence or personality, of leaders and nonleaders to determine if certain traits predicted effective leadership. Research into the *trait theory of leadership* was done mostly between the 1920s and the 1950s. Although it often found certain traits, such as self-confidence and ability to influence others, in leaders, it uncovered no characteristics that could definitely predict leadership. Other traits found more in leaders were the ability to give guidance and be decisive.

The people centered leader is much more sensitive to subordinates as humans and is generally considerate and concerned about people. People-centered leaders are often participative or democratic leaders as well: they involve the employees as much as possible in relevant job aspects, and employees participate in the decision-making process. Although people-centered leadership does not always improve productivity, it does enhance employee and group satisfaction. The task-centered leader, on the other hand, is highly concerned with getting the job done, so this behaviour includes assigning tasks, explaining how to do them, and stressing the importance of meeting deadlines.

The task is more important than the person to the task-centered leader, who may also be an autocratic leader. In an autocratic style of leadership, the leader makes decisions and gives orders without any input from employees. The autocratic leader may be referred to as a dictator or authoritarian. Certain task-centered leadership behaviour, such as directing and structuring, is associated with productivity; being autocratic is not. Most task-centered leadership behaviour diminishes employee and group satisfaction, except in letting people know what is expected of them.

Some leaders can act in both task- and people-oriented ways. Research by Robert Blake and Jane Mouton shows that leaders who are both highly task- and people-oriented attain more productivity and employee and group satisfaction than ones who are not as highly oriented in both areas. Blake and Mouton devised

The *Managerial Grid,* which shows the possible combinations of leadership with regard to concern for staff and concern for production. Situational leadership refers to leaders who change their orientation in order to adapt to a given situation. In the situational leadership II model, developed by Kenneth H. Blanchard, there are two dimensions of leadership behaviour: task or directive and maintenance or supportive. Task behaviours are used to get work done, such as telling an employee what to do and how to do it. Maintenance behaviours are supportive behaviours, such as listening and encouraging. High or low levels of these two dimensions can form the basis for four leadership styles.

Depending on the development level of the employee, a manager can determine when to use which of the four leadership styles. If an employee is enthusiastic about doing a job but not very competent, as can be the case with new hires, a directing style, emphasizing high task behaviour, is appropriate. A coaching style is preferable when the employee has some competence but less enthusiasm or commitment. If employee ability is high, but commitment is variable, a supporting style is suitable. Lastly, when an employee is both highly competent and committed, a delegating style is appropriate.

The hospitality industry has traditionally hired people from many different cultural and ethnic backgrounds, as well as women. Particularly within hotel and restaurant companies with international operations, managers have had to deal with cultural diversity in the work force and among guests. Yet even in domestic companies, members of various ethnic and cultural groups are at work in the different departments, as any walking tour demonstrates. It is obvious that effective managing of this diversity is a requirement at all levels of a hospitality organization, and that the companies in the forefront of managing diversity will have a competitive edge. How to manage diversity in the work force requires careful examination. Of related interest are selected aspects of managing certain groups that are 'specially protected under the law, such as senior citizens and the handicapped.

Development of the multicultural workplace

The majority of the work force was composed of white males, who dominated all aspects of management. Some organizations are still at this stage of development. Research in this area describes organizations as being in one of three developmental stages: monocultural, nondiscriminatory, and multicultural. Monocultural organizations are dominated by white males, who set the pace for everything that happens within the organization, Women, minorities, and other socially oppressed groups are either not hired at all or must abide by the system set in place.

The nondiscriminatory organization has a genuine desire to get rid of the majority group's unfair advantage; however, this is done without significantly changing the system. With the civil rights movement of the 1960s and resulting Equal Employment Opportunity legislation, the struggle was to eliminate racism and prejudice through ignoring differences. Equality of the races was translated to mean sameness. Many civil rights advocates at that time down-played the cultural heritage of the blacks.

The problem with the nondiscriminatory stage is that although an organization may hire more minority members and want to promote an unbiased atmosphere, the majority culture is still seen as the standard to which everyone, regardless of differences, must conform. For example, when women entered the work force in large numbers fairly recently, many felt they had to become like men in order to find a place in and measure up to the white male standards; they started wearing dark suits, talked about sports, and became more competitive and assertive. The final stage of development is the multicultural organization. This type is not blind to differences among cultural groups, but rather acknowledges and builds on them.

Management values such diversity and seeks to derive the benefits of these differences. Power is shared, and different cultural groups in the organization contribute to its goals. An organization at this stage also recognizes that there is much diversity within a group as well.

Managing the multicultural work force

Many Americans have already become aware of different cultures through eating or working at ethnically oriented foodservices, whose numbers have recently been increasing; they include, for example, Mexican, Japanese, and Vietnamese cooking. Multicultural awareness is the first step to becoming culturally effective and thus better able to communicate and motivate across different races, genders, cultures, ages, and life-styles. Mistakes due to cultural fumbles, whether in human resource management, customer service, or wherever, are costly to a company in terms of lost business, managers who leave, and poor morale. To increase awareness of other cultures, a manager must first acknowledge and understand the effects of his or her own culture. We are all culture-bound to some extent, and our culture is so ingrained in us that we think our way of talking, perceiving, thinking, valuing, and behaving are normal and right.

After becoming aware of one's own culture, the next step is to learn various facets of others. It is important for the manager to see other cultures as objectively as possible, by realizing personal cultural biases and not passing judgment. It is also important to stress the value of diversity and an appreciation of it. By learning about another culture, it is hoped that the manager will be able to understand people from this culture better, as well as to be understood better in turn. Learning an increased awareness of another culture may include some or all of the following topics:

— Myths and stereotypes of the culture
— Linguistic differences
— Nonverbal language differences
— Values and customs
— Food likes and dislikes
— Work habits and attitude toward work

A danger in learning about any culture is that the information may be overgeneralized, thereby promoting stereotypes. It is important to keep in mind that regardless of cultural background, a person is still an individual and needs to be treated as someone with a unique personality, wants, and needs.

A manager who has become aware of other cultures is ready to practice various skills designed for interacting with individuals from another culture. These skills might include either sending and receiving or interpreting both verbal and nonverbal communication, such as handing out work assignments or listening to employees. Such multicultural management skills include the following:

— Self-awareness: The recognition of one's own values, assumptions, needs, and limitations.

— Culture reading: The ability to find and trace the inherent logic in each culture.

— Multiple perspective: The ability to suspend judgment, remove one's own cultural filters, and see through others' eyes, or perspectives.

— Intercultural communication skills: The ability to send and interpret both verbal and nonverbal messages accurately across different cultures.

— Gear shifting: The ability to readjust expectations, modify plans, try out new approaches, and rebound from setbacks.

— Culture *shock* savvy: The ability to monitor one's own adjustment to a new culture.

— *Relationship-building skills:* The ability to relate to and inspire confidence in all kinds of people and to maintain a support system.

— *Intercultural facilitation skills:* The ability to manage cultural differences and use them to the operation's benefit.

Teaching methods such as role playing, simulations, or case studies can be used to increase multicultural awareness and develop skills for dealing successfully in multicultural situations.

A list of tips for working effectively in a multicultural organization follows:

— Learn how people are addressed in their own language. Be aware that in other cultures the order in which names are written or spoken is different. Some cultures give one, several, or multiple names.

— Before telling a joke, consider if the joke or how it is told could offend anyone. Humour sometimes uses satire, ridicule, or stereotyping, all of which may be offensive to people from other cultures. Seemingly harmless teasing may be completely misread by other cultural groups.

— Be patient with people who do not speak your language fluently, and do not judge how they speak, It is only natural that people from other cultures will have accents, choose different words, and speak with a different tone, rhythm, and pace.

— Be aware that other cultures may handle disagreement differently. In some cultures saying "No" is frowned upon, and other signals may be used to indicate disagreement.

— Realize that other cultures may put a different value on speaking directly or expressively. For instance, in some cultures it is considered impolite to complain or admit to not understanding something.

— Get different cultural groups to work together on projects. This is an excellent way to promote understanding and friendship.

— Be cautious about the use and interpretation of gestures. Gestures, such as thumbs up, and body postures are by no means universal. For example, in the United States, a customer may gesture "one" to a server in a restaurant by putting up an index finger. In some

— Watch other people's reactions to use of space, and refrain from touching anyone until you understand the use of touching in their culture.

Managing protected groups

Protected groups are those employees who have been

given special legal considerations derived from civil rights legislation or Equal Employment Opportunity regulations. Some of the protected groups are racial or ethnic minorities, women, older people (over forty years old), and the handicapped. A myth concerning protected groups is that it is illegal to discipline or terminate them. This is incorrect. Protected groups must simply be treated on an equal basis with other employees in these matters. A manager should apply the so-called OUCH test when taking any type of disciplinary action:

O = Objective

U = Uniform in application

C = Consistently applied

H = Have job relatedness

This will help prevent any discriminatory actions against protected group members-and others as well.

Racial or ethnic minorities

In addition to previous observations about taking note of cultural diversity, some additional techniques can help to facilitate communication with employees for whom English is a second language:

1. Be simple and specific when speaking. Do not talk for too long, and encourage two-way communication. Avoid slang and figures of speech, as they may be confusing. Speak slowly and clearly. Summarize the conversation.
2. Ask for feedback. Don't ask yes or no questions, as these words are used differently in other cultures; for example, some Asians avoid the word no. Ask open-ended questions so the employee has to verbalize his or her understanding of the matter.
3. Provide employees with written communications

before and after meetings. This technique should help to minimize misunderstandings.

Women

The Equal Employment Opportunity Commission issued guidelines in 1980 on sexual harassment, indicating that it is a form of sex discrimination under Title VII of the 1964 Civil Rights Act. Any employer who knows about or should have known about such misconduct and fails to correct it is considered guilty of sexual harassment.

The employer is basically responsible for guarding against sexual harassment of both female and male employees. In cases where a supervisor commits sexual harassment, the employer is guilty regardless of whether it was known or should have been known. Of interest to the hospitality manager is that employers are also guilty if they allow nonemployees, such as guests or individuals making deliveries, to harass employees sexually without immediately taking corrective action. If the employer genuinely did not know that sexual harassment took place, liability can be averted if the company has an adequate sexual harassment policy, if the employee did not use existing grievance procedures, and if the situation is corrected immediately. If found guilty, the employer may be liable to reinstate the employee and pay back wages, lost benefits, interest, and legal fees. Research indicates that perhaps half the women in the work force experience sexual harassment at some time.

One study of the tourism industry demonstrated that sexual harassment is clearly a problem: 46 percent of the respondents reported having been subjected several times to "unwanted teasing, jokes, remarks, or questions of a sexual nature". If a hospitality operator wants to avoid being charged with sexual harassment, it is best to develop and implement a specific sexual harassment policy, which should include the following:

— An easy -to-understand definition of sexual harassment including the right of all employees not to be sexually harassed

— Clear-cut disciplinary guidelines for those found guilty, with flexibility for different degrees of harassment

— A formal complaint procedure, with provisions for speedy resolution

— A statement assuring protection for those who make charges, and barring any retaliatory action

Once a policy is formulated, it needs to be publicized to all employees. In particular, managers should receive in-depth training on what constitutes sexual harassment, how to prevent it, and how to investigate it when charges are made. An organization's human resource department is normally very involved in this entire process.

Older employees

The Age Discrimination in Employment Act of 1967 allows older employees to work as long as they want to in most occupations. Older employees now represent a new labour source for hospitality operators; fast-food restaurants are actively recruiting older individuals to work part-time. However, this is hardly the case in the hotel industry, where due to negative stereotypes, there is little interest in hiring employees over age sixty-five. Myths associated with older employees involve lowered productivity, higher health insurance costs, higher rates of absenteeism, and a lessened ability to train. Following are some tips for supervising what some people call Grampies: Growing number over sixty who are Retired, Active, Monied People In an Excellent State.

1. Let older employees know what is expected and how

well they are performing. Note that they prefer consistency in terms of job requirements and work schedules, and generally prefer part-time hours.

2. Make them feel like part of a team, perhaps by pairing with a younger worker for training. Involve them in decision making when possible. These efforts will probably yield excellent results, as these workers need to feel accepted in the workplace and may feel inadequate compared to younger workers.
3. Recognize performance, to motivate older employees.
4. Older employees may be better matched to jobs in which the ability to work without close supervision and reliability is important, rather than in high-stress or hazardous working conditions such as unloading trucks or working on wet floors.
5. Discuss with older employees any performance or other problems. Don't have higher expectations for this group than others. Offer assistance to help resolve any problems, such as training—which is key to this group.
6. Don't patronize your older employees. Treat them with dignity and respect.

Many of the tips for supervising older employees are simply good supervisory techniques.

A handicapped person is defined as someone with a physical or mental impairment that significantly limits one or more of life's major activities. The Rehabilitation Act of 1973 only requires federal contractors, not private employers, to hire the physically or mentally handicapped. Another legal issue with regard to handicapped employees deals with *reasonable accommodation* which also applies to other protected groups. This refers to making adjustments, without undue hardship to the employer, in the work situation so that someone who is handicapped can satisfactorily perform a useful task. Handicapped employees do generally require more training than normal, but once trained, they tend to be very dependable and reliable.

The hospitality industry has traditionally hired people from different cultural and ethnic backgrounds, as well as women. Particularly within hotel and restaurant companies with international operations', managers have had to deal with cultural diversity in the work force and among guests. Yet even in domestic companies, various ethnic and cultural groups are represented in the different departments, as can be seen in any walking tour. It is obvious that effective managing of this diversity is a requirement at all levels of a hospitality organization, and that the companies in the forefront of managing diversity will have a competitive edge.

Many of the methods used to deal with problem employee performance can be viewed as either negative or positive, depending upon the intent and how it is carried out. If the intent is punishment, it is viewed as negative. If the intent is to help the employee change behaviour, it is viewed as positive. A positive approach is preferable, although there are certainly situations when punishment is appropriate.

It is important to remember that many times when employees make mistakes, it is not their fault. Why don't employees do what they should? Here are some common reasons:

— They don't know what to do: Their training was perhaps poor or nonexistent, or performance standards were not made clear. Before asking an employee to perform a job well and follow the organization's rules, the manager must communicate all expectations and check that the employer actually does understand them. A well-written job description is a start.

— They don't know how *they are* performing: Employees need feedback while they are working in order to understand what constitutes appropriate and inappropriate behaviour. A performance management system that includes strong informal review goes a long way toward making employees aware of their conduct. Positive reinforcement, such as praise, increases the chances of their repeating the right behaviour. When managers ignore problem behaviour, they are allowing incompetence, which is really their fault.

— They don't know why they are doing it: If employees understand why a certain task has to be done, or why it should be done a certain way, they are much more likely to do it right.

— Expectations are unrealistic and unreasonable: At times, due to job design or lack of supplies or equipment, managers ask employees to perform jobs that simply can't be done. For instance, banquet cooks may be asked to prepare a meal that requires more oven space than the facility has; when there are complaints of cold food from a few guests, it is blamed on the cooking staff. It is unrealistic to expect an employee to accomplish more than can reasonably be done or to work under poor conditions.

— There is a mismatch between the employee and the *job:* The employee may be overqualified or underqualified for the job, resulting in poor performance in either case. In the hospitality field, sometimes an employee who prefers to work alone is hired to work directly with guests. This problem will come out soon and may be blamed on the employee, rather than the selection of the wrong employee for the position.

— They are not properly motivated: The reasons for this can range from being lazy to being bored and not seeing any chance of growth. In some cases, managers can do much to improve an employee's motivational level; in other cases, very little.

In almost all these situations, management can do much to correct the problems.

Establish nature of problem behaviour

Problem behaviour runs the gamut from excessive tardiness to theft of the employer's property. Besides attendance problems, there are typically concerns about performance and honesty. Some organizations categorize disciplinary problems as minor infractions, major infractions, and causes for immediate discharge. Minor infractions do little harm to the operation but can be serious if they occur frequently or together with another infraction. Examples include unexcused absences or latenesses, leaving the work area without permission, or taking long breaks. Major infractions interfere substantially with operations; they might include discourtesy to customers or refusal to do something. Causes for immediate discharge may be actions that are illegal or put someone in danger, such as theft or possession of drugs on company property.

Set disciplinary guidelines

Disciplinary guidelines stating how to handle each problem or each category of offenses should be written in unambiguous language for managers and employees alike to read and use. They should also be fair, realistic, and reasonably related to the safe and efficient operation of the business. It is unlikely that any set of guidelines can cover all circumstances that may arise; on the other hand, they should not be too general. When establishing disciplinary guidelines, most employers use a progressive discipline system. Progressive discipline applies corrective measures, such as counselling, in increasing degrees or steps. In other words, an employee is rarely terminated for a first offense; instead, the worker is given several opportunities to correct the behaviour before anything like suspension or termination would occur.

The purpose of progressive discipline is to get the employee to correct behaviour voluntarily. An example of a progressive discipline system is to use first oral warnings or counselling in response to problem behaviour, then a written warning, suspension, and finally termination. At each step in the progressive discipline, the intent is to help the employee get back on track. Any system of disciplinary guidelines must include a procedure so that an employee can appeal a disciplinary decision. Appeals are also called *grievances,* a term used more frequently in unionized organizations.

Managers, particularly supervisory ones, need training in how to handle grievances. They also need to encourage the use of an appeal process when an employee does not feel he or she has been treated fairly, as well as to assure employees that there will be no retaliation for making an appeal. Some organizations attempt to resolve grievances through what is called an open-door policy, in which managers above the immediate supervisor are identified as the people whom employees may contact with a grievance. The purpose of an open-door policy is to increase communication and give employees the feeling that they can resolve problems at work even when the supervisor is not supportive. Unfortunately, this policy frequently has problems with it, because either managers don't really keep their doors open or the employees feel awkward using it; members of the management team also may be inconsistent in giving decisions, which employees might then use to their advantage. In order for an open-door policy to work, there must be managers who support the policy and are consistent, fair, and open-minded.

Investigation

The purpose of an investigation is to get the facts, not to draw conclusions; that will come later. Remember, an employee should be considered innocent until proven guilty. An investigation into misconduct should be addressed as soon after the fact as possible, obtaining information from anyone who can provide any. Review the person's employment record, including recent performance evaluations and documentation of any prior problems. Discuss this person's performance and work record with any former managers and human resource managers. Consider an employee's overall employee record and contributions to the employer.

Interview

Before going into an interview, an employee may ask to bring a representative along. Both union and nonunion employees have the right to have a representative present for an investigatory interview if it may result in discipline. Of course, this is necessary only if the employee requests it. Of key importance in this process is to sit down with an open mind and discuss the situation with the employee. This should be done in a timely manner, as it is not fair to inform an employee that there was a concern, say, three months ago. But if the situation was somewhat emotional and, for instance, tempers flared, it is best to wait until everything has cooled down.

The steps in the interview process are to state the problem, listen to the employee reach agreement on the problem, derive a solution to which all parties agree and set a follow-up date. When opening the interview, try to create an informal and nonthreatening atmosphere. Remember to criticize not the person but the behaviour, and always work on maintaining the employee's self-esteem. Also keep emotions under control, don't argue, and stick to the subject matter at hand. Be sure to preface the statement of the problem with an explanation that the employee will get to tell his or her side next.

Present the problem and any pertinent facts in a nonjudgmental fashion, and explain how the problem relates to the expectation of the employee; for example, "Are you aware that we have found an unusually high number of errors in your night audit over the past few weeks?" Next, ask the employee to give his or her side, or view of the problem and its causes. The manager needs to sit back and listen with an open mind, asking open-ended questions to clarify as needed, such as "What are the circumstances that may be contributing to this?" Discuss the reasons for the problem and factors that affect it, trying constantly to reach an agreement.

Employees may mention personal reasons as causes; if so, refer the worker to an employee assistance program counsellor, if one is available. If not, and the problem is minor, such as the employee is late due to a car that's in the shop for a few weeks, the manager may be able to help. If there is no agreement on the nature of the problem, such as employee rudeness to guests, the manager will have to end the meeting, reach a decision about what to do, and get back to the employee. Even if there is agreement, the manager may want some time to decide how to handle this situation. The manager may also decide to continue with the discussion and assist the employee in thinking of possible solutions.

The primary responsibility for this is on the employee, who needs to show commitment during this phase to resolve the problem. This includes developing a plan of action, including how and when follow-up will be done, with the manager again assisting the employee in the process. Before ending the meeting, it is a good idea to ask the employee to state his or her understanding of the problem and the plan of action. This helps reinforce ownership of, or responsibility for, the problem. If no agreement is possible on a plan of action, the manager will have to decide what to do.

Decision making

Before making a decision, the manager should thoroughly discuss the situation with other managers, including a human resource manager if possible, to ensure that any actions are consistent, fair, and appropriate within the organization. If decisions are not applied consistently, employees will be uncertain about what types of behaviour are unacceptable. Inconsistency and excessive discipline also weaken employees' trust in the fairness of the manager and commitment to the organization. Also consider whether the employee has been adequately forewarned about the consequences of such behaviour. Especially in the case of termination, if the employee was not forewarned, the termination would probably be reversed in court.

Additionally, if employees are surprised by disciplinary measures, it creates distrust and sometimes fear. Extenuating circumstances need to be examined as well. Perhaps a manager or another worker provoked an employee's behaviour, for instance. Also consider to what extent the behaviour varies from desired performance and how significant such behaviour is. When making an employee aware of the decision, the manager should explain the reasons for it, too. The manager also must always invite the employee to use the appeal procedure, and explain how to do so.

Documentation

Documentation of the entire disciplinary process is a vital managerial function. Adequate documentation is needed in order to terminate an employee and make it hold up in court, if necessary. Documentation is also essential for a successful performance appraisal system. Following are tips on how to document:

1. Document performance as quickly as possible and date it.
2. Be specific about what the employee did and the circumstances under which the behaviour occurred. Be accurate and behaviour-oriented. Document thoroughly and include who, when, where, and how. Only include relevant information.
3 Opinions and hearsay have no place in documentation; note only facts, behaviour, and direct observations, not inferences or impressions. Strive to be objective and clear.
4. Be consistent by recording both positive and negative performance, and by documenting in the same manner for all employees.
5. Describe the significance of the behaviour as compared to expected performance.
6. Document all information revealed in the investigation as well as obtained from the employee during the interview.
7. Document any disciplinary action or action the employee must take, as well as consequences if improvement is not made. Make note of a follow-up date.

8. Employees should be encouraged to make written comments on all written disciplinary notices.

Termination

Termination refers to an employee leaving his or her job. There are five types of termination: Voluntary termination, such as quitting or retiring; termination due to employee's failure to meet expectations; firing or immediate dismissal; layoff; and position elimination. In a layoff, an employee may be recalled to work. In a position elimination, a recall will not occur. The relationship between employer and employee has long followed the *employment-at-will doctrine*. This doctrine states that either the employer or the employee is free to sever the employment relationship at any time, without notice or reason, as long as there is no employment contract requiring a specific duration of employment.

The courts have made judgments fairly recently that erode the employment-at-will doctrine. The courts have supported employees who were dismissed for refusing to behave illegally or for acting in the public interest. Employees have also found support when they were terminated in spite of an implied contract between employer and employee that employment was to continue unless there was a just or reasonable cause or when termination was motivated by bad faith or unfair dealing.

Other employers prefer to apply and uphold a just *cause* standard in their discipline and discharge policies. This approach is certainly the best for the employee. It is also the best approach for the hospitality employer, who is sure to lose applicants if they are required to sign at-will statements or are told that their jobs can be terminated at any time. Remember, too, that the objective of a disciplinary procedure is to retain the employee, because it is expensive to hire and train workers. Termination should be used only when the employee has destroyed his or her ability to contribute to the organization.

The courts have never denied the right to dismiss an employee for just cause. When doing so, the manager needs to be able to answer yes to each of the following questions:

1. Considering the employee's past record and any possible extenuating circumstances, does termination fit the infraction?
2. Did the employee have advance notice of the rules, and was he or she forewarned of the consequences of violating them?
3. Were management's expectations of the employee reasonable?
4. Did management make a reasonable effort to help the employee resolve the problem before termination, and is there proof of this?
5. Was management's investigation of the final offense made in a fair and objective manner, and did it involve someone other than the employee's direct supervisor?
6. Has this employee been treated like others in similar circumstances?

Another thing to consider before terminating an employee is to look at other alternatives; these might include transfer to another position or demotion. Some employees may do very well either in a different position, which may even be in another location, or in a less demanding and stressful job. If, however, termination proves necessary, the manager should follow these guidelines for conducting an effective termination meeting:

1. Hold the meeting in a private place where there will be no interruptions. Such privacy is unlikely in one's office, so choose another room.

2. Check the timing of the meeting. Don't have the meeting on a holiday, the employee's birthday, or any other special occasion. Also avoid termination when the employee has recently been involved in union organizing, has filed a complaint with the EEOC, or is able to become eligible for a company-sponsored benefit, such as becoming vested in a pension plan. Although Friday seems to be a favourite day for terminations, probably a better time is earlier in the week, to allow the employee the opportunity to get right to the task of finding another job. Choosing a time at the end of the day is probably best, as it allows the employee to get belongings together without undue attention from peers.

3. Before having the meeting, be sure there is confirmation for the action from top management, and probably human resources. Be sure all the paperwork for employees leaving the company, such as benefit continuance forms, is completed.

4. Plan to have another manager or human resource person present as a witness during the meeting. Keep news of the impending termination as private as possible.

5. State directly the decision to terminate and the reasons for it. Be firm yet tactful. Discuss some of the employee's good qualities and skills. Make it clear this decision is final. Explain when it is effective.

6. Expect the employee to be upset, emotional, and irrational. Let the employee vent some anger, and listen. Answer any of the questions the employee may have. Treat the employee with respect.

7. Explain how reference inquiries will be handled and give the employee the opportunity to speak to someone in human resources or a supervisor, if the individual so desires.
8. Explain when any benefits will run out and the terms, if applicable of any severance pay. Keys must be turned in and so forth. It may be best at this point to let someone from human resources handle the situation.
9. Management may want the employee escorted out, by someone from human resources, for example, if it is felt the individual may cause problems.

Some managers also feel it is a good idea after terminating someone to let other employees know informally that it occurred and why. This will clear the air and offset rumours.

Manager's role in discipline

The manager plays a most pivotal role in administering discipline fairly and consistently. Unfortunately, many managers don't want to discipline, for example, the server who comes in late several times a week or the maintenance person who never seems to get anything fixed, yet uses excessive overtime.

Managers often want to be a "good guy," and think that the employees will dislike them if they follow the disciplinary guidelines. It is also difficult for many managers to confront an employee with a problem, and because many managers have been unable to do so in the past, that only makes it harder for one to do so in the present. Managers may also feel inadequate about how to handle disciplinary problems if they have had little training in this area. Managers, particularly supervisory ones, can do much to reduce disciplinary problems. Here are some managerial techniques that can help prevent disciplinary problems from happening:

1. Be thorough in the selection process to ensure hiring the right people. Use techniques that make the process more foolproof: longer interviews, multiple interviews and interviewers, early-morning interviews (if the applicant is late, forget about that person), and thorough reference checking.
2. Be sure to have a probationary period for new employees, in which either party can terminate the relationship for any reason during a specified period of time, usually the first sixty to ninety days. Use the probationary period to weed out employees whose performance is borderline or worse. If in doubt, extend the probationary period.
3. Be visible and build a positive atmosphere. Be friendly and approachable, and talk to all employees as equals.
4. Respect the employees and treat them like adults. Don't have favourites.
5. Make sure all expectations and standards are known and are in writing. Also be sure consequences are communicated.
6. Give plenty of praise. Always praise in public and criticize in private.
7. Communicate on a regular basis to all employees.
8. Set a good example.
9. Orient and train all employees adequately. Give employees the opportunity to learn more and better themselves in the organization.
10. Have strong supervisory managers who practice fair and consistent management and are not afraid to confront problem performance and behaviour.

Positive discipline

Positive discipline is based on the idea that employees

are responsible for their own conduct, including correcting it when appropriate. In other words, employees are treated as adults. This type of discipline has been used with professionals as well as nonsupervisory employees. Instead of threats and punishment, it relies on encouragement, and instead of reprimands, it uses reminders. It also means praising employees when they do something right. With negative discipline, employees do things mainly because they have to, and the organization loses the benefits of individual commitment and acceptance of personal responsibility. Positive discipline is also progressive in nature.

The first step involves a counselling session between the employee and the manager to identify the problem and find a solution. The manager does not reprimand the employee or threaten further disciplinary action. Instead, the emphasis is on confronting the employee in a mature and supportive manner with the need to change, by reminding the worker that appropriate performance and behaviour are his or her responsibility.

A note of this meeting is put in the manager's file. Upon follow-up, if the problem is not resolved, there is a second counselling session, in which the manager mentions again that improvement is the employee's responsibility, then helps to work on a solution. The manager draws up a written solution and gives it to the employee. After the second conference, if the problem is still not resolved or at least, improved, the employee is allowed a decision-making leave of one or more days with pay. The purpose of such a leave is to remove any hostility and show the individual that the organization wants to help.

The employee is given the time off to decide if he or she is willing to meet the standards. Upon return from the leave, the employee is asked to advise the supervisor of a decision-either to try to meet the standards or to resign. If the employee stays but problems continue, termination is the next step. Because positive discipline has a just cause focus, such terminations will stand up in court.

Organizations using a positive discipline system have received certain benefits as a result. There are fewer disciplinary discussions, problem situations get addressed and resolved faster, and managers report less immature and emotional behaviour when confronting employees as mature adults. Because these managers are no longer required to be punitive and judgmental, they tend to deal with problems more quickly. In general, unions support the idea of employees being responsible for their own actions. Employees also like being treated as adults and being recognized for good performance. Perhaps most important, because the emphasis is on building commitment rather than mere compliance to rules, employees are more committed to high performance and achieving the goals of the organization.

Managing Service

Service is as different from the production of goods as factories are to the farms that preceded them. The primary output of a service is not a product or a construction. Instead, the output is consumed when produced, and value is added to the output in an intangible way, such as added convenience.

A service can't be kept in inventory and the person receiving it is left with only a service experience. Due in large part to these differences, the way service companies are structured and managed needs to be different from that of companies producing goods. Customer service refers to satisfactorily meeting customer needs and wants with products or services. Service management is much more comprehensive and involves "a structured, systematic approach for planning, organizing, and controlling the development and delivery of a product or service that promotes superior customer satisfaction and superior results for the organization". Service management is emerging as a way for a hospitality operator to deal with competition. If service is managed properly, it can give the customer more value for his dollar. Good service is frequently the main reason customers frequent certain hospitality operations, and poor service the major reason customers try the competition. Interestingly enough, most customers who are unhappy with service never complain to the company; they simply tell their friends and go to the competitor.

If a customer complains, it is far cheaper and better business to try to please that customer than to find a new one. Service management is first a philosophy, a set of values and attitudes, which must be translated into a set of methods. It can benefit from, among other things, an examination of characteristics of successful service organizations, as well as specific steps to manage service in the hospitality industry.

Nature of service

The exact nature of quality service varies according to an individual customer's needs, expectations, definition of good service, and perceptions of service. Someone's expectations of service will obviously be different if walking into a luxury hotel than into a budget facility. Expectations of restaurant customers identified in a National Restaurant survey included employees who smile when greeting customers, put customers at ease, check if the meal is fine, explain how long the meal will take to be served, and are knowledgeable about the menu and food preparation.

Nevertheless, every customer defines and perceives overall good service differently. This explains why some customers appear to be very demanding; they simply may have a different definition, perception, or level of expectation for service. The critical point of service occurs when the customer comes in contact with any aspect of an organization and is left with an impression of the quality of its service. This has been referred to by Jan Carlzon of Scandinavian Airlines as "the moment of truth". Every service business has anywhere from one to thousands of moments of truth every day. It is at these encounters that customers are won, maintained, or lost. Service can be split into two dimensions: tangible and intangible.

The tangible, or physical, aspects of service in hospitality include the meal, the hotel or motel room, any other facilities or equipment the customer can use such as a hotel pool, and the cleanliness of the operation. Despite these tangible aspects, the guest is left with nothing tangible. The intangible dimensions of service include reliability, assurance, accuracy, responsiveness, and empathy. Reliability refers to the service being delivered dependably and consistently. Assurance looks at how the service employees relieve customers of any uncertainties and put them at ease; in a restaurant, for instance, servers need to assure customers when their table will be ready or when entrees will be served.

Accuracy involves being attentive to details and following procedures correctly; for example, servers need to follow precisely the order of service in a dining room, as well as other procedures there. Responsiveness refers to prompt, timely service. The last intangible dimension of service, empathy, relies on many interpersonal skills of the employee. It refers to the ability to imagine any service encounter from the customer's point of view. It encompasses a caring attitude, attentiveness, courteousness, and awareness. Some empathic skills that frontline service personnel in the hospitality industry use include the following:

- — Greeting customers promptly and keeping them informed as to when a service will be performed.
- — Giving personal attention, such as calling customers by name when appropriate, and giving undivided attention.
- — Being aware of and anticipating customers' needs.
- — Being natural, courteous, and friendly.
- — Being aware of how the customer views the level of service.
- — Explaining when there are delays or problems.
- — Communicating clearly through verbal and nonverbal language.
- — Maintaining a calm, relaxed tone of voice.
- — Being helpful and going beyond the call of duty.
- — Handling complaints in an effective and timely manner.

Many of these skills can be taught or reinforced through training.

Characteristics of service organisations

Successful service organizations share several characteristics. First, management has formulated and supports a policy statement providing for excellent customer service. Unfortunately, some companies make profits their primary objective. When customer satisfaction is most important, profitability will follow. It is one thing to state that customer service is important, however, and another actually to put this into effect. Often parts of the organizational culture may block efforts.

A certain level of teamwork, cooperation, optimism, and loyalty is necessary for success. Management also needs to be sure that sufficient steps have been taken to implement the program. In addition, management sets a model for excellent guest relations. The managers who are to implement the program are also given the appropriate authority and can change it as needed, within a certain framework. Successful organizations design systems for the convenience of the customer, not the operator. Two examples include drive-through windows in fast-food operations and express checkout procedures in hotels. These organizations put the customers first and know their customers' needs, attitudes, values, and perceptions.

Another important characteristic is that frontline service employees are given latitude to satisfy the customer; they do not have rigid rule books detailing how to do everything, so the customer does not hear the otherwise familiar refrain "I'm sorry but that is our policy." For instance, at Stew Leonard's, when a customer realized she had no money with her to pay for groceries, the cashier simply took her name and address and asked her to pay for them the next time she came in. The customer was so shocked that she asked to see a manager before she would leave the store without paying for her groceries.

In all ways, in fact, frontline service employees are customer-oriented. How employees treat customers reflects, to an extent, how management treats the employees. If management maintains a healthy work environment, in which employees are respected, involved, and rewarded for providing quality service, good customer service is more likely.

Steps to manage service in the hospitality industry

The first step in managing service is to make it an

important part of the mission statement of the company. A mission statement typically describes what kind of business the company is in, what its mission, or purpose, is, and what it believes in. For instance, the Holiday Inn chain of hotels offers convenience at a moderate price. The hotels are conveniently located near airports or city centers and either have a restaurant or are near eating places; the rooms are clean and comfortable. Implicit in its mission are various service objectives. In order to develop a mission statement and service objectives, the organization must be sure to know and understand its customers.

Once the mission statement and service objectives are clear, a service strategy must be developed to clarify and implement them. A key part of the plan should be to establish service performance standards. Performance standards translate work requirements into levels of acceptable or unacceptable performance, and they need to be built into job descriptions and evaluation forms. For example, these are sample performance standards for a server:

1. Customers are greeted within one minute of sitting down.
2. Customer complaints are resolved immediately, and the dining room manager is notified.
3. The server looks directly at the customers when speaking with them.
4. The server checks back with each party at least once during the meal.
5. Meals are accurately served.
6. Refills are taken care of before the customer orders them.

7. The server correctly answers all questions on the menu.
8. The server accommodates at least 80 percent of customers' special requests.
9. The server is rated as "friendly" by at least 90 percent of customers on comment cards.
10. The server is always in proper uniform.

The next step in managing service concerns educating everyone in the organization about the program, especially the frontline service personnel, Because they are the ones who manage the moments of truth, it is crucial to give a lot of attention to their training, hiring, and orientation. When hiring employees who will deal directly with customers, it is important to look for empathic people who have good interpersonal relationship skills and self-esteem. They also need to be flexible in dealing with the many different situations that present themselves in hospitality and effective in communicating, both verbally and nonverbally. Preemployment testing can help determine some of these qualities.

During the interview, open-ended and situational questions can be used to get an idea of the person's personality and interpersonal skills. The importance to the job of good customer relations should be stressed at this time. During orientation and training, customer relations need to be given prominence. Training topics may include why customer relations are so important, an explanation and discussion about performance standards, and such skills as showing empathy and handling complaints and breakdowns in service. So-called smile training and attitude training, however, have not worked to build customer relation skills. If it is necessary to teach a new employee how to smile or make eye contact, perhaps the wrong person was hired; and attitude really means nothing until it is displayed in behaviour and actions, which can then be observed. Useful training methods include role playing, behaviour modelling, and performance tryout. In order for the hiring, orientation, and training process to pay off, the employees must be well managed.

Management needs to maintain good communication with and supervision of the frontline service personnel, reward employees when appropriate, involve them in decisions, promote from within, set a good example, clearly communicate expectations, and evaluate performance periodically. There must be a more-than-satisfactory quality of work life as well as a motivating environment. Within hospitality organizations, many frontline customer contact positions are entry-level jobs for which wages are far from outstanding, so good management is vital to good service. Performance needs to be measured and monitored to determine if the standards are being met. This can be accomplished by various methods, including *service audits,* checklists, overall supervision, and customer feedback. Service audits examine whether standards are being met, by either rating this or judging the frequency of such success.

A service audit may examine, for example, the timeliness of service. The amount of information from customers will vary depending on the complexity of the business and size of the effort. Hot lines are phone numbers customers can dial if there is a concern. Focus groups involve a trained interviewer meeting with a small group of customers.

3

Staffing and Training

Staffing is a major function within human resources management and probably the area in which the hospitality manager interacts the most with the human resource department, where one exists. Staffing has three basic components: human resource planning, recruiting, and selecting. Each component warrants separate discussion, along with the laws and guidelines affecting staffing.

Staffing and the law

The selection of applicants must be based on the person's abilities, experience, and education as they relate to the job standards and requirements. Any criteria used in the selection process must be consistently and directly related to job performance. The only exception to this law is the case of a *bona fide occupational qualification (BFOQ)*. A BFOQ is a job requirement to which the *Equal Employment Opportunity (EEO)* laws do not apply. For example, an attendant in a men's restroom has to be male. In order to meet legal requirements, a BFOQ must be a business necessity; in other words, the business would be negatively affected without such an exemption from the law. In 1978 the EEOC and three other government agencies—the Civil Service Commission, Department of Labour, and Department of Justice—presented a unified federal position on nondiscriminatory employment practices: the *Uniform Guidelines on Employee Selection Procedures*. This document applies to private employers who employ fifteen or more employees for twenty or more weeks in a calendar year, as well as to federal, state, and local governments.

It was designed primarily to show employers how to comply with EEO laws. It also asks employers to be able to demonstrate that selection procedures are job-related and valid—that is, reliable in predicting good job performance. This can be useful if an employer is taken to court and the plaintiff claims there is *adverse impact* (or unequal effect) on a protected group. Some of the key terms contained in the guidelines are defined below.

Adverse impact: A substantially different rate of selection in hiring, promotion, or other employment decisions that works to the disadvantage of members of a particular race, sex, or religious or ethnic group. Some of the key terms contained in the guidelines are defined below:

— *Substantially different rate of selection:* The agencies have adopted a rule of thumb under which they will generally consider a selection rate for any race, sex, or ethnic group to be substantially different if it is less than four-fifths, or 80 percent, of the highest selection rate for any other group. This 80 percent rule of thumb is not intended as a legal definition, but rather a practical means of keeping the attention of the enforcement agencies on discrepancies in rates of hiring, promotion, and other selection decisions.

— *Compliance with these guidelines:* Use of a selection procedure is in compliance with these guidelines if it

> has been validated—if it does not result in adverse impact on any race, sex, or ethnic group—or, in unusual circumstances, if use of the procedure is otherwise justified in accordance with federal law.

The intent of Equal Employment Opportunity laws is the employment of individuals in a fair and non-discriminatory manner. EEO laws also try to correct special problems of protected groups such as members of minorities, women, older people, and those with physical disabilities. All employers with over 100 employees must submit annually an Equal Employment Opportunity report, referred to as the EEO-1 report. In this report, all employees are first classified into job categories, and each job category is separated into gender and minority status. This form is examined by the EEOC in the event of a discrimination claim, to see if the composition of a specific group in the operator's labour force is at least eighty percent of the normal rate for that area.

In order to obtain the data needed for this report, employers are allowed to collect minority group data on job applicants as long as any form requesting such information is kept separate from the application. To be prepared for possible claims of discrimination and show support of equal employment opportunity, operators should keep records of all recruitment efforts for one year, including advertisements, referral sources, and so on. Going beyond EEO, *affirmative* action is a policy that requires organizations to correct past discriminatory practices by making extra efforts to recruit, hire, and promote qualified members of protected groups. This is implemented by having organizations set up affirmative action programs to ensure a balanced and representative work force.

Affirmative action programs are required for employers with federal contracts over a certain amount, as well as employers who have been found guilty of discriminatory employment practices; such programs are also freely developed by some employers. In developing an affirmative action program, a company will generally take the following steps.

1. Issue a written equal employment policy and affirmative action commitment.
2. Appoint a top official with responsibility and authority to direct and implement the program.
3. Publicize the policy and affirmative action commitment.
4. Survey present minority and female employment by department and job classification.
5. Develop goals and timetables to improve utilization of minorities, males, and females in each area that has been identified.
6. Develop and implement specific programs to achieve goals.
7. Establish an internal audit and reporting system to monitor and evaluate progress in each aspect of the program.
8. Develop supportive in-house and community programs.

On occasion, the existence of an affirmative action program has led to an accusation of reverse discrimination, which is when an unprotected individual, such as a white male, charges an employer with discrimination because a member of a protected group received preference of some kind. Besides federal laws, state and local governments also have *fair employment practice acts (FEP)*. They are patterned after federal legislation and often extend antidiscrimination laws to employers with just one or more employees. They might expand the definition of discrimination to include such factors as physical appearance or marital status. State and local agencies such as the Michigan Department of Civil Rights are set up to administer the fair employment practice acts.

Child labour provisions of the fair labour standards act

The Fair Labour Standards Act is a federal law applying to child labour. For minors, there are laws restricting maximum work hours, night work, and jobs involving certain types of equipment and the serving of alcoholic beverages. The federal child labour laws are described below; however, if a state or local law is stricter than the federal one, the state or local law must be followed.

Minimum Employment Age: fourteen years old

Minors fourteen and fifteen years of age may not do any of the following:

— Cooking (except at soda fountains, lunch counters, snack bars, or cafeteria serving counters) or baking

— Work requiring the use of a ladder

— Occupations that involve operating, setting up, adjusting, cleaning, oiling, or repairing power-driven food slicers and grinders, food choppers and cutters, or bakery-type mixers

— Work in freezers or meat coolers or in preparation of meats for sale (except wrapping, sealing, labeling, weighing, pricing, or stocking when performed in other areas)

— Loading and unloading goods to and from trucks, railroad cars, or conveyors

— Work in warehouses, except office or clerical work

Minors sixteen and seventeen years of age may not:

— Operate elevators or power-driven hoists

— Operate power-driven shearing machines or bakery machinery

— Operate circular saws or band saws

— Drive certain motor vehicles (without restrictions)

Maximum work hours

— *Ages fourteen and fifteen:* on school days, three hours per day, eighteen hours per week; on nonschool days, eight hours per day, forty hours per week. Also work may not begin before 7 A.M. nor end after 7 P.M., except from June 1 through Labour Day, when evening hours are extended to 9 P.M.

— *Ages sixteen and over:* no restrictions on work hours

Immigration reform and control act (1986)

Under the Immigration Reform and Control Act, employers must verify the identity and employment eligibility of all individuals hired after November 6, 1986, and who continued to be employed after May 31, 1987. This is accomplished by filling out Form I-9, Employment Eligibility Verification. In order for someone who is not a U.S. citizen to work in this country, the employee must have an Alien Registration Receipt Card.

Form 1-9 must be filled out completely by the employer and new employee within three business days of the hire date and kept on file for three years, or one year after an employee is terminated, whichever is later. The new employee must supply documents to establish identity and employment eligibility as listed on Form 1-9.

Although employers are not required to keep copies of the documentation presented, if documentation is kept for one employee, it should be kept for all employees. If the paperwork is not done correctly, the first-offense maximum fine is $1,000 per instance. In cases where unauthorized aliens have been hired, the first offense has a $2,000 maximum fine, the second offense a $5,000 maximum, and any further offenses a $10,000 maximum.

The labour market

It is a sad fact that many hotels, motels, and eating establishments are having problems getting qualified employees. For instance, a 1988 study that the National Restaurant Association commissioned found two problems in particular: fewer qualified applicants overall and fewer applicants for hourly jobs. The selected employment characteristics lead to several explanations for the current labour shortage:

1. The Bureau of Labour Statistics projected that by 1990 there would be 11 percent fewer workers ages 16 to 24 than there were in 1984. After 1990 the number is expected to continue to decline, but at a lower rate, and in 1995 the number will stabilize. These young people represent an important component of the hospitality job force. The decline in this group has occurred because the post-World War II baby boom ended by the mid-1960s, and the birthrate declined throughout the 1970s.

2. Competition for the 16-to-24 age group from retail and other industries is and will continue to be a concern (National Restaurant Association 1988).

3. The average wages paid in the hospitality industry are significantly below the average hourly rate for nonsupervisory jobs (excluding the agricultural sector), which is $8.76 (National Restaurant Association 1988).

4. The high yearly *turnover* rate, especially for eating and drinking places, makes the labour shortage even worse because of the increased frequency of having to find replacements. Turnover refers to the loss of an employee who must be replaced. Turnover, defined as a percentage, is calculated as follows:

$$\text{Turnover rate} = \frac{\text{Number of replacement}}{\text{Average number of employees}} \times 100\%$$

5. The hospitality industry continues to grow and therefore to have more jobs that need to be filled. Since 1970 the number of jobs in the foodservice industry has more than doubled. Similarly, the demand for lodging has increased, due to overall population growth, business expansion, and rising income.
6. Tough new immigration laws have decreased the number of applicants for some operators. The 1986 federal Immigration Reform and Control Act prohibits employers from hiring illegal aliens and fines them heavily for doing so.
7. The unemployment rate is not high in most places, although teenage unemployment, especially for black teenagers, remains high.
8. Last, but not least, is the negative view some people have of working in a hospitality position.

In the restaurant business, about half of all separations—such as resignation or termination—occur within the first thirty days. Nation ally, the Bureau of National Affairs reports for 1987 that half of all types of employees left their jobs in the first year.

Turnover is high in the hospitality industry, and with that comes certain costs. Hiring an unskilled hourly employee who does not work out may cost between $400 and $1,500 per employee, or typically up to about one month's pay. In two surveys of hotels, the cost of hiring and training non managerial employees was between $1,100 to $1,500 each. These figures can go up to $2,0,00 to $3,000 for skilled employees such as line cooks and servers. This basically covers the expenses for recruiting and selecting a new candidate, doing all the necessary paperwork for the new employee such as payroll and benefit records, training the worker, and covering overtime costs incurred while the position is vacant, as well as any severance pay.

It often takes at least five weeks for a position to be filled when taking into account getting the paperwork done, recruiting, interviewing, selecting, and then giving the new employee time to leave the former job and be trained for the new one.

The cost of filling positions can go higher the longer the position goes unfilled and the more skill and training are required. And worse than the dollar cost incurred is how high turnover tends to lower both employee morale and quality of service and to cause stress for managers. Unmanaged turnover can cause a significant loss of customers.

Turnover can occur due to either voluntary or involuntary reasons. When an employee leaves a job voluntarily, it may be a blessing, if the worker created problems, or a misfortune, if he or she was a good worker.

Good employees might be leaving to make more money elsewhere or to get what they think will be a more interesting and challenging job, perhaps in a better working environment. In many cases, through good selection processes and management, ways can be found to keep desirable employees. Problem employees might also be indicative of poor management procedures, in that frequently they prove to have been hired due to poor selection procedures. Employees also leave jobs involuntarily, due to termination or layoff. Termination, too, can usually be traced to poor selection procedures. Causes of turnover, therefore, may include poor employee selection, wages that are not competitive, few opportunities for advancement, inadequate orientation and training, poor supervision, and unfavourable working environment.

Industry approaches to the labour shortage

In order to attract more employees and hold onto them—a decrease in turnover referred to as *retention*—employers are offering better advancement opportunities, higher starting wages, more orientation and training, regular job evaluation, flexible schedules, transportation to work, improved benefits, child care assistance, greater employee involvement in operations, recognition programs, and profit sharing or stock option purchase plans. Other methods being used to reduce turnover include good communication of rules and regulations to employees, accurate job descriptions (listing of job tasks) and job specifications (listing of worker requirements), a process for resolving employee complaints, cross-training or training employees to do more than one job, and effective supervision.

Hospitality operators should conduct *exit interviews* when employees leave, to help determine the reasons for turnover. Be aware, however, that employees are not always honest about why they are leaving a job; they may state they are leaving for a better job, for example, when in reality they are having problems with their supervisor.

In addition, some operators are redesigning their facilities and jobs to require less labour. For instance, Dunkin Donuts is emphasizing drive-through instead of sit-down service. Also one fast-food operator is using an automated beverage dispenser that does everything but put lids on the cups. Another fast-food chain is testing a device by which customers enter their own orders at a computer terminal. In the end, however, finding and retaining good employees is crucial.

Recruitment

Recruitment refers to the search for individuals from both inside and outside an organization in sufficient numbers and with appropriate qualifications to apply for the jobs that need to be filled. Keep in mind that in the 1990's most of the growth in the labour force will consist of females and minorities.

In an organization large enough to have its own human resource department, a human resource manager will usually assist by having hopefuls fill out application forms, by advertising for positions, and by posting vacant positions in-house.

In the case of a human resource department, the recruiting process is typically started with the hospitality manager filling out and forwarding to it—with the appropriate approvals—an *employment requisition* form; this is much like a purchase order and functions as a control mechanism to make sure managers are filling approved positions. Many organizations have a policy of *promoting from within*, also referred to as internal recruiting, whenever possible. This policy has the advantage of rewarding and motivating employees, giving them something to work toward. At times, though, it may be wiser to hire people from the outside who have new ideas and a different perspective.

Many employers post vacant positions, meaning that openings are listed in designated locations, such as a bulletin board outside the human resource department. Some companies maintain on computer a complete record of qualifications of every employee so that when a position becomes vacant, the human resource manager can obtain a list of people within the company who could fill the position.

For companies looking outside the organization, there is a wide variety of recruitment methods and sources, including the following:

— Advertising

— In-house publicity

— Employee referrals

— Walk-ins and unsolicited applications

— High schools, vocational-technical schools, colleges and universities

— Job fairs

— Various organizations, agencies, and associations such as those for senior citizens, women, the handicapped, veterans, minorities, and local businesses

— Professional and trade organizations and societies (national, state, and local)

— Branches of the military

— Federal government (veteran and youth training programs)

— State employment service or job service center

— Private Industry Council

— Private employment agencies

— Temporary agencies

— Leasing companies

— Prisons (work-release programs)

— Vendor referrals

— Labour unions (if unionized)

Advertising to fill job openings is often placed in newspapers, usually on Sunday, but also can be done through television, local cable, radio, and professional organizations' publications.

Domino's Pizza ran a well-received recruitment advertisement on television, featuring a model store in Plexiglas, upbeat music, and neon signs flashing messages such as "Earn Cash"—all, of course, targeted to young people. Due to the high cost of advertising and the need for it to be impressive and effective, some operators hire agencies with expertise in recruitment advertising.

When choosing a newspaper, it is important to examine and compare the area where it is distributed, its circulation, characteristics of the readership, and advertising rates. The ad itself should include basic information such as the position title, company name, and location of job. Information to help sell the job includes competitive pay, a complete benefits package, free meals, flexible work hours, or the opportunity for advancement. Be sure to do the following in any advertising: use a company logo when possible, be specific about how people should apply, keep files of all advertising and how many applicants responded to each one, and avoid wording that refers to one sex only, such as busboy or waitress.

In three studies of newspaper recruiting advertisements by Kohl and Stephens in 1984, 1985, and

1986, hospitality firms (along with trade companies) had the highest percentages of questionable or illegal advertisements. Most were discriminatory in using gender-specific references, such as waiter, busboy, maid, or host. Preferable terms would be server, bus help, housekeeper, and host or hostess. Jobs can be publicized in many other ways. An in-house publicity program can include a message on place mats, receipts, table tents, and outdoor signs. Notices also can be posted in health clubs, supermarkets, churches, and community centers. Job fairs can be held on or off the company's premises to attract interested possible applicants.

Tours can also be offered to potential employees. Employee referral programs, in which a current employee refers an applicant to the company, are used very successfully by some operators to draw in new workers. Good employees often bring in talented applicants; likewise, poor employees often refer poor applicants.

The employee who made the referral is rewarded with a cash bonus or some other type of incentive. When implementing such a program, it is important to include all employees, ask them to fill out a referral or recommendation form, require the referred applicants to undergo and pass the normal selection procedures, and set a period of time for the new employee to work before the other employee receives the entire or partial reward. Rewards vary from a 10-cent hourly raise to a $250 cash bonus, radios, tickets to sports events, or points toward merchandise.

The rewards are often given when the new employee completes the time requirement but are sometimes provided in installments. The program may be limited to certain positions and time periods. Employees can also be recruited through nepotism, which refers to hiring relatives of an existing employee. Operations may have policies that either allow this practice or discourage it. Some employers allow relatives to be hired but require them to work in a separate area or department from other relatives. Educational institutions are an excellent source of potential employees. Many hospitality operators have work-study, co-op, and internship program arrangements with various colleges and other schools.

Many also recruit at and send job notices to a school's placement office. Operators can publicize their job openings through career days at local high schools, guest lectures, and posters. Advertising can be done on college campuses through school newspapers, sporting events, or bag stuffers at the bookstore. Many organizations, associations, and agencies can be a source of potential applicants. Some operators recently have made a lot of effort to attract applicants from women's, senior citizens', handicapped, veteran, minority, fraternal, and business groups, and there are many others.

Women's groups include Displaced Homemaker organizations, the National Organization of Women and Weight Watchers, which is predominantly female in membership. Senior citizens' organizations include the American Association for Retired Persons; names of other groups can be obtained through the local Chamber of Commerce or Office on Aging. Sources of handicapped workers include state rehabilitation agencies, job service centers, and nonprofit organizations such as Easter Seals and Goodwill Industries. Sources of veterans include the Veterans Administration and the local Veterans of Foreign Wars and American Legion. Organizations such as the Urban League and state job services are sources of minority employees.

Fraternal organizations include the Elks, Girt and Boy Scouts, and church groups. An excellent business group to contact for information on applicants is the local

Chamber of Commerce. It is to a hospitality manager's advantage to network with local businesspeople who may be able to help with recruitment and other problems. Among these groups, hiring retirees is becoming more common, as seen in a McDonald's television commercial. In their McMasters program, McDonald's offers jobs and training to persons older than fifty-five.

The over-sixty-five group will increase to 20 percent of the population in 2020 from 12 percent in 1987. Retirees tend to be loyal, dependable, and service-oriented, but they also tend to need more time off due to illness, work more slowly, and require more training. Most want to work part-time not so much for the money as for the socializing. Because most are receiving Social Security benefits, they do not want to work too many hours and earn too much money; otherwise they would have to pay some money back to Social Security. According to the Vocational Rehabilitation Administration in Washington, D.C., approximately 18,000 people with disabilities are currently working in foodservice. There are many more who are able and willing to work in food service but can't find employment.

Although often they take longer to train and their productivity is lower, handicapped employees tend to be dedicated, hardworking, and reliable individuals who stay with their jobs. Other sources of information for recruiting include government agencies. The U.S. Department of Labour can be contacted about specific employment and training programs. State employment services are involved in recruiting, testing, and training unemployed people so they can return to work; state agencies also maintain a job bank, or list of open jobs, in their local offices so employers can register jobs with them. The Private Industry Council administers many government-funded services and programs on a local level; businesses often contribute money toward worthy projects such as job training. City and county governments also sometimes set up job placement assistance programs. Private employment agencies, in a contingency search, charge a fee to the employer, which the agency does not collect until they place an applicant. Often, if a newly placed employee leaves the job during a specified period of time, referred to as the guarantee period, the agency must find a suitable replacement or return the fee. Usually the amount of the fee is based on a percentage of the employee's salary, although fees are often negotiable.

Private agencies prefer to be used exclusively during a job search; however, if they are not providing good results, it is best to ask another agency for applicants as well. Often a private agency will advertise for the company. Temporary agencies can provide hospitality employees who will stay for as little as one day, or as long as they are needed. The agencies charge by the hour. Although their hourly rates range from 50 to 150 percent higher than a typical salary for the position, this can be offset by not paying this employee any benefits. The higher rate also covers the agency's overhead and profit. There are a small number of temporary agencies specializing in filling positions for hotels, restaurants, and caterers.

Temporary agencies seem most able to fill seasonal and emergency fill-in personnel and entry-level utility workers. When evaluating temporary agencies, find out how the agency selects and trains employees, if the employees are bonded and covered by liability insurance and workers' compensation, and if there is a money-back policy if an employee does not work out. Leasing companies are a new concept being used as a source of employees on a more long-term basis than temporary agencies. Typically these companies hire employees who are trained and leased to the hospitality operator. The leasing company essentially acts as the human resource department for the operator, takes over the function of staffing and payroll, and charges a monthly service fee for the leasing service.

One Chicago leasing company reports saving restaurants about two percent of their gross payroll. Employees generally like to work for leasing companies because they frequently offer better benefits and more variety in work settings. Another source of employees—not always considered—is the prison system. For instance, a major airline and a hotel chain both use inmates to handle reservations.

Other methods, such as setting up industries in prisons and placing offenders in the community with a job, are being used to respond to the rising prison population and the increasing financial burden this causes. Not all convicts are hardened criminals, and many are looking for jobs in order to begin reentering society. Some ex-prisoners have useful work skills, including some learned while in prison, and want to hold onto a job.

A poll taken by the Florida Prison Industries Placement Service showed much greater employer receptiveness to the idea of hiring ex-offenders than popular opinion might suggest. Most problems that might occur due to hiring ex-offenders can be resolved by using good hiring and record-keeping practices and providing proficient and fair supervision.

Selection

The selection process involves matching the right person to the right job. Two documents crucial to selection are the *job* specification and job description. Applicants should be matched with the requirements listed in the job specification, and their knowledge, skills, and abilities matched with the tasks detailed in the job description. Good selection practices increase organizational productivity, decrease turnover and replacement costs, and increase job satisfaction. Steps in selection typically include getting potential employees to complete an application form, screening applications, interviewing, conducting preemployment testing, and making background checks. Once these steps are performed, a selection decision can be made.

Interviewing

Purposes for an interview include reviewing and verifying education and prior work history, asking for additional information of knowledge and skills, observing poise and communication skills, drawing out character traits and motivations, and informing the applicant more fully about the job and the organization. Interviewing is a skill that requires practice. Before interviewing, preparation is needed.

Review the application once again in order to jot down any specific questions for the applicant. Also review the job description, job specification, wages, and benefits. A prepared list of general questions for applicants can be helpful and lends consistency to the process. Select a quiet place that will be private and without distractions or interruptions during the interview. Alert anyone else who will be involved in the interview process.

The interviewer should always start the interview on time, greet the applicant warmly by name, and introduce himself or herself by name and title. A seating arrangement that does not put a desk or table between interviewer and applicant is also conducive to developing rapport. At this point, it is a good idea to describe what will occur during the interview, such as discussing the applicant's qualifications, the nature of the job, and the company and answering questions. To conduct the actual interview, it is important first to understand the types of questions that can be asked. Open questions require the applicant to discuss something about himself or herself.

On the other hand, closed questions can be answered with a yes or no. Direct questions can be answered with a specific piece of information. Reflective questions restate what the applicant said in order to gain more clarification. Probing questions seek more information. Situational questions ask what the applicant has done in certain circumstances in the past or would do in hypothetical situations.

Loaded, or leading, questions give the desired answer to the applicant; they should be avoided. Depending on the type of information desired, different types of questions can be appropriate. To learn the most about an applicant, open, reflective, probing, and situational questions should be emphasized. To save time and avoid discrimination, standardize the types of questions asked for a particular job, and be sure to base questions on job duties and requirements. During the interview, information is gathered about the applicant's background, and qualifications, the job is fully explained, and often a tour of the work area takes place.

The applicant should be made fully aware of job tasks and responsibilities, work hours, overtime requirements, policies and procedures, wages and benefits, company history and structure, and any probationary period. Both the applicant's suitability and his or her desire to perform the job within all its constraints need to be assessed during the interview. In closing the interview, there should be time for the applicant to ask any further questions. At the same time, the applicant should be asked for any feelings about the job, and told when a decision will be made and how he or she will be notified.

Tips for interviewing include the following:

1. Be nonjudgmental during the entire interview process. Accept what is said and don't jump to conclusions. A poor interviewer reaches a decision in the first five minutes.
2. Recognize any personal biases and try not to let them be influential. Do not look for clones of oneself, and do not look for the same kind of person for all jobs.
3. Spend most of the time listening.
4. Listen for clues to the applicant's needs, wants, and motivating factors.
5. Make notes openly so that vital information is not forgotten.
6. Repeat or paraphrase the applicant's statements to attain better understanding.
7. Use pauses to allow the applicant to open up.
8. Respond to what the applicant is conveying through words and body language.
9. Paint a realistic picture of the job. Be honest. Make no promises that cannot be kept. Provide information freely.
10. Avoid halo error, which is when the interviewer judges an applicant favourably due to only one strong characteristic. The opposite of this can be called horns error, in which the applicant is rated poorly due to one weak point

Preemployment testing

Preemployment testing covers a wide variety of testing devices that are used to help select the best candidate for the job. Psychological, performance, and intelligence tests are some examples. All tests must meet guidelines for nondiscrimination according to the EEO Uniform Guidelines on Employee Selection Procedures. Tests must be related to successful performance on the job—in other words, valid—and yield consistent results—in other words, reliable.

Tests are available that are either commercially made or custom-made. Each needs to be evaluated in terms of legality, cost, time to administer, and corporate policy. Most psychological tests are paper-and-pencil tests designed to measure aspects of personality that affect performance. They include attitude, honesty, and personality tests. The former measure attitudes, feelings, and beliefs. Honesty tests are the most commonly used psychological tests. They are paper-and-pencil tests used to locate high-risk applicants for positions in which dishonesty would be damaging to the organization, particularly in which dishonesty would be hard to detect. They are relatively inexpensive, not offensive to candidates, and quick to administer.

One example is the Reid Honesty Test, which is a four-part paper-and-pencil test requiring forty-five minutes. It asks questions about personal honesty, drug use, and attitudes toward punishment of theft. Personality tests, such as the Minnesota Multiphasic Inventory, are designed to reveal psychological characteristics felt relevant to a particular job. Different tests focus on psychological characteristics such as emotional stability or ability to handle stress. The London House Corporation has designed a paper-and-pencil test for hourly employees; referred to as the personnel selection inventory, it is available in ten different test forms. It tests for some of the following: honesty, drug avoidance, customer relations attitudes, emotional stability, safety, employability index, and detailed personal and behavioural history. It costs under twenty dollars to administer and can be completed in less than an hour.

The test meets the Uniform Guidelines of Employee Selection Procedures regarding the construction and validation of psychological tests. Performance tests require candidates to perform part of the job for which they have applied. For example, an applicant for a cooking position may be asked to prepare a given recipe; a front-of-the-house employee in a restaurant may be asked to set a table after being shown how it is to be done. At the end of 1988, the Polygraph Protection Act took effect the intent of this law was to forbid the use of a *polygraph*, or lie detector, to screen job applicants, a practice some hospitality operators previously used.

The lie detector can still be used to investigate theft, if there is reasonable suspicion and advance notice is given. A last form of testing some employers use involves medical examinations. State or local agencies may require them for food handlers, and many health care institutions require them for all new employees in the foodservice department. Some medical exams include drug testing, usually through urinalysis. Drug testing is probably the most controversial preemployment test. Some states have laws regulating its use, but generally the courts have upheld drug testing.

Selection decision

Once information is compiled on various candidates for a job, it must all be evaluated in order to determine whom to hire. Some managers evaluate candidates by examining what is referred to as *can-do* and *will-do* factors. Can-do factors are covered in the job specification or requirement form. Job specifications spell out the knowledge, skills, aptitudes, and work history considered important to successful job performance. Will-do factors include motivation, work interests, and personal characteristics. In the hospitality industry, for example, the latter might include the ability to communicate with guests and work under pressure. In many entry-level hospitality jobs, the candidates can do the job but lack the motivation or interest required so that they will do it very well. A written evaluation of each applicant should be written to help ensure that each person was given fair and equal consideration. If the selection process is neglected and employers make a practice of just hiring "warm bodies," they are leaving themselves open to being sued for *negligent hiring,* in addition to previously mentioned undesirable results such as high turnover rates and poor-quality products and services. In the past ten years, lawsuits for negligent hiring have increased tremendously.

The employer has the duty of due care, which means taking reasonable and appropriate precautions to avoid hiring and retaining employees who might harm other workers or the public as in assault and battery. To avoid liability for negligent hiring, the employer can do the following:

1. Conduct a thorough background check of job candidates. Verify employment, education, and residential background. Also require veterans to provide a copy of their DD214 form, which shows an honourable discharge.

2. Check out gaps in employment and short residency periods.

3. Examine state laws on hiring candidates with criminal records. Check for a criminal record if felt to be needed.

4. When checking out work references, ask about problem behaviour such as excessive absenteeism and lateness, lying, violence, inability to get along with others, and drug or alcohol abuse.

Once the candidate is selected, the person must be notified and a job offer extended. This is typically the responsibility of the human resource department, which should confirm the job title, working arrangements, wages, and starting date with the selected candidate. The person is also normally asked to make a decision within a certain period of time. If there is no human resource department, it is preferable for the manager supervising the new employee to make the offer.

Training

Training requires a time commitment, which is tough to find in a business with so much time pressure. So if someone does not find the time for training, what happens? Managers will lose control over some very important aspects of their business, such as work methods, quality control, quality service, and performance standards. In other words, the housekeepers might all clean the rooms differently, the cooks might each provide different-sized portions for the same menu item, and the guests might not be welcomed quickly or treated very well. Therefore, the need for training, learning, and coaching is clear.

Training means to instruct and guide the development of a trainee toward acquiring knowledge, behaviour (skills), and attitudes to meet a specific need. Most training in the hospitality industry is centered around orientation, job skills, and attitude development for both new and current managers, supervisors, and hourly employees. The overall goal of training is to bring about a desired level of work performance.

Learning refers to knowledge the trainee gains through observation and study, resulting in a change in behaviour or attitude. Coaching reinforces the learning acquired in training and is usually done on the job. It is important to examine why training is important, how adults learn best, and how to develop a training program, as well as keys to excellent training programs and resources.

Training has a variety of objectives:

— Orienting new employees to the organization and their jobs

— Helping employees perform their current jobs well

— Helping employees qualify for future jobs

— Keeping employees informed of changes within an organization

— Providing opportunities for personal development

Training increases productivity because employees do their jobs more efficiently. Now management can spend more time planning and organizing and less time putting out fires. With good training programs, there are fewer errors or problems such as accidents, which are counterproductive. Instead, the quality of both products and services is more consistent. Costs also are lower, due to less waste, fewer accidents, less breakage, and so on. Both employees and guests end up more satisfied due to training. If employees are doing their jobs well, the guests know that, which decreases complaints and also makes them more likely to return.

Employees are more confident and proud of what they are doing and make fewer mistakes. They are more likely to feel they belong to the organization—in other words, loyal—which can translate into lower absenteeism and turnover rates and lower recruiting and training costs. In essence, training gives the employee a dual message: "You are important to this organization, and we care about how you do your job."

How adults learn best

Many tips and tricks for teaching adults are derived from research and *adult learning theory*. They can be categorized into three areas: the motivation of adult learners, the design of training programs for adults, and classroom work with adults.

Motivation:

— Adults can't be forced to learn,

— Learning is not its own reward; most adults seek out learning because they have a use for the knowledge or skill being sought.

— Adults pursue learning experiences in order to cope with life-changing events such as a promotion, termination, or move to a new city.

Training programs:

— Material for learning should be relevant, realistic, and practical. Adults prefer a straightforward, how-to style of teaching,

— Adults come to the classroom with much prior experience, so they need to integrate new ideas with what they already know. Information that differs radically from what they already know will be integrated more slowly, as the old information has to be reevaluated.

— Adults like to know what the purpose of the training is and how it will benefit them.

— Adults learn best when given the big picture first. Next the material should be split up into small doses, going from simple to complex.

— Adults generally like to participate in training and to practice new skills.

— Adults learn best using different teaching methods and audiovisual or visual aids.

— Material should be presented at a speed that permits mastery.

— Being very self-conscious of errors, adults tend to take fewer risks in training sessions. They also do not like to compete with one another.

— Adults prefer self-directed learning over group learning led by a professional. The self-directed learning is not necessarily isolated and still includes contact with people.

— The adult learner should be involved in the development of training programs in order to make the programs more acceptable to them.

Classroom:

— The learning environment must be comfortable, informal, quiet and without interruptions, and well lighted; surroundings should be pleasant.

— Adults have much life experience, which can be tapped in the classroom to add to the class.

— Adults need to be treated as adults in training.

— Classes should not be too long-fifteen to thirty minutes is adequate in most cases.

— Repetition and feedback such as praise are two valuable tools in the classroom.

Although these tips can't be universally applied to all adults and all training situations, they are true in the majority of cases.

Orientation

Orientation is a specific type of training designed for new employees. Its purposes are to make new employees knowledgeable about their new job and at the same time give them a feeling of belonging to a competent organization where procedures and standards are important. If a new employee starts and is asked to begin working with another employee immediately without any formal orientation, the new employee is likely to feel somewhat confused and bewildered.

When a manager takes the time to greet new employees and go through orientation procedures, it gives the employee the message that both he or she and the job are important. The following topics should be discussed during orientation:

— The history, organization, and objectives or philosophy of the company

— Policies and procedures such as dress code, conduct, work schedule and breaks, tips, and parking

— Performance specifics, including job description, detailed position description, performance standards, and performance evaluation

— Training programs

— Disciplinary procedures

— Pay and benefits

— Immediate training concerns-for example, sanitation and safety

The orientation session itself should be held preferably on the employee's first day of work. Depending on its length, it may be split into two or more sessions. The new employee should not be overloaded with too much information at once. Either the employee's supervisor or another manager can conduct the session. The best way to cover the needed information is to devise and use an orientation checklist of all the topics to be covered. Another feature of the checklist is that upon completion of orientation, it should be signed by both parties. The checklist then becomes documentation that the employee was oriented to the new job.

Upon completion of part or all of the listed items, the employee should be taken on a tour of the facility and introduced to other employees. It is important for a manager who takes a new employee around to meet others not to express any opinions about anyone. This is unfair to new employees, who need to form their own opinions.

Once the orientation process is completed, the employee should receive an orientation packet, which is basically written information about everything covered during orientation. It should include benefit forms and literature, the job description, a listing of performance standards, an evaluation form, a work schedule, information on company holidays, an organization chart, a listing of pertinent policies and procedures, material on sanitation and safety basics, a union contract (if applicable), and a map of the facility and parking lots.

Conducting a needs assessment

The first step in developing a training program is to make a *needs assessment,* or determination of what training is needed. Training programs should be designed both to orient new employees and to train them to perform any job. This second type is referred to as job skills training, which can also be used to retrain current employees when it is found, for instance, that the quality of service has decreased. Evidence that training is needed includes unhappy guests or employees, low productivity, low sales, high costs, poor product quality such as unappetizing food, or a high accident rate.

Techniques that are used in needs assessment include observing performance and comparing it to previously established standards, checking key indicators such as the evidence noted above, or surveying employees and managers as to where more training is needed.

Developing the overall training program

Once the broad objectives for the training program are determined, the following need to be identified: the specific content matter, how much is to be taught at a time, and when, where, and to whom it will be taught. Costs must also be considered during this process.

The first step in a job skills training program is to analyse the job, if this has not already been done. Each task or distinct work activity needs to be identified, and its procedures and rationale explained. This then becomes the content of the training program, which very often is derived from established policies and procedures within the organization. If developing a training program on sanitation and safety, for instance, the manager may wish to consult several books on these topics, in addition to looking up any relevant policies and procedures. Determining how much to teach at a time and when to teach it depends on many factors. Employees should not be inundated with too much information in any training situation, either on the job or in the classroom.

Classroom training sessions lasting from fifteen to thirty minutes are generally in order, and should be arranged when employees can afford to leave their work location without undue concern about their job not being done. If this is never really possible, training can be done at the beginning or end of a shift or another time; other employees can also be scheduled in advance to cover the positions of employees who need to attend training sessions. When deciding where to hold the training, consider whether the work location or a classroom environment would be best. It is also necessary to decide which group of employees to target for the training-in other words, for which employees the training will be relevant.

Developing individual training lessons

By this point the objectives and content are detailed for each training lesson. Teaching methods, audiovisual aids, and a trainer are still needed. Audiovisual aids have sound and visual characteristics that make teaching and learning easier. They include films, slides, slide tapes, flip charts, transparencies, boards, simulators, and videotapes. Audiovisual hardware is the equipment used in presentations, such as a slide projector. Audiovisual software, also referred to as off-the-shelf training programs, run through the hardware. When choosing audiovisual software, consider such factors as cost, availability of the hardware, durability, portability, and ease of use.

Also consider that in order to be effective, visual presentations should be simple, concise, uncluttered, relevant, realistic, colourful, easy to read, and accurate; pictures should be used to supplement words. Whereas content represents what training is meant to convey, teaching methods involve how the content will be conveyed to the employee successfully; in other words, it changes behaviour or attitudes or both. The selection of an appropriate teaching method is crucial to the success of a training program. Probably the most common teaching method used for employees is what is commonly referred to as *on-the-job training* (OJT). With this method, the new employee works with a peer or a manager or supervisor on the actual job. *OJT* is of little use if the employee is put with someone who either can't or doesn't want to train a new person or if the structure of the training is loose. Although this method has the potential to provide good hands-on experience, it has been badly abused in what has been referred to as the "buddy system." What happens here is that the job takes priority, so that the trainee may not get much explanation of what to do and also may spend too much time doing menial jobs Without any significance, such as running for supplies.

OJT can work well when certain conditions are met. First, the trainer must be Willing and able to train a new employee. Next, the training should be structured with specific tasks to be accomplished within certain time frames. Procedures, along With their rationale and performance standards, should be taught and the trainee allowed to do parts of the job of the trainer, when ready.

Table 1

Teaching methods as related to level of learner participation

Level of Learner Participation	Method
Learners listen and watch	Lectures, demonstrations
Learners listen, watch, and read	Programmed instruction
Learners listen, watch, read, move, write, or respond	Structured discussions, behaviour modelling
Learners manipulate	Performance tryout
Learners make decisions	Brainstorming, case discussions, role playing, simulations, games

The trainee should be frequently questioned for understanding and trained off the job as well for the best results. Other teaching methods are described below. Most are used with groups, but many can also be used in one-on-one training.

The methods vary in terms of how much the employees can participate. Participatory techniques are good to use with topics that are open to discussion and analysis, or when teaching new skills that can be demonstrated and practiced. When using any technique in which employees are asked to discuss and analyse chosen topics, the group members must be ready and willing to participate and the trainer must be skilled in group dynamics. In the lecture method, the trainer does all the talking, making for a relatively passive and unstimulating experience for employees unless the trainer has exceptional presentation skills. While providing much information quickly, it does not encourage retention.

Lecturing is a good method to get basic information across to a large number of people. This method is better when combined with teaching aids, questioning of both trainer and employees, and structured discussion. With demonstrations, the trainer shows one or more trainees how to perform a specific skill, such as checking in a hotel guest or starting the dishwasher. It is suitable for learning many procedures and skills. Demonstrations typically are followed by performance tryouts, during which the employees get to practice the skills demonstrated. These methods work best when the skills are presented one step at a time and the employees practice after each step. This method is excellent at getting employee involvement, but requires some time to do properly. A traditional approach to training developed during World War II uses the three methods discussed up to this point. The combined method has four steps: tell (lecture), show (demonstration), do (performance tryout), and review. It is an excellent method to teach new skills. It is also used to learn new behaviour, under the name *behaviour modelling. The* first step in behaviour modelling is to explain the behaviour needed to perform a task, such as how to deal with a complaint from a guest.

Next, the trainer may demonstrate the desired behaviour or use a medium such as video to do so. The employees are then asked to practice the procedure, and they receive feedback on their attempts. Behaviour modelling is an excellent method for employees to try out new behaviour in a safe environment. This method requires some time investment as well as a skilled trainer to oversee it.

Programmed instruction uses a manual or teaching machine such as a computer, instead of a trainer, to present programmed material, or subject matter with organized, logical sequences that demand continuous responses on the part of the employees. After being given a small chunk of information, the employees must each answer a question, by either writing it down or pushing a button on the machine. If the answer is right, the employee continues to the next segment of information. If the response is wrong, the employee must try until he or she gets the answer right.

Programmed instruction is useful because it involves the employee, feedback is instant, and each employee can select his or her own pace. Structured discussions are conversations between employees aimed toward meeting specific predefined objectives. In a class on kitchen safety, for example, employees may be asked to split up into small groups and develop ideas on how to prevent common kitchen accidents such as bums, falls, and fires. These ideas are usually read back to the trainer, who writes them down for all to see. The trainer must be skilled at keeping the class on track.

Brainstorming is a form of discussion in which employees are asked to generate ideas spontaneously on a given topic without evaluating them. For example, a group of cooks may be asked to brainstorm ideas on how to save energy. Next, the group analyses the ideas and decides which ones they want to use to develop a plan of action.

Case discussions use case studies, or descriptions of real-life situations, which the employee or group studies, discusses, and answers questions about. For example, with a case study about an outbreak of food-borne illness, employees may be asked to determine what led to it. Case studies allow for analysis and application of information. As in brainstorming, there must be ample time for this method, and the trainer must be skilful in leading discussions. In role playing, employees simulate a specific real or hypothetical situation involving two or more people. In health care, for example, employees may reenact delivering the wrong meal to a sick patient. This technique can be used to examine current behaviour or try out new ones to build skill and confidence.

The role playing itself is usually followed by discussion and analysis. It also requires much time and a skilful trainer, particularly because adults often do not want to participate. Simulations duplicate a general real-life job situation. For instance, a simulation of a hotel front desk can be made, at which employees can practice their skills without causing any problems for actual guests. It is an excellent method, if a simulation model is available, to provide realistic job-related learning experiences. Games may be simulations that are made competitive. Games may also be like those for children—that is, they have a set of rules and a defined objective to meet. They may be designed for one person or for groups. Good games are hard to develop but are generally fun for employees.

A final method to be discussed is really not a separate method, but some hospitality people think it not only is one but also is the be-all and end-all of training: videotapes. Videotapes are an audiovisual aid that can be effective as a medium to help accomplish learning objectives. They are useful in demonstrating behaviour and dialogue as well as content that is hard to explain verbally. They are also useful in giving a consistent message within a large organization, such as a hotel chain with many different locations. They are not as useful when the material is very technical or thorough or if it is not appropriate for the employees' educational level and previous experience. Like any audiovisual aid, videotapes must be relevant and accurate in order to succeed. Home-made videotapes are not so well received, because employees will compare their quality to the better quality they see constantly on television.

Conducting the training

Selecting a trainer and training that person to do a good job may be difficult. Ideally a manager or supervisor is probably the best choice for training. In the case of on-the-job training, if a competent employee can train, it is advisable to compensate that person in some way, because the employee is being asked to take on another significant responsibility. Examples of rewards for trainers include pay increases, a bonus, a new title at a higher level, special privileges, or some mark of distinction, such as a pin.

Being a good trainer requires a variety of characteristics; the person should

— Knowledgeable
— Enthusiastic and interested
— Funny
— Clear and concise
— Responsive to employees
— Sincerely caring in attitude toward employees
— Patient
— A good role model
— Organized

— Able to put employees at ease
— Good at asking and answering employees
— Good in classroom management skills
— Good in reinforcement skills

All training sessions should be documented as to what was taught, who attended (confirmed with signatures), and date and time. A training record for each employee should also be maintained. These records are useful for monitoring an employee's performance and also as backup in employee discharge cases.

Evaluating

Making an *evaluation is* the crucial process of determining if training objectives were accomplished. It can occur both during and after the training. Formative evaluation uses observation, interviews, and surveys to monitor training while it is going on. Summative evaluation measures the results of the training after the program is completed, looking at it in five different ways:

1. *Reaction:* Did the employees like the program?
2. *Knowledge:* Did the employees learn the information taught?
3. *Behaviour:* Are the employees using the new skills or behaviour on the job?
4. *Attitudes:* Do the employees demonstrate any new attitudes?
5. *Productivity:* Did the training increase productivity, and was it cost-effective?

Various techniques can be used to answer these questions. Evaluation forms can be filled out anonymously by participants, to determine what they liked and did not like about the training. Tests are frequently given at the end of training sessions to determine if the employees know the information or skills covered.

For instance, a dishwasher may be asked the correct temperature for the final rinse and then asked to demonstrate how to pick up dishes without contaminating them. Results can also be measured through observation of employee behaviour and monitoring of critical indicators such as the number of guest complaints, level of repeat business, and so forth. Questionnaires can be used with both guests and employees to collect information. After collecting information from various sources using different techniques, the person doing the evaluation needs to compare the results to the learning objectives to determine if the training indeed succeeded in bringing about the desired changes.

Following up

Of all the steps in training, the follow-up is perhaps the most important. Unless there is follow-up to ensure that employees are using what they were taught, the expense and efforts made to train may be lost. Follow-up can be accomplished through *coaching,* which is a two-step process. First, job performance is analysed. Next, performance is reinforced or corrected face-to-face. Coaching is a continual process that checks the results of training and also the progress toward goals set in performance evaluation sessions. Following are some coaching tips:

1. Be a coach, not a drill sergeant. Don't stay constantly on employees' backs, watching or criticizing everything they do. The purpose of coaching is to help employees grow and improve their job performance. Being friendly and using praise does wonders.

2. When analysing someone's job performance, if there appear to be problems, find out the possible causes. Be sure to discuss the situation with the employee. Does the employee know-and understand clearly-what to do? Does the employee know his or her performance is not satisfactory? Ask the employee questions, preferably open-ended, in an' effort to help, not punish.

3. When job performance is found to be in need of correction, first get an agreement with the employee that a problem exists. Next, discuss together some possible solutions and mutually agree on action to correct the concern. Follow-up is of course necessary. Recognize achievement.

4. Listen to the employee during the coaching session. Be supportive and helpful.

5. Correct errors promptly and in private. Employees are very sensitive about being told in front of their peers that they are doing something wrong. Unless the error could have grave consequences, wait at least to pull the employee aside long enough to tell him or her how to correct it.

6. Recognize when someone has reached his or her potential.

Managerial and supervisory training

Training for managers and supervisors follows the general guidelines discussed up to this point. Some additional methods of training are used for these people. They include job rotation, self-study, special projects and assignments, and mentors. Often a hotel or foodservice company will begin a new manager by training the person to work in all areas or departments. This is referred to as job rotation.

Self-study might include correspondence courses. Special projects and assignments are non-routine tasks that expose the person to new areas. A mentor is someone who develops another individual and assists that person in a career within the organization, mentors serve as role models and teach, guide, coach, and counsel their subordinates. In this manner, mentors help an organization by having skilled and knowledgeable subordinates.

The mentor also benefits by receiving admiration and seeing his or her managerial methods used. There are no formalized systems for mentors in the industry except for apprenticeships for culinary professionals. In a survey sent to two hundred general managers in hotels, approximately two-thirds of respondents reported having had a mentor.

The study showed that general managers who had mentors progressed faster in their careers than those who didn't. It was reported that mentors helped subordinates feel confident and provided guidance about career moves. In another survey of foodservices, including those within hotels, it was found that the average length of managerial training was thirteen weeks. The most popular teaching method used was on-the-job training. Management training cost an average of $1,250 per week. Domino's Pizza operates 3,800 stores within and outside the United States. Franchisees own about 70 percent of all Domino's outlets. Training at Domino's is decentralized in structure and responsibility. There are regional training centers, which are used for its manager-in -training programs; about 85 percent of all training for employees is OJT. Thirteen regional training directors train supervisors, who each oversee six to eight stores. Supervisors then train store managers, which takes about ten months, and the latter then train their employees.

There are five distinct employee jobs at each store, and employees are cross-trained to handle all of them-phone answerer, pizza maker, oven tender, router, and driver. Each store has a videocassette recorder, and for a minimal cost any of fourteen video training packages on subjects such as orientation, delivery, and pizza making can be bought. Managers are taught to use the "tell, show, do, review" approach in training employees. Domino's also uses visually appealing posters with work-related tips, posted in appropriate Places. Near the oven, for example, is a poster showing the perfect pepperoni pizza, which serves as a useful reminder to the oven tender. Domino's franchisees can either send their managers to regional training centers or do all the training themselves, but all trainers must be certified by Domino's. In order to teach the manager-in-training program, the trainer must attend a course on how to teach the classes and then actually teach them before receiving certification.

After certification, the trainer is continually monitored, and certification will be-and has been-taken away if standards are not being met. Most franchise contracts in the industry require the franchisor to provide a certain level of training before a new franchise opens. This is often supplemented with regional meetings and national conferences once or twice a year.

Keys to excellent training programs

Employees need incentives to learn new skills-or anything else. The incentive could be simple praise or recognition, for example by giving the employee a certificate or pin, or could include a pay increase, job title change, or better benefits. Training programs need to be planned in advance. This can help in terms of allowing enough time for the program and getting support for it. Trainers need to be carefully selected and taught to train effectively.

Top corporate management must support training programs, which, after all, better enable employees to absorb the mission and guest-service philosophy of the organization. Top management can support programs by helping to find the time, money, and expertise to get them going. Likewise, managers and supervisors need to reinforce what was learned in training, after employees return to their work stations, and they need to create a motivating work climate. Managers also need to be good role models, by being enthusiastic, competent, calm, organized, consistent, fair, visible, and respectful of guests, employees, and peers.

Hospitality industry training resources

Many resources are available to help someone who is setting out to develop a training program. It is a waste of money to develop a training program and related materials from scratch if something already exists that may be adaptable to the person's specific needs. Following is a list of resources-places, people, and materials-that may be helpful:

1. Local colleges, universities, and vocational-technical schools that have a foodservice or culinary curriculum; they typically provide credit and noncredit courses in many areas such as business, management, supervising, training, and foodservice topics. Faculty members and graduate students can also help in developing and implementing training programs.

2. Industry associations such as the Educational Institute of the American Hotel and Motel Association (AHMA), the Educational Foundation of the National Restaurant Association (NRA), and the American Management Association, which offer a variety of seminars, correspondence courses, books, and training materials.

3. Professional training societies, such as the Council of Hotel and Restaurant Trainers (CHART) and the American Society for Training and Development (ASTD).
4. The local Red Cross and police and fire departments.
5. State and local health departments, which can be valuable resources for sanitation and safety programs.
6. Sales representatives of food products, supplies, and equipment; they may have training materials available.
7. Training consultants; ask the local branch of the AIIMA or NRA for information.
8. Packaged training programs, which are available from a variety of vendors including the AHMA and NRA.

Most training in the hospitality industry is centered around orientation, job skills and attitude development for both new and current managerial, supervisory and hourly employees.

4
Human Resource Management

Management policies must then have a style and content that suits the needs of a stable workforce. While it is easy to imagine the relationship between job satisfaction and labour turnover, the relationship between job satisfaction and commitment is more complex and is, in some respects, rather surprising. One would expect labour turnover to decline as job satisfaction and commitment increase.

However, what is the direction of influence between job satisfaction and commitment? If an employee is more satisfied are they also more committed or does commitment cause satisfaction? To understand the relationship between this trio of concepts it is necessary to start with one behavioural aspect, that of people leaving. Whether they leave or stay does act as an indicator of both job satisfaction and commitment. However, the key to this matter is the pivotal concept of job satisfaction. It is pivotal because it will be shown that both labour turnover and commitment are dependent upon it. If a new perspective is taken on job satisfaction, one which is not concerned with questions of what motivates, then the role of job satisfaction becomes clearer. The new perspective is to see it as a process, not just as content which gratifies needs.

Job satisfaction as a process

Motivation theory shows us what elements of employment and work can motivate. In motivational theory, individual differences between people and changes within the same person in different circumstances and over time are explained by different levels of individual need and changes in those needs. What has to be explained is how changes come about. Accepting changes in personal need, how does the individual construe these changes? There must be a process at work here involving both personal needs and situational variables.

Note what is being said here, that job satisfaction is not just a matter of satisfying needs but also of making the social and physical environment work for them. Every individual makes his or her own satisfaction. The individual puts together their psychological and social needs with all the elements of the situation as they find it and produces a concept of job satisfaction of their own. In other words, job satisfaction is manufactured. Very much a bespoke creation.

The assumption is that, even if individuals are not rational or realistic, the situation imposes both on them. Whatever satisfaction there is to be had must lie in their objective situation. In other words, it is only their situation which can satisfy their actual needs. It cannot come from anywhere else. Even ambitions and dreams have their centre of gravity in the person's current situation. The expression 'Where do we go from here?' captures this notion of things being rooted in the reality of the present. This is not to say that everybody will be able to create an acceptable level of job satisfaction. For some the level of satisfaction created remains unsatisfactory, which may in turn lead to labour turnover.

There are five processes that enable people to create their own satisfaction. Each of them works through either changes of needs or are responses to stimuli from the work environment. The processes are:

— Information processing.

— Selecting particular attributes.

— Ordering attributes.

— Trade-offs.

— Reselection and reordering over time.

For the purposes of understanding these processes, it would be useful to work from a hypothetical example. An individual has some personal needs which relate to work. These needs are expressed in a range of job attributes which they look for in selecting a job and hope to find in the job. Not all attributes of a job are selected and those that are, exist in a rank order of some kind, for example, working in a stimulating group comes before pay which ranks above interesting tasks, etc. All very well, but how does it actually work?

As the sole source of satisfaction is the working environment, the individual takes in the information that is there, then reassesses their range and rank of favoured job attributes. No good wanting autonomy if the place runs on close supervision! What then happens when some of the favoured job attributes are not available in that particular environment? One solution is to leave, but another is to 'trade-off' the costs and benefits in order to get a 'working set of job attribute satisfiers'.

For example, the pay is poor but the boss is nice, the group is attractive even if the work is boring, etc. In this way, job satisfaction is manufactured by the individual. It must be said that if there are particular and intensely felt needs that are not available, then the most likely form of behaviour is to leave.

Commitment

Commitment is a conscious affirmation of loyalty to something or somebody. As commitment in secret is rather a redundant idea, the concept implies some form of behaviour which substantiates this state of loyalty. It may be as mundane as not leaving or something more affirmative such as extra motivation. A further complication comes with the focus of commitment. Within the work environment there are many potential targets:

— Job commitment.

— Tasks within a job.

— Occupational commitment.

— Career commitment.

— Organizational commitment.

— Work group attachment.

— Commitment to a profession.

It would be easy to fall into the trap of thinking that because the organization is the actual situation for all these types of commitment, they are all variations on the theme of organizational commitment. They are not. If the primary aim is to create organizational commitment, then loyalty to a task, an occupation, a profession, or to personal advancement, can run counter to the concept of the organization as the' emotional home and source of stimulus.

Organizational commitment

Definitions *abound, but* perhaps the clearest way to describe organizational commitment is to draw a picture of the behaviour that is likely to be found in an employee who is specifically committed to an organization. Beyond the obvious likelihood of punctuality, reliability and cooperativeness, three deeper aspects of commitment may be present and visible. These are:

1 Art emotional attachment to the aims and values of the organization. This attachment is often expressed through pride in the name of the company.

2 A willingness that goes beyond normative expectations.

3 Being prepared to push instrumentality into the background. Notice, pushing it away from performance but not abandoning it!

In a sense, commitment has one advantage for management over motivation, in that while motivation has to be demonstrated to be acknowledged, commitment actually has to be openly declared in some way by both parties. Commitment implies going public.

The definitions themselves, while various, are fairly coherent. Some emphasize the connection between organization and personality and between group and personality. For example:

> 'The willingness of social actors to give their energy and loyalty to social systems, the attachment of personality systems to social systems to social relations which are seen as self expressive.'

One element expressed in all the definitions is congruence, the process by which the goals of the organization and those of the individual become increasingly integrated or congruent. For example:

> 'A partisan, affective attachment to the goals and values of an organization, to one's role in relation to goals and values, and to the organization for its own sake apart from its purely instrumental worth.'

However, some writers recognize that the *instrumental worth* of an organization can never be dismissed.

A common theme that runs through the ideas on commitment is the concept of exchange, that is, giving energy and time in return for rewards. This brings together the basic ideas of motivation theory with ideas on work environment, in that people come to organizations with needs, desires and skills. If the organization provides the opportunity for abilities to be utilized and for some needs to be satisfied in a consistent and dependable way, then the possibility of commitment is enhanced. By contrast, when this is not the case, then the chance of achieving commitment is diminished. This idea of exchange not only reconfirms that the instrumental nature of employment is never far from the surface but also that it fits exactly into one of the key elements of the job satisfaction process - that of exchanging attributes. Here we have stumbled upon the link between job satisfaction and commitment.

The exchange idea must, in operation, be a judgement made after some time; for example: 'Let's take a rain check. I'm giving this much and I'm getting this back. Yes, it's worth committing, no it is not worth it.' The process of forming a judgement by summing up both sides of an equation is only possible through the job satisfaction process itself. In other words, only after manipulating and altering valued attributes through an exchange process and then seeing if satisfaction is attainable is a decision to commit made. If this is true, then we would expect to see *commitment following job satisfaction with perhaps a small time lag*. This is indeed the case, but there is an extra twist in the tail.

If the progress of an employee is examined over a period of time, starting from the moment they agree to join the organization, then a pattern emerges that slightly changes the relationship between job satisfaction and commitment just described. At this point two new terms are introduced —entrenchment and re-commitment.

A brief overview of the progress of a newcomer into an organization would be through a series of stages:

Stage	Behaviour
(a) Pre-entry stage	Anticipation
(b) Early stage	Initiation through socialization
(c) Settling in	Time to evaluate job satisfaction
(d) Settled in	If job satisfaction is high, then the employee re-commits If job satisfaction is low, then the employee does not re-commit.

What is happening here is that commitment is dependent not just on job satisfaction but on job satisfaction being maintained to the time when a reappraisal or 'taking a rain check' takes place. In other words, achieving job satisfaction at the very beginning is good but not a precursor of commitment. If, and only if, job satisfaction is maintained does the employee commit. What follows this commitment is a form of entrenchment whereby the employee, so to speak, puts down roots.

Psychological value

The real value of organizational commitment is in its capacity to facilitate change. If the individual is focused on the organization rather than the job or the career or profession, then the reception accorded to change is slightly different than if commitment was not present. If we expand the concept of motivation a little, a number of questions appear. When applying an incentive, what are we trying to achieve? To get people to work harder? Be more loyal? Be flexible? Be prepared to abandon old skills? Be prepared to learn new skills? The last three objectives all carry the fear of change and require cooperation. The committed environment has an advantage over mere 'good motivational practices' in this important area.

Empowerment

In order to understand what empowerment is, it is necessary to recognize that it is about organizational behaviour and about change. It is a new form of organizational behaviour and structure which has come about because of a perceived need for organizational responsiveness and which is itself the mechanism that enables organizations to be responsive.

The idea of empowerment is perhaps often misunderstood. Such misunderstanding has led to cynicism about the 'authenticity' of empowerment schemes. Responsibility without power is one cynical view. In a sense, this scepticism is justified because to work properly empowerment has to be done well. This requires management to realize what an enormous change is required of the incumbent of an empowered role. For empowerment to work properly, both managers and workers have to understand the real implications of what the change actually means. Empowerment is incorporating into an employee's role the authority and means to be responsive to customer requirements. It enables the employees to be responsive by ensuring that the necessary rules of order within the organization do not interfere with the performance of a task which the customer requires. Put simply, this means that empowerment is giving the employees the right to 'break the rules' to serve the customer. In a real sense this is a risky strategy for management because 'rules' are always necessary to an organization. It is a balance between organizational rules and discretion which must be available quickly. The idea that employees should have authority and take responsibility for their actions is not new, but it has never before been allied to a business objective, that is, ensuring customers receive a defined quality of product or service. What is new about the empowerment movement is that it takes a basic idea from motivation theory, that is, that employees respond to autonomy and achievement, and places it in an overall design of the production or service. Here human performance is built-in to the product or service itself, rather than being just a factor of production like working capital.

Logic

Perhaps the best way to see the differences in philosophies between straightforward good management of workers and the empowerment idea is to see how the empowerment movement came about. The logic of giving employees authority stems directly from three factors which have come together simultaneously. These are:

1 The advances in computer and telecommunication systems have led to an increased ability to communicate and an increased ability to specify and control the content of people's jobs.

2 Technology has granted the ability to specify and therefore to standardize a product or service. At the same time, market competition has led to the need to use that ability to specify and standardize to create product differentiation through added value.

3 A desire to get closer to the customer. The idea that companies must understand the needs of their

customers has led to the simple conclusion that means getting dose to them.

These three 'big' ideas have led to a number of organizational changes:

(a) The height of the organizational pyramid is being lowered. Organizations are getting flatter, with fewer and fewer levels of authority between the strategy decision-makers and the shop floor.

(b) If being able to respond to customer needs is the aim, then flexible work practices are essential. The implication here is that roles need to be defined broadly and must 'not be set in stone'.

(c) If understanding the customers' needs is the aim, then those people who deal directly with the customers are important employees. The new emphasis is to focus on the performance of those employees who deal directly with customers.

(d) To take advantage of the flatter organization, the flexible work practices and the feedback from customers there has to be an organization culture that values change.

In a sense these organizational changes are 'the context' of empowerment rather than leading directly to it. What the organizational changes imply is good human relations management with a focus on development and on individuals. What leads directly to the notion of empowerment is the realization that it is never easy for an organization to be responsive and that there is no one ideal structure that will guarantee such responsiveness.

Organization theory has in the past suggested two polar types of organization: the bureaucratic structure and the organic structure. While the former is 'rule bound,' the latter is more open, less rule bound, and capable of rapid change. Obviously the organic model is more responsive than the bureaucratic one. However, the question remains, is it responsive enough? The modem answer to this question is No! Organizational structures need rules, need goals of order, otherwise nothing can be achieved. By definition this places a limit on how rapidly a structure can change itself. It is this reasoning that has led to the conclusion that people can be more responsive than structures and that therefore to 'go that extra mile' for the customer requires a personal response rather than an organization response. This is the heart of empowerment. This is the logic that leads to the idea of giving people the ability to override organizational rules and norms to meet specific customer needs.

Limitations

It must be clear from the context that empowerment is not about management giving up their responsibility and giving away their authority to employees who can do what they like. This is a recipe for chaos. What empowerment is about is giving employees authority and decision-making power within parameters defined by two variables, which are:

— The definition and nature of the actual product and service being offered.

— The boundaries of customer perception of that product or service and the probable range of discrepancy between the organization's definition of product and service and the customers' definition.

In other words, the employee cannot change the product or service but they can intervene between the organization's idea of what the product or service is and the customer's perception of it. Where they disagree is where the responsiveness of empowerment plays its major role. Differences in expectations, the requirement for minor changes and for minor additions, the idiosyncratic nature of feedback on satisfaction, all these aspects are best handled by a person rather than by a set of rules and roles. The real limits on empowerment come in two forms:

— Control over resources.

— The scope of the product and service itself.

Phony empowerment is when the employee only has the 'power' to make a profuse apology' but cannot put the problem right. There must be sufficient resources under the control of the person to be able to put things right. The danger here is that they may promise more than can be delivered or that they may extend the product or service beyond that laid down (and costed) by management. The resource problem in the context of empowerment requires a closer relationship between managers and workers.

Management-worker relationship

There is a strong element of trust required by the idea of empowerment. This is why the concept is so closely linked to the policy of encouraging organizational commitment from employees. Commitment and trust come out of the same knapsack. Where there is a blurring of boundaries and rules and where there is a high level of subjectivity, trust becomes the significant element in the manager-worker response to the customer. However, trust is not all that is required: knowledge of the product/service and knowledge of the organization form the background to trust. If an employee is going to respond to a customer, they must know:

— What the product or service is! This means knowing its limits and its position in relation to other products or services.

— What the organization can and cannot do! False promises end in tears. There are limits in terms of production and its terms of costs.

— The rules and norms of the organization. To be sensitive to the areas of discretion.

— This knowledge cannot come about by accident. It requires careful role definition and training.

Change and learning

The logic of empowerment is based on the idea that organizations, even organic organizations, cannot be quickly responsive to customers. There are limits to how adaptive an organization can be. This is also true of individual managers. They cannot do everything, know everything. It follows therefore that encouraging learning by employees takes away from managers the potential burden of knowledge overload. Even if they have the knowledge, managers cannot remember or be aware of everything at the moment it becomes required by a customer.

In terms of technical production, the normal situation would be managers laying down the product and system, and faults being picked up as they occur. This is a 'deficiency based' approach to quality. The problem is that it is 'backwards facing. When a problem occurs, it is handled. The empowerment approach is the key to prevent problems, to be proactive in terms of quality. The approach required here is one of continuous learning by the employee. The development of this learning begins with training employees to reflect on the quality of their own work. This is followed by giving them the authority to change their own work methods to improve the product. The final stage is to incorporate the capacity to reflect and change into the definition of the product or service itself.

Flexible people

A set of people who are multi-skilled and who are willing to change their job content on a contingency basis. This kind of constant change provides interest and challenge for the worker who has to cope without diminishing standards. In reality, flexible workers have to be able to cope emotionally with moving from a pleasant skilled task to, perhaps, even a demeaning unskilled task. This kind of demand on workers makes their attitude as important as their skills and training. For this reason, the concept of flexible people is linked with that of empowerment.

Nuclear flexibility

Numerical flexibility meets the need to adjust short-term labour supply by such means as:

— Temporary workers.

— Part-time workers.

— Overtime.

Earnings flexibility

Here, adjustments in labour supply are achieved by linking pay to performance. In this way the cost of labour is automatically adjusted to the level of business. Tipping can be seen in this light.

Functional flexibility

Functional flexibility meets the needs for adjustment to demand by adjusting the content of jobs:

— Boundaries between jobs are broken down.

— Related jobs are joined together by common skills.

— People are trained to perform a wide range of skills (flexible people).

In a very real sense functional flexibility is the tough one because the others are easier to implement and often act as a deterrent for introducing functional flexibility. If any organization is operating with a weak internal labour market, then it finds altering numbers of workers by manipulation recruitment and labour turnover and having a self-adjusting pay system very easy to implement and very successful. The problem is that numerical and earnings flexibility are possible enemies of quality. Think of the tired chambermaid on overtime cutting corners to get home. It is the ideas of flexible people and functional flexibility that connect to quality in a positive way.

In other words, these four forms of flexibility are not always compatible and are in fact rivals, with numerical and earnings lining up against people and functional. When variations and fluctuations in customer demand are extreme, such as when there are daily, or even hourly, fluctuations, then from the point of view of the manager, the task of juggling people, jobs, skills and costs, while trying to maintain quality, is a difficult one. It requires a coping strategy. This volatile contingency behaviour is associated with direct service industries such as retailing, hotel and catering, and various forms of tourism business.

One argument, which is discussed later, is that functional flexibility begins life as another item to juggle, part of coping, *but which over time becomes a stabilizing strategy* which decreases the variance of labour supply and reduces the need for the alternative forms of extended labour supply such as casual labour and overtime. Indeed, the rationale for functional flexibility is that it provides an alternative form of coping with business variation to numerical flexibility, which alters numbers employed, and to earnings flexibility, which alters individuals' pay.

There are two forms of functional flexibility. These are, first, *whole job substitution* where workers take over other jobs when required and, secondly, *boundary-loosing approaches* where parts of jobs become merged so that the task can be moved from person to person instead of the person moving to the task.

Barriers to functional flexibility

Functional flexibility is about changing people's jobs! There is always a resistance to change, but this in itself is not the main barrier. There are three serious problems with loosening an organization's job boundaries:

— The skiff mix.

— The size of skill differentials.

— Group competition.

It is easy to talk about multi-skilling, but it is not so easy to apply. If the skills of the proposed 'merged jobs' are numerous and of high contrast and variety, then it may be difficult to train people in so many tasks. A mixture of manual skills, people skills and data skills at several levels might make for interesting work but it may give recruiters and trainers headaches! If there is a wide gap between skilled occupations and unskilled occupations it may be impossible to 'merge' jobs across such a gap. In this case the organization has to accept that functional flexibility can only occur within particular areas. A more human barrier comes with the existence of groups who function competitively within an organization. Work processes often range groups of workers against each other. For example, reception want the rooms now, housekeeping want them really clean! Drivers of excursion coaches much leave on time, guides do not want to hassle their clients! This kind of pressure is natural, but it does not make it easy to merge jobs.

Substitution, quality and strategy

The principle relating technology to external labour markets is known as the substitution principle. However, exactly the same principles apply within an organization's internal labour market. This is problematic for a strategy which encompasses standards of quality, because some of the principles of substitution have the effect of pushing quality downwards. The argument here is that as substitution presents dangers to quality, they need to be encompassed within the same strategy. An organization's ability to substitute one person for another increases when the following apply:

— The more unskilled the job.

— The more training is offered by the organization.

— The more personal attributes count in a job.

— The less dependent the job is on previous knowledge.

— The more knowledge can be substituted by — information.

— The less the degree of specificity.

In a real sense the second of these principles, that of training, can—if it is contained within a strategy—offset the adverse effects of the others. The danger is, however, that without planning and without specifying what is required in terms of knowledge, skill and personal attributes, these aspects will be determined by market forces and cost reduction economics. It is worth pointing out that quality strategies have to be able to defend themselves from economic imperatives.

One such argument from economics would suggest that functional flexibility has to be cheaper than its more established alternatives. Even if this were possible in the long term, it is an unfair argument because, unlike numerical and earnings flexibility, functional flexibility is umbilically linked to the maintenance of quality. Quality measures and functional flexibility must both share the same policy and strategy framework because they are mutually dependent.

Strategy for implementation: plan or let it happen organically? Two interesting choices exist here. First is the requirement for training. In this approach, multi-skilling is done through training. This requires planning and careful application. Someone who does a job occasionally needs to be as good as someone who does just that job every day. The second approach is more organic and suggests that boundary loosening is the easier way to overcome barriers and that after a time the new flexibility becomes institutionalized not through policy but through daily experience.

Here the approach is to encourage people to do part of each other's work, so that gradually everyone can do everybody else's job. In a way this is a dangerous approach because it is difficult to control. It does, however, have the merit of getting the concept accepted without the negotiation that would be required by the planned approach and without engendering the fear that follows the public announcement of change.

The theoretical framework for the idea that a once highly volatile situation can be turned into a stable one comes from some experience of seeing it happen to an external labour market. Unstable labour markets can gradually be tamed by increasing bureaucracy within organizations. This argument is founded on the idea that people become more responsible when they are managed more responsibly.

There are parallels here—enhanced skill and empowerment may have the same taming effect. Once functional flexibility takes hold, it can overcome the many barriers that confront it and directly challenge economic arguments, not on the grounds of being the cheapest form of enhanced labour supply but by its ability to reduce the fluctuations within labour supply. If consumer demand and labour supply are seen as conflicting, then functional flexibility can be seen as a conflict resolution mechanism, being so automatic as to be almost unnoticeable.

The starting point of training

The planned approach to a commitment to functional flexibility means a planning process and training.

The planning process

1 Identify which jobs can be part of the programme.

2 Sort the jobs into broad levels of skill. This banding ensures that people can be matched to their right level.

3 Within each job, identify: systems and sequences, technical knowledge, routine and variable tasks, and tasks containing a degree of personal judgement and decision-making.

4 Identify common tasks between jobs.

5 Identify common knowledge between jobs.

6 Identify core skills and knowledge.

If functional flexibility is achieved, then the organization structure and, more particularly, the wage structure will change radically. To speculate on this requires the abandonment of two accepted ideas and their replacement with two others. If we abandon the concept of the job as a defined occupation, and if we abandon the idea of people choosing a job being based mainly on job content, and instead substitute the idea of the flexible job and add that job selection may be as much influenced by the convenience of the hours of work as by the job content, then the wage and skill structure simply has to change. Contrast the pyramid on the left, which has a traditional structure of pay differential based on occupations and their skills, against the one on the right where there are only three skill levels. Within the lower level the differentials are based on time at which the work takes place. It is the acceptance of the concept of unsocial hours which is so important to the reform of pay in labour-intensive service industries. Career management is about matching the organizational needs with employee aspiration while keeping one eye on the external labour market supply conditions. But in more practical terms, it is about 'traffic' management-matching opportunities to potential, and identifying growth factors—what causes potential to be realized later? In other words, there are two inseparable concepts involved in career management—planning and *management development*. What is illustrated here is that each concept has its own special problems.

In the case of career planning, the long term meets the immediacy of a vacancy and rarely is the timing perfect so potential rarely dovetails perfectly. So it is not just a case of identifying potential but 'storing' it. In 4 sense, 'storage and growth' is the key concept in career planning. It is pointless having people with potential waiting around in jobs that do not develop them towards their potential.

The special problem of management development is recognizing potential, and what causes it to grow, against the background of young managers recruited from the labour market doing very different jobs from the jobs of senior managers in the organization. The interests of planning and management development coincide in identifying jobs which contribute both the storage and growth functions of careers.

Career planning

The career planner needs to have information in four key areas:

— Organization pay structure.

— Pay levels of competitors.

— Business plans and their impact on opportunities.

— Identified potential.

Putting aside, for a moment, all considerations of quality, what the planner needs to know in respect of identified potential is:

— The number of people identified as having potential.

— Where these people are in the organization. How old they are.

— What they earn.

— The existing channels of promotion.

— The key stages in development

— How long people stay at each stage of a career path.

— Dead-ends or blockages.

If a career planner had all this knowledge it would still lack direction. What gives it all meaning is having target occupations. It is no good talking about future managers—what are they doing? You need to specify the target occupations you are engineering paths and devising personal development programmes for, for example unit management, financial controller, sales manager etc. These targets are not ceilings for the individuals concerned, but do give the system some focus without being inflexible.

What has to be understood is, first, that whether or not an organization has a formal promotion policy, one will exist through custom and practice, second, that single promotion affects all other promotions and finally, that even in the most organized scheme there will always be a difference between the policies and what happens in reality. It follows from this that the first task for the career planner is to find out what is going on. All this points to the need for some career analysis. Like other functions, career analysis needs some clear information including:

1 What is happening at the moment (examination of current labour supply and the working of promotion criteria)?

2 How effective are the organization promotion policies?

3 How realistic are the promises made to aspirants?

4 What is the effect of existing policies and intended policies on all other personnel policies such as pay structure, pensions and status?

Manpower flow approach

The best guide to analysis is to examine the career of the target occupation. When this is compared with some hypothetical career path it is even more effective. If, for example, it is assumed that all the sales managers in a hotel company come from a reception background because of the experience that would give them of handling customers, and that they would also have had a hotel school education, then this can be tested by focusing on the career histories of those in the position. The result is a comparison between two manpower flows.

Age distributions

An age, distribution is simply a way of distributing a population between defined and meaningful grades or levels on the basis of age. It uses proportions of people in grades at particular ages to describe the population. The basic needs of career planning are to display paths, identify stages of development and indicate timespan. Here, for example, if you haven't progressed from grade 1 to grade 2 by the time you are thirty-five, you are unlikely to do so. A more useful form of the age distribution is the biographical age distribution. The great advantage of this technique is that it is independent of rates of mobility and, therefore, can operate at any velocity of labour turnover.

Biographical age distribution

Here, the conditions are changed from describing different people of different ages in different grades to describing the same people at different ages in different grades. In other words, the distribution now looks backwards over the career histories of a sample of a target occupation. To bring that order to this distribution two conditions are desirable: first, that the sample is all in the same occupational level or grade, and second, that the sample should be the same age. By these means, the distribution has a standardized starting point.

However, the first condition is easy to meet, but the second is almost impossible. This means that the sample will decline to the right of the distribution. This in itself is harmless, but it does mean that the capacity of the sample to answer questions is limited to the *left of the age of the youngest member of the sample.* The target group is represented by the white space. What is important here, is how quickly people become assistant hotel managers, which appears to be the only route to becoming a general manager. In this form of analysis, the longer a person stays in a particular grade, the more important it is deemed to be as a development stage. By this token, department heads and supervisors stand little chance of making it and these roles are not seen as development roles. The merits of this form of age distribution are that it:

— Identifies career path.

— Identifies stages which are crucial to development.

— Is independent of levels of mobility.

— Is an investigation technique.

The danger of this technique, however, is that it does not measure the recent past. If things have changed dramatically in the target occupation this technique will miss them.

Management development

The real problem with management development is that it is never easy to say what it is that constitutes good performance. In other words, what is a good manager? It is easier to point out good managers than it is to say why they are good. It is even harder to generalize what you see in good individuals into something you can select for or develop people towards. There are so many types of manager and they do so many different things, how can we pull out some common factors? In fact, management development is really an organizational concept because at least when placed within this framework it might be possible to judge good performance.

Management development varies between companies because their jobs are different, their needs are different and their assessment of performance will be different. While it is obvious that the knowledge base of someone at the junior level of management will be different from a very senior manager and that, at least in theory, the difference could be made up by training, what concerns management development is being able to identify those people who can change sufficiently to become capable of managing at the higher level. In its early days, management development tried to identify psychological traits which were common between aspirants and successful managers. A less ambitious and more practical approach is to look for skills. Like anything else skills have levels, but at least some will be common to both junior and senior managers and their application to different levels of management can be measured.

If there is a criticism to be made of this approach, it is that there has been a bias towards people- handling skills rather than decision-taking and analytical skills. The problem for investigation is always that the type of decision tends to change with the level of authority. In a sense, this is a clue to how skills can be revealed. The focus of attention must be the target job and the skills they use. Techniques are available for investigating management skills, but the basis must be to find out what the superiors of the target job consider to be the attributes of good performance. The approach to this problem which follows is in two stages.

Stage 1

1 Find out how the superiors of the target job differentiate between existing incumbents of this job.

2 Test to see which dimensions are related to good performance by asking the superior to rank the present incumbents or to use similar data from the appraisal system.

3 Check for the degree of consensus between the superiors.

Stage 2

1 Investigate the actual work of the target job by:

(a) Observation

(b) Critical incident technique.

2 Use superiors to identify what would constitute good and bad practice.

3 Ask superiors to identify what skill would be necessary to achieve good practice.

Stage 1 looks at people and stage 2 at jobs. When brought together they should help to identify and authenticate required skills and good and bad performance of those skills. It must not be overlooked, however, that management is not just a bag of skills, there is the question of knowledge and can it be implanted by experience or education and training. There has been a tendency to overlook the actual human being who is trying to build a career. While the goal of the planner and the developer might be to have any person with potential in the right job, getting satisfaction, growing and not being tempted by the labour market, individuals may perceive their own careers in a variety of ways.

Motivation again is central to the concept of management development. The basis of Schein's argument is the experience of work which people have and which forms their orientations. Three other pressures on personal aspirations can be identified:

— The compatibility of the career with the style of life the person desires.

— How far they have already travelled. Satisfaction with career is often correlated with how far back they started.

— People always remember what attracted them into the career in the first place. Often motives for behaviour can be traced back to those original purposes.

Careers in the hotel and catering industry

Management careers exhibit a number of conspicuous features:

— There are a lot of career opportunities in management. The industry displays a rate of promotion to management far in excess of most industries.

— There are two streams of management - those based on experience only and those based on vocational education and experience.

— Careers tend to be developed through a mixture of company career structures and labour market mobility.

— Because there are two streams of management career with one offering the opportunity to rise from the lower ranks the salaries of all junior ranks tend to be pulled down by this connection to the working ranks.

— This restriction does not apply to levels higher than junior managers and management salaries show a wide dispersion.

— Career structures vary from company to company.

Perhaps the most obvious structural feature of the hotel and catering industry is its fragmented small unit structure. We have to add another vital variable: companies or organizations. While most companies mimic the structure of the industry in that they have numbers of units plus a head office with perhaps some intervening levels of management, how they actually operate in terms of how authority and responsibility are distributed and how roles are prescribed is likely to vary from company to company.

Influence of structures

Given the structure of the industry, the obvious target

occupation for careers would be unit management: hotel manager, restaurant manager, catering manager etc. This is clearly a large proportion of the management population of the industry, but the opportunities don't stop there as line management extends up to the corporate level. Functional specialisms at head office and within larger units offer alternative careers.

However, functional specialization is, by its nature, a smaller population than line management. To understand career paths to unit management it is helpful to recast the skill pyramid showing the direction of the flows. Two points need to be made here. First, the 'store and grow' stage is clearly the role of the assistant manager. Second, and of great importance, is the assumption which underlies the whole edifice, which is that some of the knowledge at the bottom is needed at the top, or to put it another way, managers have to have technical knowledge of the operation they are managing.

Influence of role changes

This assumption is coming under pressure from two fronts - a business orientation and technology. Information technology is allowing more things to be controlled in terms of the unit by head office and by the manager within the unit.

To use the benefit of this technology managers are being granted autonomy within specified parameters and hotel activities are being turned into cost centres. In tandem with this is an emphasis on selling. The result of these changes could be a change in organization structure, with autonomy being given to department heads reporting directly to the manager. This diminishes the role of the assistant manager. It is possible to envisage a generalized customer care role here.

The point here is that if you change a job, you

change the knowledge base of the job and, therefore, you change the career path needed to reach it. Organizational change produces career changes. Similarly, changes in the unit-head office relationship affect the role given to functional specialists such as marketing, finance and personnel. Examples can be found of companies which favour head office as the locus of these functions and others that deploy them in the units or area office. The message is basically that variations in company philosophy on organizational structure produce variations in role description, which alter career paths.

However, it is worth considering whether the changes discussed above are changes or additions to the knowledge base of managers. Does the need for increased business skill and information technology skill deny the need for the technical skills of hotel and catering? Notwithstanding the pressures for change, the industry is, to a very large extent, reliant upon the assistant manager to provide its stock of managers.

Most managers have served three appointments as assistants, but the jump from assistant to sole charge is always a large one. No matter what technical knowledge and people-handling skills are accumulated on the way up, the individual's ability to grow as a decision maker will not develop unless he or she is given the chance to make decisions. It is at this point that corporate development plans are in the hands of existing unit managers. A corporate culture of development, delegation and appraisal is essential if the 'unassertive copilot syndrome' is to be avoided. If the assistant simply carries out decisions already taken, the assertiveness so essential to sole charge will simply wither. It is worth exploring this idea further.

As in any activity, speculation abounds as to the merits of the past versus the future. Such speculation usually uses stereotypes as its currency. In the hotel industry the 'old-fashioned' manager is ranged against a modern business person with ideas about standardization and costs. Sometimes this comes out as an amateur versus professional argument. A more detailed version suggests that the host spends too much time making the guest happy at the expense of profits and that the manager of the future would be in the office doing some long-term thinking and planning.

These kind of arguments infiltrate the dialogue between industry and education. Like many of its kind this debate is based on the false premise that these approaches are mutually exclusive. They are not. These aspects of looking after guests and doing some business planning are simply two parts of one activity - managing. They are only separated by size of operation. The hotel manager of the future has to have traditional knowledge of the profession and modern business skills.

What links both the so-called, traditional knowledge with the modern world is innovation and imagination. If we say that, the modern manager should:

— Know how customers differentiate between hotels.

— Be able to lead customer taste.

— Know how to design a system.

— Be able to assess the capacity of people, groups, systems and machines.

That is, know what is possible; what can be done. These capabilities can be achieved solely by experience (a lot!) and solely by scientific management (market research, systems design, work study etc.) but *they are best activated by both.* This argument is an advert for both experience and education but there is something missing! How do you know that you need these capabilities? The answer is you won't know unless you have an imagination and are an innovative person. To a very large extent innovation is dependent upon assertiveness. Some recent work in management development has classified managers in terms of innovators and adaptors. The first are not dependent on existing knowledge to handle situations and are prepared to go outside the known parameters for a solution.

The adaptor uses initiative but thinks within the known constraints. Both require willpower and assertiveness. To return to the assistant manager, if he or she cannot change something, cannot exert their will, then eventually they will begin not to see the need for change. Seen as a development process, lack of assertiveness can turn an innovator into an adaptor. Taken to its logical conclusion a lack of assertiveness makes a person leave management altogether.

The point being made here is that the role of the assistant manager only works as a development process if *it is made to work in this way*. The problem is that the role contains tendencies that can work against personal development. First, and most obviously, if the manager has not given the assistant responsibility and authority then the young person's, opportunity to develop assertiveness and decision-making ability will simply be choked off. Second, and quite independent of the attitude of the manager, is the 'here and now' nature of the work. Constant pressure from guests with problems and staff with problems can make the assistant manager see their role and management itself as a problem-solving, short-term activity. This process is reinforced by the variety of the work being in itself an attractive aspect of the work. Constant variety and 'never a dull moment' can be fun but there is a drawback if it makes the person forget the long term.

Finally, assistant managers need eyes in the back of their heads! The sheer complexity of running at least four types of work process (cleaning rooms, serving drinks, serving food and producing food) and undertaking probably several managerial functions (sales, personnel, training and accounting) all in the same day would make adaptors of us all! With such variety the assistant manager is dependent on systems and procedures but as has been said many times before, standards are subjective and therefore the qualitative control of standards requires constant judgements. It doesn't have to happen but all these characteristics can lower the person's perspective. What the role is good at is developing people- handling skills.

Constantly talking to guests and staff should instil both confidence and skill into an individual's make-up. It is sometimes argued that these skills are only for junior ranks and are not necessary for higher management. This of course is nonsense. To take just two aspects, listening and persuasiveness are skills as much in use by company chairmen as by junior managers.

However, whether a person becomes good at handling people is dependent on whether they are given clear authority to decide matters. In reality, the problem is not so much that the assistant manager does not get the chance to make decisions but that these decisions are confined to guest relations and operational tuning problems. When do they learn about business? Exactly when or how these skills are developed are important questions for career planners. The use of managerial assessment is helpful in this respect because it tells the planner how far individuals have developed. The question of how far managers need to know the technical aspects of running their operation is often debated. This question is part of the wider debate referred to earlier.

In fact, it is quite obvious that managers must know about what they are managing and the depth of technical knowledge only improves their capacity to make good business decisions. At the very least technical knowledge has four distinct roles:

— It forms part of the basis of personal authority.

— It forms a central part of the individual's occupational identity.

— It grants the ability to assess the personal capacity of workers in an industry where personal productivity matters.

— It grants the ability to recognize the open-ended aspects of business such as service and food and beverage and how they can be developed to increase sales.

Organizational change

No-one doubts that organizations change. Sometimes the change is in the nature of an upheaval and at other times it happens gradually. Change can be deliberate and planned but it can also be enforced and reactive. Not too many years ago the academic discipline of organization theory used to concern itself with two broad modals, the bureaucratic form with its rules and defined roles and the organic form which was less rigid. To a large extent these forms are still the basic currency of organizational structure, but the plot has changed. It has become more complicated. The idea of thinking of organization structure as the result of influence by other factors has not changed, but our thinking about what constitutes 'structure' has changed. It can no longer be confined to elements such as hierarchy, roles, power, authority, groups. Now we must also think of less tangible dimensions such as culture, leadership, information, behaviour. Structure, meaning form, is now only one of many ways of perceiving organizations. Indeed, change itself has become a focus of attention, suggesting that organizational change is the result of larger changes in the social and industrial worlds. Organizations are the entity which conducts the transactions which make up the economic activity in all its forms. It is in organizations that goods and services are produced, work provided and value enhanced. Such is the complexity of technology, markets and finance that no one individual can cope with the attention they require. To cope with such a division of labour requires a unified entity, which is the organization.

Organizations are also social entities which contain relationships of various types. Life within organizations contrasts with social life despite both pervading the other's territory. We speak of organization decision-making but, in a purist sense, only people can make decisions! Yet, such is the significance of the context of organizations that we can indeed speak of them in decision-making terms. When individuals make decisions in organizations they are, to paraphrase Abraham Lincoln, for the organization, by the organization.

Organizations like individuals, have self-interests, the most important of which are to survive and grow. Organizational theory is a body of knowledge which attempts to explain the structure of organization, the behaviour of organizations and the behaviour of people within organizations. It combines ideas of form and structure with human factors and environmental factors such as markets, society, law and politics. At its centre is a concern to explain how the work involved in making things and supplying services is organized. By inference, there is the suggestion that it is also concerned with how things should be organized. The idea of an 'ideal' modal is always around. More suggestive than prescriptive.

The main concepts in organizational theory are:

— The division of labour, the complexity of the production task and the degree of specialization.

— Centralization or decentralization of authority.

— Communication and information distribution.

— Technology, task scope routineness.

— Labour and labour cost.

— The degree of environmental complexity and uncertainty.

— The degree of competitiveness and cooperativeness in the environment.

— Culture and values.

All these dimensions can be studied in a number of ways. For example:

(a) We can take an intra-organizational perspective.

(b) We can adopt inter-organizational approaches which are concerned with competition and integration and, in a comparative sense, with diversity versus convergence.

(c) We can look at organizations in their social and political environments by looking at how organizations adapt to changes in the market, technological and political environments.

Although change is a matter of intra-organizational concern, in effect the concept of change cuts across all these perspectives. The need to change may stem from within, but may equally be caused by something external - it may be initiated by the organization or by outside forces, it may be voluntary or inevitable. For the management of any organization there are always two types of goals based on a concern with, on the one hand, 'order' within the organization and, on the other, with expansion and productivity. These might be termed goals of order and goals of productivity. Clearly they are related. Nothing can be produced in chaos and indiscipline. A degree of order is always necessary. Productivity itself is a source of order as it brings economic benefits. These two goals can be incompatible when the value of production is not distributed in some acceptable way.

Goals of order concern such aspects as fairness and equity in the distribution of rewards and in the application of authority, group identity, competition, values, discipline. Goals of productivity concern incentives, motivation, leadership, job design, differentials. Both sets of goals overlap in terms of organizational structure and human resource management policy.

The pressures to change

External factors

Changes in the economic, legal, political and technological worlds can force change on an organization. However, it must be said that organizations themselves are part of the environment they live in and continuously attempt to exert influence.

— Internal factors

— Inadequate output.

— Inadequate profits.

— Competition.

— Technological change.

— Low performance in terms of innovation, efficiency and adaptiveness.

— Inadequate utilization of plant, support systems or maintenance.

— Low morale.

Achieving change

Putting aside for a moment the actual causes and purposes of change, it is possible to make some assumptions about organizations:

1 How organizations are structured affects performance and outputs.

2 The values of the dominant coalition also affect performance and outputs.

3 The environment sets limits on how organizations are structured.

4 People who lose status or power resist change.

5 The more exposure to change, the more the acceptance of it.

The opportunity to start from scratch is rare, so organizational change is always a matter of some form of *intervention* in the status quo. The nature of this intervention is the material for strategy. There is, however, an original sin in the field of organization change which is, to expect training to do all the work. It is a very common occurrence to find a belief that training alone will change attitudes and thus enable other changes to take place. This is a fallacy. Training can never be that powerful and it can never work alone. In fact, no single technique can work on its own. In a way, it is not surprising that so much faith is placed in training because at a very fundamental level change is about job redesign, new attitudes and new expectations.

Approaches to organization change and key issues

— Changing attitudes through training. Redesigning jobs.

— Redesigning the structure and therefore roles within it.

— Strategic vision and will.

— Out of chaos; letting the organization change in an organic unplanned way.

— Making structure serve objectives.

— Preparation for responsiveness; making ready for unspecified change.

— Changing people and/or skills; technological change and human capital.

— Changing key people.

No single one of these approaches can affect change. Strategy has to encompass a coalition of these approaches. However, some approaches are always there. All strategic approaches are dependent on three main components. First, is the vision and willpower of top management. Without this, very little will actually happen and strategy may remain at the level of plans. Secondly, there must be a change in key people and thirdly a role change. It is an inevitable outcome of organization change that roles will change. At its simplest, strategy has five tools which it can use to implement change:

1 Policies.

2 Structural changes.

3 Appointing new people.

4 Procedures, systems and plans.

5 Tactical interventions.

These are the means, the active ingredients of strategy. It is likely that they will all be used within a strategy. For example, the very purpose of appointing a new person would be the expectation that they would have new policies, change existing systems, change roles and make new appointments of their own. At the general level, however, the key debate is between the school of thought that argues that attitudes and behaviour will change when roles are altered and the school which argues that when roles change attitudes and behaviour remain the same unless role change is accompanied by training.

Organizational change usually implies an intervention which covers the whole organization, though this is not necessarily always the case. It follows that if the whole organization is changed, then the relationships it has with other organizations will be changed as a consequence.

The human process of influencing change

A change 'agent' has to work to achieve change and does so by being sensitive to the needs and desires of others and being sensitive to the alliances and coalitions they make as part of organizational life. Persuasion is a word which conceals an enormous amount of effort. Persuasion has numerous tasks, which include:

— Sense needs.

— Amplify understanding.

— Build awareness.

— Create credibility.

— Legitimize viewpoints.

— Generate partial solutions to problems.

— Broaden support.

— Identify opposition.

— Identify areas of indifference.

— Clarify the risks.

— Encourage flexibility.

— Put forward trial concepts, i.e. fly kites.

— Create supportive groups.

— Eliminate undesirable alternatives.

— Crystallize the issues and the debate.

— Seek consensus.

— Establish and maintain coalitions.

— Formalize what is agreed.

This is what persuasion actually entails! It is not surprising that it is so often associated with leadership.

Resistance to change

It is easy to imagine that change is greeted by resistance. It is also wrong. Often change is welcomed. It depends on the culture of the organization and on the degree of threat implied by the change and on society's general attitude towards change.

A conceptual framework, often referred to as the 'iron cage', sums up the dimensions of resistance. The key 'enforcers' of this attitude are investment in training and society's approval or disapproval of change. In behavioural terms, resistance can be more complicated. Behavioural reactions can include:

— Enthusiasm.

— Disillusionment.

— Panic.

— A search for the guilty who support change.

— Punishment of those who sit on the fence.

— Praise for those who resist.

— Reinforced by society; negative attitude

The key to understanding reactions to change lies in timing. There is a clear distinction between first reactions and reflection and between the hope that it may not happen and the acceptance of its inevitability. Action taken too early could be damaging. The positive acceptance of change depends upon the degree of insecurity which accompanies it and with the degree of investment made in the 'old ways'. Management have to appreciate that when workers have made sacrifices to learn skills they are unlikely to surrender them without regret. The policy implications of this are:

1 There has to be a culture of change based on openness.

2 Consultation is a part of the change process.

3 Incentives have to be built into retraining packages.

It is also necessary for managers to realize that the acceptance of change does not automatically mean that the old ways are forgotten. Regret about 'the old days and old ways' is a serious motivational issue, and not one that can be ignored

Developing tabour strategies

Labour strategies are largely dependent on business strategies. The business strategy decrees to the labour strategy:

How many workers are needed.

— The proportion of fixed to variable employment.

— The proportion of added value available for wages.

— The type of people the business needs.

— The type of skills the business needs.

Two factors dominate the relationship between business strategy and labour strategy, these are:

— The pattern of demand by customers.

— Technological change.

Despite this relationship, labour strategy has a life of its own quite distinct from business strategy. You don't change your staff every time your business strategy changes, nor do you restructure your organization with every change of plan. In other words, labour is usually more permanent than the duration of business plans and it is for this reason that the problems of attracting, retaining, sustaining and motivating a workforce need consideration independently in their own right.

Strategy

Usually the word strategy is associated with the word planning. This is correct, but strategy means more than designing a programme of action for the future. Such programmes require objectives—where do these objectives come from? For the business, it may well be that the objectives come from alternatives derived from market information. But here, strategy comes from the pursuit of targets. This is not the case with labour strategy. Here the concern is with continuity and change and in this respect labour strategy is more architectural in tone.

The central element to all strategy, which precedes the planning process, is the creation of a vision. Put simple what do we want my organization to look like in the future?' The creation of a vision is never easy. Like any building their quality and quantity are interrelated and interdependent, therefore any vision and consequent design must examine the interconnections between all these parts of the organization. What is more, organizations live in labour markets, therefore the vision should embrace the relationship between the organization and its labour markets. To pick your way through this maze requires a particular questioning technique, which at its simplest argues that the objectives of your labour strategy come from asking:

— What do I want?

— Why do I want it?

— What does it assume about technology, labour markets and the behaviour or people?

— What would need to change from the present position?

These questions need to be addressed across a range of organizational issues.

Strategy and coherence

One reasonably safe bet is to bypass all the issues on motivation and to say that whatever you are doing to motivate your staff only has a chance of success if it makes sense to the individual employee. If your labour strategies are coherent, then the individual is more likely to 'sense' what you are doing than if he or she is being pulled in two different directions at the same time. If, for example, an individual is given close supervision and is expected to show initiative, or has insecure tenure of employment and is expected to be committed to the organization. Such contradictions are often only apparent to the individuals concerned, but they undercut management's efforts to motivate.

The process of developing labour strategies

There are three major stages in developing labour strategies. The first two are directly concerned with the business strategy but the third is concerned with the type of organization which will meet the needs of the business strategy. The stages are:Review the pattern of technological change

It is important to be clear about what is meant by 'technological' in this context. Here the word is used to describe any work process not necessarily done by a machine. To change the service in a restaurant from silver service to a self-service buffet is a change in work process and is as much a technological change as replacing manual work by machine.

The *technological assessment* which precedes labour strategy development has, itself, three components each with a different significance for strategy.

Technological change

Looking into the future, what rate and type of change do you envisage:

— Steady state (i.e. no change).

— Gradual change built on existing knowledge and skills.

— Gradual change based on new knowledge and skills.

— Incremental change built on existing knowledge and skills.

— Incremental change built on new knowledge and skills.

— Revolutionary change.

Examples of incremental change might be computerized reservation systems, sous vide and microwave cookers. The impact of these changes is not just on the numbers of people employed, but on the type and depth of skill required.

Technology and the labour market

The nature of jobs determines their labour market characteristics, therefore what has to be assessed is the nature of the jobs to be done, because such an assessment is the primary influence on future recruitment policies. What has to be assessed for each work category is:

— The degree of specificity to the organization.

— The level of training, education and experience.

— How far personal characteristics count.

— How far knowledge can be substituted by information.

Technology and control

The assessment here is primarily concerned with how far performance standards can be measured and what value management place upon employee autonomy and initiative.

Develop strategies for organizational behaviour—attracting, sustaining and motivating the workforce

At the heart of this approach to developing strategies is a questioning framework. The assumption of this framework is that strategies begin with the question 'what do I want?'. This emphasizes the importance of managerial 'will' in strategy. It also argues that the starting point is a vision of what the organization ought to be like in the future. The emphasis is on values and primary purposes.

Note also that the planning process in the conventional sense begins at the fifth point and that 'means' enter at the next stage. The means can be structures, systems, specific appointments, policies etc. Remember that this framework is simply a sequence of questions, but what are these questions about? Where do you start? What you are trying to do is to get to the fundamentals then to examine your position on the fundamentals of organizational design. There are six, which are:

— Stability Concerned with the mobility of the workforce and the relationship between the organization and its labour markets.

— Incentive Concerned with rewards—attraction, motivation and retention. Control Concerned with style of authority and questions of autonomy.

— Order Concerned with differentials of all types between members of the workforce.

— Communication Concerned with the degree of openness and knowledge distribution.

— Location Concerned with significance of the location of the organization in the local society.

All this does is identify areas of concern - how do we get at meaningful questions? The technique recommended here is to take, for each area, extreme policy options (EPOs). Examples would be high job security policy, or pay market leadership, or strong worker autonomy or single status. By taking an extreme policy option you can explore your thinking in each area. An example would be appropriate at this point.

Example: An extreme position on Stability

Original purposes and values

I want a stable organization with a constant workforce and minimal labour wastage. This requires a strategy to produce job security for the workforce.

Rationale for the original purpose and values

Why do I want Stability?

— I don't anticipate fluctuations in demand.

— I anticipate regular technological change.

— I need to increase the value of human capital because the new technology develops from existing knowledge.

— Existing skills are very specific to the organization.

— I want to avoid a difficult labour market and heavy recruitment costs.

— I want to avoid high training costs.

— I want loyalty and commitment.

— I think that I will get an emphasis on quality if I offer security.

— I want flexibility and adaptability in my workforce.

About people

— That the investment already made in skill is not a barrier to learning or, if it is, that a job security policy will overcome it.

— That people will be prepared to pass on their skills to others-willingly. Again, the relationship between their own investment and job security policy is crucial.

— That by taking the sacrifice out of learning people will be prepared to abandon old skills for new.

— That by feeling secure people will show more commitment to their work and to the firm. In other words, security motivates.

— That in the long term people will find their own ways of doing things, therefore detailed specification of end (quality and quantity) is probably better than tight control of means.

— That there is a danger of dependency which matters if technology grants workers a degree of autonomy.

— That people will value long-term personal relationships with co-workers.

— That people will either consciously or unconsciously, forgo their labour market power - weaken it in return for security.

About the labour market

— That you won't be able to find the skills you need at a price you are prepared to pay.

— That the jobs you have cannot easily be substituted by people with different skills.

— That after a while your firm will not be 'visible' in the marketplace.

About technology

— That the type and rate of change can be handled by workforce.

— That no revolutionary change is on the way.

Objectives

What must/do?

— Ensure I have a retraining capacity.

— Ensure that productivity improves consistently.

— Apply pay levels that will prevent temptation to leave. (Do I want to become a market leader?)

— Offer a package which is unconditional on performance.

— Ensure managerial control over the deployment of skills. Promote from within. Reduce ports of entry to the necessary minimum. Negotiate a flexible union agreement. Lower manning levels.

— Possibly build a buffer of non-secure part-time employment to account for fluctuation in demand.

— Grant a degree of autonomy as to means while keeping controls of ends. Develop a style of supervision suitable for long-term relationships.

— Develop a communication policy that assumes that people are interested and involved.

A complete review of strategy requires this process to be carried out across all the fundamentals of organization design using, in each case, appropriate extreme policy options (EPO). The whole purpose of following the exercise is to make your labour strategies coherent. Extremes are valuable in two ways. First, they point out the underlying assumptions about behaviour so that you can cross compare these assumptions to see that they don't contradict each other.

Second, you modify your position from the extreme but do so with the knowledge that you know the implications. In the example given you may not really want a high job security policy, but a more moderate version of it, but you are clear now as to why you want it and what it implies. In real terms, you are likely to have strategies in areas like recruitment, pay, status, promotion, selection and training.

Although they exist in their own right, these strategies should flow from the analysis of the fundamental. That way they should display coherence. Once you have decided what you want and why you want it, and have refined this down to some objectives, then one additional consideration arises - by what means are these objectives to be achieved? Obviously, the actual means used will depend on the objectives, but broadly speaking labour strategies can be implemented in a variety of ways.

— Through policies, procedures, systems and plans.

— By altering the organizational structure.

— By appointing specific people to implement objectives.

— By making tactical interventions without altering policies or structures.

Thinking the matter through is one thing, but once you reach the point of considering means then simultaneously you have reached the point when you have to consider how to communicate the strategy.

The great danger with strategic matter is that it is long term and it is about change, there is simply more time available for misinterpretation by the workforce. In other words, whatever the strategy, the communication of it, both intended and unintended, must be thought through. So far, the only criterion for judging a labour strategy has been coherence, but as everything depends upon the authority of management, this too could be a minimum requirement of any strategy -that it enhances the authority of management.

A direction for HRM

It will be recalled that right at the beginning of this book there was a lot of talk about the 'immediacy' of the industry - the focus on the here and now. Yet, here we are at the end talking about strategy. In fact, there is nothing incompatible here. True, strategy is commonly associated with the long term, but it *always embraces the immediate.* It is a fatal flaw to think of strategy as long term and in broad outline.

Real strategic thinking and planning starts from where you are now and projects where you want to go to. If there is a real criticism to be made of labour management, whether it is in the guise of personnel management, industrial relations, manpower planning or whatever, it is its failure to achieve completeness. The failure to think and plan in detail. In a sense, trying to answer unanswerable questions like what motivates and what the industry needs in terms of specific workforce requirements, have prevented management from trying everything and from trying to give everything a coherence. Giving workers a gleaming new canteen, plenty of scope in their work, harsh supervision and poor pay, is not telling the same story; neither is good pay, no autonomy, poor conditions and good supervision. They cannot have everything! Maybe, but if what they have points in the same direction, is coherent, then management's motivational exhortations may stand a better chance of getting a response. If it is a game of chance and you don't want to bet on all the horses, at least you can make it a handicapped race! Applied motivation in the future is likely to be about putting attributes together into employment and motivational packages which tell a story to the worker. Without doubt, the technique of the future will be employee attitude surveys. If convenience is going to be a major factor in the decision to work in a leisure society, then 'motivational packages' will be built with regard to how people live as well as what they do at work.

The industry values part-time workers, because they are convenient to the economics of labour supply, but such workers will have to be valued for much more than this. They are at the cutting edge of productivity. Time and effort spent in motivation here is well spent. Perhaps the future is organizing different employment packages for skilled full time, unskilled full time and unskilled part time, irrespective of what job they do. Hotel and catering units almost always exist in a labour market surplus might strike a discordant note. Running around hoping to keep up with the labour turnover doesn't 'feel' like a surplus. Yet it is.

The labour market is tough enough without making it harder for yourself with stereotyped notions of what you want. The search for 'good people' is not helped by a myopic vision of 'willing flexible souls'. Looking for good people means constantly looking at job content. It is not just the person to fit the job, but the job itself to allow the person to be maximally effective. If a genuine shortage exists in the labour market then management are forced to look at job content, but a modern approach to FIRM embraces this as naturally as expert selection procedures. When it comes to evaluating competence and effectiveness, the focus is on job content rather than the personal qualities anyway. Why not make it a central focus in recruitment and selection? One of the more tedious debates which permeates the industry and vocational education is whether the skills of managing are more important than knowledge of hotel and catering operations. The argument is destructive because both are necessary and complementary.

Good practice in HRM assumes that everyone who manages has the skills to do so. HRM has contributed to these skills by devising methods of measuring competence. This process is linked to managing by objectives, but the future will go beyond setting objectives and measuring defined competences to researching and prescribing 'how' things are to be achieved. Again, we see detailed thinking coming to the aid of effectiveness. This is not Taylorism making a comeback in a suit and tie, but a balance between researched methods of achieving objectives in management and encouraging managers to have initiative to go on and find even better ways.

One thing is certain, the structure of the industry being as it is, nothing can be achieved in HRM strategy without stable, motivated and skilled unit managers. There is undoubtedly an HRM movement in corporate life—uncodified but nevertheless an observable trend towards an emphasis on the long term, on getting commitment from people, and encouraging flexibility and quality in general.

5

Hotel Operations

The importance of this job is suggested by the observation that many traditional hotel departments have been reorganized so major functions now report to the controller's office. The prime example of this is the front office, where previously the front office manager supervised the activities of the night audit staff, cashiers, and other front desk clerks. Increasingly, hotel firms are transferring the responsibility for night audits and cashiers to the accounting office, with the ultimate responsibility for these information-gathering and controlling functions resting with the hotel controller.

Another increasingly important department in the hotel is one that coordinates and supervises all the electronic data processing (EDP) or management information systems (MIS). In many instances, EDP and MIS functions are now also the responsibility of the hotel controller. This recognizes the training and the ability of hotel controllers to provide for the structured accumulation, storage, and reporting of data in forms that are most useful to the operating departments and other executives of the hotel.

The success of hotel firms in the modern era will depend on how well they manage, control, and utilize the information that is available to them for their own operations. Managers also need to develop other sources of information in the business environment that affect their regulatory structure and their competition.

The hotel controller

The 1989 survey on hotel controller was based on a questionnaire mailed to 750 members of the International Association of Hospitality Accountants (IAHA) who were identified as working in hotel accounting positions. We received a total of 319 responses, representing a response rate of 42.5 percent. More than 90 percent of the controllers who responded have at least an associate's degree and nearly 20 percent have at least a master's degree. Those findings are similar to those of the 1983 study.

The shift can be viewed also from the demand side—perhaps hotel companies now recognize the value of hospitality management training and operations experience in the controller's position.

In 1989, the most frequently cited areas of knowledge were computers, cash management, and internal controls, each of which was claimed by more than 90 percent of our study sample. As with the 1983 survey, although cash management was considered important by more than 90 percent of the respondents, controllers do not appear to have significant authority over the two critical cash management functions of investing (46.4 percent) and borrowing funds (20.4 percent). More controllers became familiar with taxes and computers between 1983 and 1989.

The controllers' knowledge of taxes went from 60 to 75 percent of respondents reporting tax knowledge, and the percentage familiar with computers rose almost 30 percentage points (from 70 percent to 97 percent). In the latest survey we asked the controllers to grade themselves on two new areas of expertise: Financial Accounting Standards Board (FASB) pronouncements and risk management.

Only 18 percent were up to date with the FASB, while 36 percent said "yes" to having knowledge of risk management. Also, "auditing" and "internal control" were listed as separate categories in 1989, whereas they were combined for the 1983 survey. More than 90 percent of the respondents indicated that they have responsibility for such standard accounting functions as general accounting, receivables, payables, and payroll, a finding virtually identical to that in 1983. Other major areas of responsibility shared by most controllers include night and income audits, cashiers, and food and beverage controls. There are some indications that controllers are becoming increasingly involved with the operational aspects of their hotels. More than 50 percent of the respondents indicated that their responsibilities included purchasing, receiving, and storage (inventory).

The number of respondents responsible for the storage function increased 18 points from 1983 to 1989, going from 34 percent to more than 52 percent, and a purchasing function was claimed by 60 percent of the respondents, which is ten points greater than in 1983. Responsibility for hotel security, the least commonly shared function among the controllers, more than doubled in the last six years, growing from 9 percent in 1983 to almost 22 percent in the current study. The controllers' role in electronic data processing (EDP) and computer system management grew by leaps and bounds during the 1980s.

In 1989, more than 87 percent of the respondents

indicated responsibility for the computer systems used for accounting functions. Additionally, 58 percent indicated responsibility for front office and reservations system computers—systems clearly not under the umbrella of traditional accounting functions. In the 1983 study, we asked just one question about responsibility for EDP, and 52 percent of the controllers indicated that they had some responsibility for EDP. It's possible, however, that the 1983 finding is understated due to the vagueness of the question. In any event, it's clear that over the years computer-oriented responsibilities have escalated sharply. That conclusion is certainly consistent with the proliferation of electronic data-processing systems in all aspects of hotel operations. The majority of controllers reported responsibility of tax returns, cash management, and beverage controls.

A substantial percentage (more than 36 percent of the respondents in each case) also indicated responsibility for internal auditors, investments, and risk management. Our supposition that hotel controllers are increasingly becoming involved with all aspects of hotel operations and, as a result, are viewed as valuable members of the top management team, seems well founded. Further evidence of this professional leap upward is found by looking at the executive committee involvement of controllers. Overwhelming majorities of controllers are involved with such key management committees as compensation, executive, long-range planning, training, and risk management. By contrast, in the 1983 survey, only 23 percent of the controllers were on compensation committees (versus 75 percent in 1989), and only 41 percent were involved with long-range planning (versus 94 percent in 1989). There were insufficient salary increments in the questionnaire used for the 1983 study, and that flaw caused some confusion in the results. That problem was rectified in the current study by incorporating a wide range of salary increments—from under $20,000 to over $80,000.

The symmetrical distribution of salaries suggests that this time we successfully captured the compensation picture. Our results show that not only have salaries kept pace with inflation over the years, but that the distributions have been skewed significantly upward. For example, the lower increments (under $30,000) include fewer than 12 percent of the 1989 respondents compared to 32 percent in 1983. Similarly, the range of $30,000-$39,900 has dropped from 39 percent to 30 percent. At the same time, the high end has expanded. The top five increments of the 1989 study (salaries greater than $40,000) comprise more than 58 percent of the respondents, which is more than double the figure for the same salary range in 1983 (29 percent). As one might expect, experience and the specific characteristics of a controller's company or hotel affect his or her salary. Here there are no surprises:

The higher the controller's position, the higher the median salary; the larger the hotel (whether measured by number of rooms or annual room sales), the higher the median salary; the higher the level of education obtained, the higher the median salary. Such results are very similar to those from the 1983 study.

Bonus points

Typically, salary structures for top management personnel include provisions for bonuses. The number of controllers receiving bonuses in the 1989 study was about seven out of ten, up from slightly more than six out of ten in 1983. The median bonus in 1989 was between 11 and 20 percent of a controller's salary. While many different factors contribute to whether or not a controller will earn a bonus, the most common basis for issuing a bonus to a controller was whether the enterprise met its profit objectives. That standard affected almost 60 percent of controllers in 1989. Other bonus determining factors may include one or more of the following: meeting sales objectives, increasing profits over those from the previous year, achieving personal objectives, accounts receivable performance, cash flow, employee satisfaction, and corporate profits. The availability of fringe benefits for controllers in the current study is quite similar to the findings of the 1983 study.

Focus of internal auditing

The focus of the internal audit function is control. In fact, the internal audit function is a control designed to appraise the effectiveness of other controls. Internal control has been defined by the American Institute of Certified Public Accountants (AICPA) as "the plan of organization and all of the coordinate methods and measures within a business to safeguard its assets, check the accuracy and reliability of its accounting data, promote operational efficiency and encourage adherence to prescribed managerial policies".

The role of the internal auditor has been enlarged due to the expanding oversight of various government agencies and the passage of new laws. Today's hospitality firm has to satisfy many different agencies at all levels of government. The business is required to comply with complex regulations issued by taxing authorities, health and safety authorities, fair trade administrators, equal rights and affirmative action units, pension plan agencies, to name a few, while meeting a host of provisions regarding licensing of activities and the conduct of business operations.

Functional role of the internal auditor

The question often arises as to how an internal audit staff can conduct audits that require such a wide range of knowledge in so many different areas. The principal reasons that professional auditors can successfully do this are:

1. Highly qualified personnel, professionally designated as CPAs (certified public accountants), CIAs (certified internal auditors), and CMAs (certified management accountants), comprise a significant portion of the staffs of successful internal audit departments. Auditors maintain and improve their competence through continuing education programs.
2. Many internal audit departments utilize a team concept in building their staffs. This concept includes persons from various academic disciplines (accounting, auditing, finance, computer sciences, management, marketing, and others) who provide a synergistic effect.
3. Consultants or specialists are employed as needed to supply additional technical assistance.
4. Internal auditors are highly trained to use standards (desirable benchmarks) against which they compare actual organizational performance.

The internal auditor is not part of the operations team. Even though it may seem to be more efficient to use internal auditors to determine account number assignments or to decide when an expenditure should be capitalized, internal auditors must maintain their independence if they are to serve as appraisers of operating activities. Secondly, the internal auditor has a staff assignment rather than a line position. Line managers have the responsibility for operations, and this should not be shifted to the internal auditor.

The findings and recommendations of the internal auditor are advisory and should be implemented by line personnel based on their merits to the operation as determined by the line personnel. In order for the internal auditing function to be independent, that is, properly detached from operations and the functional staff groups such as accounting, finance, and marketing, the internal auditors often answer to the top management such as the chief financial officer, the operating executive, or even the audit committee of the board of directors.

Recent research on internal auditors in major lodging chains revealed that:

1. 19.4 percent reported to the controller.
2. 32.3 percent reported to the senior financial officers.
3. 16.1 percent reported to a corporate executive and the board.
4. 6.5 percent reported to the board.
5. 32 percent reported to the audit committee of the board.

The independence (ability to make objective audit decisions unaffected by influence from the activity audited) of internal auditors is affected primarily by two things: (1) the organizational level to which the auditor reports, and (2) the professional training and mindset of objectivity of the internal auditor.

Internal auditing activities

Internal auditing activities may be divided into four broad categories by the financial and managerial data each examines. The four major activities are:

1. Checking compliance with internal controls and procedures.
2. Checking compliance with applicable laws and procedures.
3. Determining whether the firm's resources are being

used efficiently.

4. Determining whether the firm's resources are being used effectively.

The internal auditing activities pertaining to internal controls would generally include such procedures as reviewing the bank reconciliation (financial data) and determining that there is adequate separation of duties in the handling of cash transactions (nonfinancial data). This major activity area received increased emphasis with the passage of the Foreign Corrupt Practices Act of 1977, which mandated that businesses have adequate internal accounting controls.

The activities included under checking compliance with applicable laws and procedures also pertain to financial and nonfinancial data. For example, the financial aspect includes the review of the company's federal tax return to determine compliance with the Internal Revenue Code. A nonfinancial aspect is determining whether the food and beverage operation is in compliance with, local health department regulations.

The internal auditing activities oriented to the efficient use of organizational resources would include conducting analytical reviews of various assets such as accounts receivables and inventories (financial data) and determining the efficiency of the firm's marketing efforts (nonfinancial data). Finally, internal auditing activities evaluating the effective use of the firm's resources would include determining whether the return on investment (ROI) for a property is above the organization's hurdle rate (financial) and determining the effectiveness of community service projects (nonfinancial).

Technical approach of the internal auditor

Internal auditing activities generally include the four major steps of planning, conducting, evaluating, and reporting.

Common procedures used and an example of each are as follows:

Procedure	*Example*
Comparing	Comparison of actual room sales to budgeted room sales and reviewing explanations for significant differences.
Vouching	Reviewing suppliers' invoices to support amounts recorded as food purchases.
Confirming	Having food purveyors verify the amount of unpaid invoices at the end of the year.
Scanning	Visually reviewing cash register tapes to determine if the number of sales trans-actions and voided transactions on the resta-urant's cash register equals the number of completed or voided server checks for a given time period.
Analysing	A comparison of an operating department's labour costs to its sales for several one-week periods throughout the year.
Inquiring	Obtaining a reasonable expla-nation from the head of the maintenance department as to why maintenance costs exceeded the budget for the month by 15 percent.
Observing	Observing the complete processing of a guest's food order from the recording by the server to delivery of food to the guest to determine the efficiency of the process.
Recomputing	Adding the cost of food inventory items to verify the computer total.

The evaluation phase is critical to drawing conclusions

that are the basis for management decisions. The scope of this phase may be best understood by answering these questions.

1. How good is the result presently being achieved? The focus may be how well a procedure has been complied as a measure of efficiency or effectiveness.
2. Why is the result what it is? Related to the first question is the evaluation of why the results are as they are and perhaps why they are not better.
3. Finally, what could be done to achieve better results in the future?

The final phase is reporting the results of the audit. The report summarizes what has been accomplished and makes the results available to executive level management.

The night audit

Hotels have always needed methods for keeping guest accounts up to date and ready for submission when guests check out. Because check-outs usually occur early in the morning it has fallen upon the front office night shift—those people working from 11:00 PM to 7:00 AM—to accumulate all charges and credits guests have accrued and to prepare the bill for presentation. Over the years, the procedure has become known as the night audit, and the individual who performs it as the night auditor. As the size and complexity of hotels increased and the demands on the night auditor grew, the night audit procedure evolved from a relatively simple, handwritten process to the sophisticated electronic systems that even small hotels use today.

Part of the night audit procedure involves compiling the guest bill for presentation. These bills are the accounts receivable to the hotel and must be readied daily since guests might wish to look at their bill or check out at any time. There is, however, more to the night audit than just preparing guest bills. The main task, and the real "audit" portion of the process, is to reconcile all the accounts, ensuring that all charges are correctly posted (assigned) to the proper guest accounts. Records of each hotel department's charges are forwarded to the night auditor, who compares what has been posted to the guest accounts with what was actually charged in the department. This process culminates in the auditor performing a trial balance of all the different guest accounts, thus ensuring that all accounting transactions relating to these accounts were handled correctly.

Additionally, even a small hotel would accumulate a large number of bills in a relatively short time. For example, a 250-room hotel that was 70 percent occupied during a month with only one person per room would generate 5,250 guestdays of business (250 × 30 × 0.7). If each guest stayed for three days, that would mean there would be 1,750 different bills (5,250/3) to prepare at the end of the month! The original purpose of the night audit procedure was to ensure that the bills presented to guests were accurate and up to date. The accounts needed to be reconciled before the guest departed.

Since this was usually in the morning, and since the late-night shift at a front desk was usually quiet, it was logical that the procedure that became the night audit would be done at this time. It also allowed someone to post all the accounts that the guest accrued before the guest went to bed, including the charge for the room itself. By midnight, it could be assumed that everyone who was going to check into the hotel had.

The accounting day would end with the closing of the last department, usually the lounge, and all charges for the day could be posted. The history of the night audit procedure can be separated into three main categories: (1) the hand transcript, (2) the machine audit, and (3) the electronic audit. Each of the categories evolved as a necessary response to the increased size and complexity of hotel operations, alongside the development of new technologies to aid the night auditor. While these three categories evolved in the order presented, it should be remembered that there are a number of hotels today that use a hand transcript or machine audit and have, for good reasons, not completely adopted the latest technology.

The hand transcript

In the early days of hotels the hand transcript developed from the need for room clerks to account for the increasing number of guests hotels were accommodating. During the nineteenth century, hotels were growing rapidly in size, and it was no longer possible for a landlord or owner to perform all the tasks required as host. Traditionally, the desk of the smaller hotel, if there even was one, would close at night.

However, as the hotels became larger, the need for desk clerks and other employees increased, and the notion of a 24-hour front desk operation arose. Similarly, a need to keep track of guest accounts arose, since more and more establishments were allowing patrons to charge instead of requiring cash up front. It was no longer practical for accounts to be prepared when guests asked for them. Additionally, hoteliers in general were discovering the increased need for control over the monies that were being generated. As a consequence, the concept of the night audit, born out of these conditions, developed. The original night audit was a handwritten, manually totalled list of guest accounts. On a large sheet of paper, or in a ledger book, individual guest accounts were arranged in rows, while the different departments that a guest could charge in were arranged in columns. After guest charges were accumulated and each individual bill was tabulated, the entries on the bills were transferred to the night audit transcript.

Both debit (charge) and credit (payment) entries were included. Row totals were calculated as debits minus credits equals amount due. Column totals were calculated and represented the total charges or credits for each department. In this fashion, the auditors would be able to verify each guest's bill by comparing it to the bill as originally created. More importantly, the auditors could then compare the departmental totals with another set of totals prepared in the individual department.

The Machine Audit

As electric cash registers became more popular, specialized machines were developed for specialized purposes, one of which was a machine that would perform the mechanical aspects of the night audit. Perhaps the most famous of these were the series of posting machines built by the National Cash Register Company. Almost every front office manager or hotel manager who started a career from the 1930s to the present time has had experience on one or another of these machines. The advantages of these machines were several. First, they would automatically total the charges or credits for each department, eliminating the need for hand calculations.

Second, the folio that is the permanent guest record could be processed through the machine, providing to the guest (and to the front office personnel) complete information on charges and credits during the guest's stay, including the date of the transaction, the department involved, the amount of the transaction, and the room number the charge was posted to. This "automated" approach eliminated much of the drudgery involved in the bookkeeping aspect of the audit and freed the auditors to spend more time on the audit portion of the job-finding mistakes and correcting them.

Third advantage of the machine was that each individual posting clerk could be controlled by having separate locks on the machine. Therefore, it was easier to monitor the activity at the front desk. This became especially important as hotels grew larger and the posting clerks were made responsible for posting charges to the guest accounts as they were accumulated during the day's operation. The goal was to require the night auditor to post as few charges as possible, thus freeing time to perform the actual audit.

A fourth advantage, and perhaps the most important from the standpoint of the night auditor, was the ability to print out a form referred to as the "D" card. The "D" card, was a special form that automatically totalled the entire day's activity. This gives departmental totals for all debit and credit transactions that were made on the posting machine. This particular form was printed out while the night auditor was clearing the machine, or "zeroing out" the totals on the posting of the machine, making it ready for the next day's transactions. Obviously, this would only be done when all posting for the day had been completed.

The night auditor, who could validate the work of the posting clerks, was the only person who could reset the machine. Note, however, that this system did not apply when the night auditor posted accounts as well as verifying them. One other situation arose during the time that the posting/auditing machines developed. To this point all discussion has centered around the charges made by guests -staying at the hotel, or the transient guests. These accounts were grouped together in what came to be known as the transient ledger. However, another entire category of guests existed: guests who were not currently staying in the hotel but were nevertheless allowed charging privileges. Originally, these individuals would probably have lived in the city where the hotel was and, as a result ' came to be known as city ledger guests. The city ledger accounts were, and still are, very similar to the standard type of accounts found in any retail store since it was easier to bill them than to bill the accounts of transient guests.

Moreover, since the majority of transactions in the hotels remained transient ledger accounts, the night auditor's function was expanded to include these charges as well. This simplified the bookkeeping process by having all charges funnel into one area. In general terms, then, the job of the night auditor would include the following steps:

1. Post any remaining departmental charges to their proper accounts, whether city or transient ledger.
2. Post all room charges, including tax, to their proper accounts.
3. Perform a trial balance of accounts, to ensure all accounts are posted correctly. Make any adjusting entries necessary.
4. Finalize the audit by clearing the machine and setting it for the next day.
5. Prepare any reports that management has requested.

There were problems associated with the machine audits. First, the machines would post to whatever accounts the posting clerks entered in them. This meant that posting to a wrong account, posting the wrong amount, and forgetting to post entirely were still problems. Additionally, since any posting made was now a part of the machine's accumulated total, making changes were not simply a matter of erasing the wrong number and replacing it with the correct one.

The Electronic Audit

The final type of audit, and the type in general usage in most types of hotels today, is the electronic audit. Essentially, this evolutionary trend is an offshoot of the computer revolution. While the machine audits were much more sophisticated and had better controls built in than the hand transcripts, they were no more than specialized adding machines. While any discussion of the sophistication of the electronic audit would by necessity be outdated the moment it is written, the electronic audit has several advantages over the manual or machine audit that bear mentioning. Even with the machine audit, the job of tracing errors and proving the trial balance still fell on the auditor. Today, however, computer systems have been designed to "think" in the sense that they can be programmed to search for the posting errors within the system, thus eliminating another need for the auditor to waste time.

Most systems have commands that will allow the posting of room charges (room rate, room tax, and local telephone) to be done automatically. This in and of itself saves an enormous amount of time since the auditor does not have to post to every folio separately. There are many other ways in which these systems can save time. Perhaps the ultimate example is in the point-of-sale system, where the departmental charges are posted directly from the department cash register onto the guest folio, thus eliminating the need for the intermediary posting clerks. For example, there are point-of-sale systems in lounges and dining rooms that will transmit any charge made at the location to the central computer, which will automatically post the charge to the indicated account. What these sophisticated systems demand is a different kind of auditor, one who understands the computer process and can perform the audit functions necessary in the electronic data-processing age. There are, of course, still problems associated with computer systems, including the one mentioned above concerning an overkill of reports generated.

The problem also remains that accounts can be posted incorrectly. Many of the systems feature built-in safeguards that effectively minimize these human mistakes. One example is the point-of-sale register, which has prices programmed into it, so no pricing errors can be made. A third problem concerns the fact that electronic machinery does not necessarily produce physical copies of the hotel's records. Thus, if the system should break down and no hard copies had been made, there might be no way to reproduce guest accounts. Worse, they might all be lost. It is extremely important that the operating procedure of the system prevent this catastrophic occurrence.

It has happened that front office employees have had to literally knock on guest doors, find out if anyone is staying in the room, and then ask the guest how much his or her bill should be! There is one final caveat to all those who are learning computer, or even machine, night audit systems. Machines fail, and people who are responsible for generating the folios for presentation to the guest will always need to know how to do the job manually should the system go down. Even the most conscientious controller or front desk manager will inevitably face a crisis situation where the system cannot provide the information needed. It is for this reason all employees involved in the preparation of guest folios should know how to accumulate the required information necessary to keep open the flow between guest and hotel.

Hotel Purchasing

"Purchasing" is a term that has a variety of beverage facilities, to housekeeping, or to what meanings to different people. However, as it is generally used in the hospitality industry, it refers to the processes of buying: ascertaining need, locating and selecting suppliers, negotiating prices and terms, and ensuring adequate delivery. In addition, purchasing includes storage, receiving, incoming inspection, and capital goods procurement. Unfortunately for many managers in the hospitality industry, purchasing is often viewed as a supplementary staff activity that simply assures that hospitality organizations have an adequate supply of goods and services. In fact, purchasing is a lot more than this. It is a key business activity that not only supports day-to-day operations but has a substantial impact on a variety of major business functions ranging from profit making to competitive positioning.

Efficient operations

The enhancement of hospitality operations is probably purchasing's most basic contribution. It does this by ensuring that goods and services are purchased in the proper quantity at the proper quality, by making sure that deliveries are on time, and by managing storage in such a way that raw materials provide maximum service. The department or managers charged with purchasing responsibility make this happen by working with operations managers to ascertain needs, by selecting reliable vendors, and by developing systems to assure a smooth throughput of raw goods in the operation-from the receiving dock to the storeroom, to the food and ever operating department requires these products.

Profit

Purchasing influences profit in two very important ways. First, because every dollar saved through prudent and judicious purchasing goes directly toward the bottom line; and secondly, because the effective use of assets ultimately affects a firm's return on investment (ROI). Let's explore the relationship between purchasing savings and bottom-line results. This typical situation illustrates the profit-making potential of wise purchasing. Let's assume that the Sleep-AU-Night Hotel Company has a sales volume of approximately $267 million, of which 30 percent, or approximately $80 million, is contributed by food and beverage sales.

Material costs for food and beverage run about 40 percent on average, and pretax profit margins average around 10 percent, or about $8 million. If management were astute and able to increase sales by $20 million (25 percent), this would represent a $2 million increase on the bottom line (0.10 x 20,000,000 = $2,000,000). However, if purchasing were able to decrease the cost of sales to 37.5 percent, a 2.5 percent decrease, the $2 million saved would go directly to the bottom line and thus equal as much on the bottom line as a 25 percent increase in sales! The following simple formula can be used to determine the sales equivalent of purchasing savings:

$$x = y \div z$$

Where:

x = the additional sales volume required to produce a pretax profit equal to that produced by a purchasing cost reduction

y = the reduction (expressed in dollars) in purchasing cost

z = the firm's pretax profit margin expressed as a decimal

In the preceding example, the equation would look like this:

x = $2,000,000 - 0.10

x = $20,000,000

Thus, it would require a $20 million sales increase to equal the effect of a $2 million cost reduction on the bottom line. While a 5 percent reduction in purchasing costs would be difficult, it is not impossible. Similarly, a 25 percent increase in sales would not be impossible, but it would be a lot more difficult than achieving a 5 percent reduction in costs.

The effect of purchasing on ROA is similar, if less dramatic. To assess an organization's overall performance, it is essential to consider the rate of return produced by all capital invested in the operation. This is called return on investment. While profit margin on sales is important, it is only half the ROI equation. The effective use of the organization's resources is equally important, and the formula for ROA is illustrates why. In accounting terms ROA is equal to the profit margin times the asset turnover rate.

In mathematical terms, this would be expressed as:

ROA = operating income (i.e., profit) ÷ total assets

ROA = (operating income - sales) × (sales - total assets)

As you can see, one half of the equation is devoted to how well managers use assets in relationship to total sales and the other is devoted to how well managers control costs in relationship to sales. Let's use the following example to illustrate: A hospitality organization has operating income of $ 1 million on $ 10 million in sales, and its total assets are equal to $ 9 million. If we plug this into the equation listed above for ROA, the equation would look like this:

($1,000,000 ÷ $10,000,000) × ($10,000,000 $9,000,000)

= 0.11, or 11% ROA

Purchasing can influence both the profit side through cost reduction and the asset side through total asset reduction. Let's say that through judicious purchasing we were able to increase operating income to $ 1.2 million and to decrease the asset base to $ 7 million. Let's calculate the effect on ROA:

$$(\$1{,}200{,}000 \div \$10{,}000{,}000) \times (\$10{,}000{,}000\ \ \$7{,}000{,}000)$$

$$= 0.17, \text{ or } 17\% \text{ ROA}$$

Thus the influence of purchasing on ROA is obvious.

The hotel purchasing function

The hotel purchasing function has not changed very much in the past 15 years. Up until the late 1980s various tax advantages were the primary reason for the construction of U.S. hotels. Providing a substantial return on investment was not expected or required. In our current economy, expectations on hotel profitability have changed. Profitability is now required along with maintaining the established level of quality. This has brought about a new interest in the purchasing function and greater importance placed on cost savings.

The true definition of purchasing should be "purchasing the right product, at the right price, at the right time." The statement sounds extremely simple, but when it is applied to the 1,000 to 2,000 items a hotel purchases, it presents a great challenge for the purchasing manager. The hotel purchasing function supports virtually every department within the property, whether purchasing chemicals for housekeeping or stewarding, office supplies for marketing, computer supplies for accounting, or food and beverage products for the restaurant outlets.

The purchasing manager usually reports to the hotel controller or to the hotel's financial control division.This will change in the future because there is a need for a more operational approach to managing the purchasing function. We need to build a team that is committed to the common goal of servicing our customers. The reporting structure will begin to shift to operations, with the purchasing manager directly reporting to the general manager or to the executive assistant or operations manager in larger properties. This would help-to promote the philosophy of team building, and purchasing would support and service customers directly rather than acting as a support to other hotel departments.

With the increasing importance of the purchasing function, the utopian mission of the purchasing manager is to procure products and services cost effectively that will meet or exceed the customer's expectation. It is necessary to continually evaluate product specifications to incorporate new products and technology.

Purchasing organisation

The purchasing department can be organized into three basic areas:

— *Administrative*: This area would consist of pricing, vendor selection, and the purchase of nonstocked items. Nonstocked items are products purchased for immediate use or held in storage in other departments throughout the hotel.

— *Receiving*: There are two categories of receiving: (1) hotel goods, which are placed in storage in the purchasing area, or other items, Which are immediately issued to the requesting department, guest, or group; (2) items that have been shipped to a registered guest or expected guest or group.

— *Issuing*: Product issuing falls into two categories: (1) consumable food and beverage supplies, consisting of all food items and liquor, beer, wine, and mixes held in the purchasing department storerooms; (2) items such as office supplies, printed forms, and linen.

The staffing and segregation of duties vary from hotel to hotel, depending upon the property size and physical layout of the back-of-teh house areas.

Interdepartmental relationships

The purchasing manager develop close working relationships with key managers within the hotel. These relationships should build and demonstrate trust, confidence in judgment, and integrity. Key managers would include the following:

— Hotel general manager

— Executive assistant/operations managing

— Director of food and beverage

— Executive chief

— Director of housekeeping

Interaction between the purchasing manager and all other departments occurs on a regular basis. Verbal interaction is the most frequent either by telephone or in person. With the technological implementation of voice mail and electronic mail the communication process has become more efficient.

Most day-to-day interaction by the purchasing manager would involve some of the following key managers and issues:

— *General manager/executive assistant manager*: Issues relating to quality changes and all discussions regarding capital expenditure, food markets, quality, and availability information.

— *Director of food and beverage*: Unresolved food-purchasing issues and information related to wine, liquor, and beer purchases.

— *Executive chef.* Issues relating to food purchases. This area requires close communications regarding vendor performance, various size and physical layout of the back-of-the house areas.

— *Director of housekeeping*: Coordination and purchase of linens, paper goods (toilet paper, facial tissue, paper towels), uniforms, and laundry and cleaning chemicals.

A good purchasing manager bases purchasing decisions on the same criteria for all business decisions-data. No one can be an expert on every product available. This is where purchase specifications come into play. Written specifications must be developed for all key products. These products should also be tested periodically to verify that they meet or exceed specifications.

Purchasing sources

There are many sources of information for identifying producers, processors, and manufacturers. Technical data are also available. Suppliers are the best source of information.

The purchasing manager's day

7:00 AM. Inspect the quality of food and beverage consumables as they are delivered to the hotel. This includes rejecting incorrect or inferior products and then contacting the appropriate vendor(s) to rectify issues or determine another source, if necessary. The average daily purchase cost could vary from a low of $3,000 to a high of $50,000, depending on the size of the property and level of business.

9:00-11:00 AM. Attend daily meeting with the chef and the catering, stewarding, and banquet departments to review upcoming banquet business. Included would be a review of the room setup for each scheduled function, menus, and, most important, the guaranteed attendance numbers.

12:00 Noon. All food and beverage purchases have been received and issued. Inventory is now taken on all items in store to determine the next day's needs. After reviewing the current levels and calculating banquet business requirements, the vendors are selected. Orders are now placed with all suppliers. The number of suppliers could range from 1 to 25.

The rest of the afternoon is spent working on nonconsumable food and beverage purchases, obtaining bids, and following up on outstanding purchase orders overdue for delivery. The average work week for the purchasing manager is 50 to 60 hours and may include weekends. For the most part, normal business hours are usually 7:00 Am to 6:00 Pm, Monday through Friday, and 7:00 Am to noon on Saturday.

Cooperation and interaction

Corporate direction and control varies with each hotel company. As a rule, many hotel companies that manage rather than franchise their properties are more involved in setting policies and procedures. The corporate purchasing function is still viewed with some skepticism, although not as much as in the past.

Today, purchasing is not a profit center and is established to benefit managed properties. The idea for the 1990s is to do more with less, and this applies to the corporate level as well as to the individual properties. The most efficient method of purchasing system wide is targeting where dollars are spent and creating the most cost-efficient way to purchase high-volume items. Corporate hotel purchasing offices are currently working to accomplish this goal. Hotel purchasing must focus on and utilize resources in the most efficient manner today. In the past, a heavy-handed approach was used to resolve issues with suppliers. As we move toward building partner-ships with key vendors today, a teamwork approach provides an environment to build upon the strengths of both the hotel and the vendor.

Another key component in business today is communication, both internal within the hotel and external with suppliers. One of our national Suppliers has the capability to link their customer service for placing orders with our domestic properties through a mainframe computer network linked to each property by PCs. Our hotels can place orders directly with the supplier through the network system and receive immediate confirmation. This nationwide system allows both our properties and the corporate office to access pricing, availability, and consumption.

Vital guidelines for property

While that was happening, more positive trends were evolving in hardware, software, and market scope. This article provides a summary of developments in each of those areas.

Hardware

During the past decade, the cost of computers and peripherals (in terms of performance per dollar invested) has dropped an average of more than 20 percent a year, and the trend is likely to continue. The hottest development of 1991 was the arrival of Intel's 486 microchip-An the PMS market. The 486 microprocessor doesn't fit all PMS situations, and not all the PMS packages can use it as a platform for their software. However, the following real-world example shows what happens in a hotel situation where the 486 does fit:

— Early in 1992, a large, upscale Midwest hotel

distributed specific bid specifications for a new PMS. Hardware requirements included 26 display screens and eight printers.

— Hardware cost of the lowest bid for a minicomputer-based system was $151,610. Lowest hardware bid for a LAN-based system was $169,427.

— When the hotel decided that both bids were beyond its budget, it asked the bidder of the UNIX-based minicomputer system to rebid the hardware using two interfaced micros with 386 chips. The hardware cost went down to $105,274.

The switch from mini-computer to two 386s, and then to a 486-based hardware configuration, resulted in a PMS installation that uses the same supplier's software at less than half the original hardware price. The continuing cost reduction in microcomputer hardware is very good for hotel budgets, but it is beginning to intrude on the market base of the major minicomputer and mainframe manufacturers. It's also actually hurting many of the PMS suppliers, because their revenue stream is dependent on a percentage of the' hardware price. When hardware costs keep falling and the commission percentage remains the same, that means fewer revenue dollars for the PMS supplier. That downward trend in hardware prices is not likely to stop. For example, Intel is planning to introduce a 100-MHz version of its 486 chip in 1993, and its design engineers have already begun work on developing the next generation microchip. It will be a 64-bit reduced instruction set computing (RISC) microchip.

New software tools

For the properties it manages, Sheraton Corporation recently decided to standardize on the new UNIX-based PMS software developed by ECI Computer. It was then able to evaluate computer bids from several manufacturers before selecting Hewlett-Packard hardware for those properties. That portability wasn't always available, and that is one of the many key changes in software design that have been gaining importance during the past year. To understand the change in software tools, let's go back 20 years, when EECO (now ECI) pioneered the first successful PMS installation at the Dorado Beach Hotel in Puerto Rico.

The system was functional (but costly) and was based on proprietary components (hardware and software). Until the 1980s, any PMS developer had to decide which hardware would be used (Burroughs, DEC, Data General, Honeywell, IBM, NCR) and then develop the application using that hardware platform's proprietary operating system. As a result, the PMS developer was locked into specific (and limited) tools. In turn, the hotel's PMS was limited in growth and flexibility, and it could be run on only one brand of computer. Lodgistix's first product used the &M Series/I. Computerized Lodging Systems chose MAI/ Basic Four.

Encore Lodging Systems opted for DEC equipment. Hotel Information Systems developed the first PMS on the now long-defunct IBM System/32. EECO used a Data General processor as its base and manufactured the remaining hardware. The operating systems associated with those hardware choices had names like EDX, BOSS, TSC + RTH, SSP, and GCOS.Other important new software tools are relational database management systems and fourth-generation languages. They have these advantages for the hotel PMS user:

— Software development, enhancement, and problem-solving time have been cut to less than half that needed with previous software tools. This means savings that can be passed on to the hotel in terms of competitive pricing and faster response to requests for software modification.

— In the past, if a change was made to a hotel PMS's data base, all the programs affected by the data base had to be recompiled.

For example, if the system had ten programs that used the reservations data base, all ten programs had to be modified and recompiled. This was time consuming and prone to errors. With today's program-development tools, the same scenario involves only one program change, and state-of-the-art software does all the rest.

Market scope

The classified pages of U.S. telephone directories list 73,068 hotels and motels; however, most of them were traditionally considered to be much too small to cost-justify a property management system. At the beginning of the 1980s, no more than 400 lodging properties could possibly install one, but the steady hardware cost reductions have kept increasing the size of the potential market.

6

HOSPITALITY MAINTENANCE

The maintenance-and-engineering department has been treated as a catch-all department, which literally means that if a problem is not related to food, marketing or sales, housekeeping, or accounting, it must be a maintenance and-engineering responsibility. Many operations define maintenance and engineering by its areas of responsibility. Other operations rely on normal dictionary definitions. Regardless of the definition or responsibilities of an organization, the basic purpose of the department can be stated as: keeping the structure, its machines, its systems, and its products in an existing or specified state of readiness. This definition assumes that everything is kept in repair, that it is operating at a high efficiency level (low energy consumption), and that there are minimal breakdowns. For a hotel, it means keeping guest rooms and public space salable, at a low cost.

Future hospitality managers will have to learn basic maintenance-and-engineering management concepts, how to analyse engineering data, and most important, the language necessary to communicate with maintenance—and engineering personnel. One purpose of this text is to provide the awareness and basic knowledge needed in order to make appropriate decisions in engineering, maintenance, and energy management. Hospitality building engineering and maintenance systems include: life safety; heating, ventilation, and air conditioning; electrical; water; transportation; exterior; environment; and special facilities equipment. In this book the future hospitality manager will become familiar with each system and strategies for effectively managing each system.

There is no glamour in managing the maintenance and engineering systems in a hotel, restaurant, club, hospital, or other hospitality building, but properly managed systems from design to operation can result in considerable long-term savings; or, on the contrary, the failure to manage such systems can result in significant long-term costs. Lodging and foodservice managers know that their management role has changed because of the increasing importance of engineering, maintenance, and energy requirements in their industry.

The health-care administrator has the same building-management problems as a hotel manager, but he must also cope with complex medical equipment. Changing technology in health care has been extremely rapid. The cost of providing space for a bed in a hospital is equivalent to the cost of a deluxe hotel room. Lodging and foodservice managers have complained about the high energy requirements per customer and how energy costs have reduced profit-making potential. They are frequently amazed to learn that their counterparts in health care consume 50 to 100 percent more energy per person to provide modem health-care facility services. Many of these non-profit institutions now offer services—expensive in the eyes of patients and clients—that have resulted in shorter patient stays, quicker recoveries, higher turnover, and a rash of statistics that make health-care units look like high-occupancy transient hotels. Health-care units are frequently compared with resort hotels in terms of their services and costs. Lodging units, foodservice operations, and health-care facilities have felt the maintenance/engineering/energy crunch. Costs in these three areas have increased three to five times faster than revenue, giving rise to price increases that offset at least part of these increased costs. This solution, however, is not available for institutional buildings, which are often heavily dependent on government funding, or for clubs, which may be unable to make the necessary adjustments in membership dues. In these last two cases, it is all too easy to cut back on maintenance and repairs, to delay repairs until they are absolutely necessary or until a piece of equipment has broken down.

The money saved by postponing maintenance can be partially used to pay energy bills. To compound the problem, a large and significant number of these institutional buildings and clubs are located in areas of very high labour and energy costs. Maintenance policy and energy consumption are usually dependent on each other; for example, if a piece of equipment is not maintained, its energy consumption increases and its life expectancy declines. Delaying normal maintenance results in very short-term savings. Many clubs and institutional operations that have delayed maintenance now face abnormally heavy maintenance, repair, and equipment replacement costs.

Management factors

Whatever the job title, facility manager, chief engineer, or maintenance supervisor, management is a critical element of the job. Whereas in past years the person holding the job of facility manager, chief engineer, or maintenance supervisor could be a good technician and be successful, the investment in facilities and the costs associated with the operations of such facilities require the person holding the position today to also be a strong manager. When evaluating the effectiveness of the management of the engineering-and-maintenance unit, particular attention should be directed toward the established goals and objectives of the unit, organizational structure of the unit, budget decisions, safety and security, workload identification and scheduling, controls and reports in use, and how computers are being utilized to manage the unit.

Goals and objectives

Managing the maintenance and engineering systems for hospitality building(s) might be defined as: design, construction, occupancy and use, repair, renovation, and disposal. The manager of the engineering-and-maintenance unit will have a difficult time keeping the unit on track if there is no end goal or set of guiding objectives. It is difficult to apply a common standard to all facilities.

Goals for an engineering-and-maintenance unit may vary considerably depending on the intended use of the facility and the business of the user. However, the goals for an engineering-and-maintenance unit must conform to the overall strategy for the hospitality business and must meet two industry-wide goals. The first goal, which is both strategic and operational, is to ensure that customers, guests, employees, and other constituencies are able to visit or work in a certain type of location and, along with that, a specific type of environment. At a minimum, it is likely to include that the environment be safe and clean and that any facility-related problems are attended to promptly. If this goal is ignored, the business may have difficulty attracting and retaining employees, customers, and guests, thereby decreasing revenues and increasing costs. The second important goal should target financial performance in terms of costs per square foot, costs per employee, costs as a percentage of revenues, costs as a percentage of total expenses, and costs in relation to prior period and budgeted costs. Objectives for an engineering-and-maintenance unit typically are directed toward preventive maintenance, repair, replacement, improvement, and modification.

Preventive maintenance

Preventive maintenance is any work performed on an operational device or facility to continue operating at its proper efficiency without interruption. The interval between preventive maintenance actions on a particular device is typically established by manufacturer's recommendations or measurements that show the declining performance of a piece of equipment or facility components.

Replacement

Replacement is performed when a piece of equipment or a facility component has reached the end of its useful life, that is, when the equipment or facility component can no longer perform effectively and repair is no longer cost effective.

Typically, the replacement objective for the engineering-and maintenance unit might focus on executing a program of planned replacement of major facility components, which replaces failing equipment before failure with new or rebuilt components that have a lower life-cycle cost.

Improvement

Improvement projects enhance the proper operation or reduce the operating cost of a facility. Such projects might include the installation of energy-and utility-conserving devices or the replacement of properly operating but maintenance-intensive equipment with similar but more reliable products. Thus, the engineering-and-maintenance unit should have an objective to identify and execute any improvement project that will provide a payback of the initial investment in 3 years or less.

Modification

Modification projects alter the basic facility or facility component to accommodate a new function. Modification projects differ from improvement projects by their point of origin. Modification projects are initiated from outside of the engineering-and-maintenance unit, whereas improvement projects are initiated from within the unit. However, because modification projects are in large part driven by estimated costs, the engineering-and maintenance unit should have an objective to estimate accurately the costs of modification projects at or under budget.

Organizational structures in the hospitality industry

Lodging. On an organization chart, the chief engineer has always held a high-level position in a lodging establishment. The chief engineer appears to be part of the total management team. In the past, however, the general manager typically spent very little time discussing operational problems with the chief engineer, seldom visiting or inspecting the engineering department. Many general managers knew little about engineering, maintenance, and energy. Chief engineers tended to know even less about management and management systems. This situation persisted for years. Since 1950, the average number of guest rooms per lodging establishment has increased.

The average new lodging establishment generally has more than 100 to 150 guest rooms, with some food and beverage facilities. These new properties, as well as older units with equivalent services, require a working chief engineer. A chief engineer is normally required for a property of 200 or more guest rooms with food and beverage and meeting room facilities. All units, regardless of size and facilities, have property maintenance requirements.

Foodservice. Freestanding, or nonlodging, foodservice units seldom have a separate maintenance-and-engineering department. The foodservice manager is generally charged with this responsibility and frequently establishes a series of maintenance service contracts for the unit.

The utility designation may also mean that this person does the general cleaning of the dining areas, outside areas, and rest rooms. Most of these activities, however, are housekeeping tasks. The unit foodservice manager, like the manager of a smaller lodging establishment, must possess a variety of skills and maintenance/energy knowledge to be effective in reducing costs.

Health care. Many health-care operations have two or even three departments involved with maintenance, engineering, and energy management. The major department is plant maintenance, which is similar to the engineering department of a hotel. The other related departments, again similar to lodging, are housekeeping and laundry. Foodservice may also be included, and its problems are similar to those of a commercial foodservice operation. Health-care and lodging units have an advantage over foodservice units in that some type of maintenance-and-engineering department is frequently available on the premises. The plant maintenance department may also have the responsibility for maintaining kitchen equipment.

The engineering and maintenance functions are usually under the organizational control of an assistant administrator. The assistant administrator becomes in reality a property manager whose functions are similar to those of the general manager of a lodging unit. The intensive-care health facility is frequently organized as Alternative I or, for an operation with a smaller number of beds, Alternative R.

Clubs. Clubs vary according to the services offered to the membership. They also vary with respect to engineering, maintenance, and energy expenses. Some clubs are similar to foodservice units; others offer services similar to those of larger hotels, especially resort hotels.

The club manager is unique among managers in being responsible to a house committee. This committee sets policies, goals, and general operating procedures for the manager to follow. The committee can set maintenance and energy standards, which may be recommended by the club manager. One or more of the committee members may provide special skills and knowledge in these important areas and may be of great assistance to the manager. In addition to the house committee, the club manager can join the Club Managers Association of America and enlist in its manager certification program.

One of the requirements of the program is a standardized competence level in maintenance and energy management. Program completion is based on seminar participation, written exams, and a service record. The results of the program have been very encouraging. (Other special management areas in the hospitality industry have developed somewhat similar programs, but, in the author's opinion, the CMAA program is one of the most successful in developing a positive maintenance energy management attitude for a large and significant number of its managers and potential managers.)

Institutional buildings. Schools, office buildings, penal institutions, colleges, and noncommercial lodging units are defined as institutional buildings. The institutional area of the hospitality industry has generally given the most consideration to engineering, maintenance, and energy. One reason for this is that a large percentage of the operating cost of these units is for the physical plant. Tremendous thought is devoted to the initial design of institutional buildings, hence their often Spartan look. These buildings are very functional; the profit goal may be totally nonexistent. Many large institutional complexes still generate their own electric power (total energy systems, or co-generation). These units are concerned primarily with the generation of steam or hot water for building heat. Electric energy is a secondary benefit and, with slightly higher energy consumption, both electric energy and steam (or hot water) can be produced.

Budgeting

To accomplish the objectives of the engineering-and-maintenance unit, personnel, materials, tools, and equipment are required. Since a business does not have unlimited resources, the costs of personnel, materials, tools, and equipment must be accurately understood and predicted as far in advance as possible in order to maintain reasonable control and to apply limited resources for the greatest benefit.

The total amount of all estimated costs for a particular period comprises the budget. Expense trends developed for lodging are generally applicable to many other hospitality areas. Related industries frequently review lodging expense trends, because they are reported annually and other industries can make fairly accurate future projections based on these data. Volumes of material have been written over the past several years on trends, future developments, and operating statistics in the lodging industry, more than in any other hospitality industry.

Lodging

The average size of a lodging unit, in terms of guest rooms per unit, has increased. The average new lodging unit has about 150 guest rooms. This is very large in comparison to most international hotels. This large average size suggests that such properties usually have some type of maintenance department.

Property Operation and Maintenance (POM) Expenses. Property operation and maintenance (POM) expenses represented approximately 5.4 percent of operating expenses for U.S. hotels and motels in 1990. POM was 5.3 percent of operating expenses in 1994.

Expense Item	*Percent of total*
Property operation	43
Payroll	6
Building, general	19
Electrical and mechanical	3
Furniture	5
Grounds	4
Supplies	4
Painting and decorating	4
Waste removal	3
Other	13
Total	100
Energy Expense	
Fuel (natural gas, oil, coal)	23
Electricity	63
Water and sewage	9
Steam	5
Total	100

Fig 2: Lodging property operation and maintenance expenses; energy expenses 2-3

Engineering and maintenance employees. The number of employees in the maintenance department is influenced by the property size and the maintenance alternatives selected by the manager. Larger properties, with Alternatives I and II, will average 4.2 employees per 100 occupied guest rooms, or 3.1 employees per 100 available guest rooms. The chief engineer spends large sums of money each year. The actual amount depends on the age of the property, its facilities, and business activity level. Regardless of the measurement base-the percentage of revenue or actual dollars per room-these variables represent significant figures and have increased for several successive years.

	Number of rooms		
Type of hotel	Under 125	125-200	Over 200
Full service	$1250	$1281	$1602
Limited service	NA	688	782
Resort	NA	2218	2714
Suite	1138	1243	1382
Convention	NA	NA	1728

Fig 3: Annual energy costs per available guest room

Foodservice

Maintenance and energy expenses for a foodservice operation depend on one or more of the following factors:

1. Type of foodservice operation.
2. Basic construction and age of the building, especially whether the building is freestanding or contained within another building.
3. Sources of energy for the property.
4. Geographic location.
5. Age and type of kitchen equipment.

The foodservice manager's attitude, knowledge, and maintenance/energy skills are probably important.

	Number of rooms		
Type of hotel	Under 125	125-200	Over 200
Full service	$1157	$1229	$1879
Limited service	597	711	861
Resort	NA	NA	2714
Suite	1183	1365	1644
Convention	NA	NA	2963

Fig 4: Annual property and maintenance expenses

Unlike the lodging manager, who is dependent on a separate department to carry out maintenance tasks and an energy-management policy, the foodservice manager is responsible for these items. If the manager is fortunate, and if the operation is large enough, the manager may be justified in hiring a maintenance person to perform minimal tasks. Foodservice managers must generally develop and administer a series of maintenance service contracts for the major electromechanical parts of the building. Without such contracts, a manager must be prepared to contact local tradespeople directly whenever a repair is required. As most foodservice operations are open during the early evening hours, dependable, qualified tradespeople must be available when they are needed. It is very important for managers to develop good working relationships with maintenance contractors and tradespeople who understand the special needs of foodservice operations and can respond quickly in an emergency.

The National Restaurant Association (NRA) has researched the energy requirements of various types of foodservice operations. The NRA foodservice categories are: cafeteria, full-menu dinner house, limited-menu dinner house, expanded-menu fast food, limited-menu fast food, coffee shop, and pizza unit. Energy consumption data for these operation types will be reported in the next section.

Maintenance and energy expenses. Until the 1970s, maintenance and energy expenses in foodservice were very low when expressed as a percentage of sales. They were so low that management was not concerned if energy costs increased by one-third or one-half (33 to 50 percent). Energy expenses were around I percent or less of sales. During the early 1970s, the costs of energy doubled in one 3-year period, then doubled again in less than 5 years. As a result, energy costs are now anywhere from 2 to 8 percent of sales, depending on the type of table service and menu theme.

Maintenance expenses have risen but not as fast as energy costs. One reason for the large increase in maintenance is that many smaller operations have hired a maintenance person. The result is that maintenance expenses, on average, may now be 2 to 6 percent of sales. In most cases, that part of the kitchen steward's time that is spent on maintenance of kitchen equipment is still not charged to maintenance. The foodservice industry continues to spend about 3 percent of its sales for the purchase of new equipment in an effort to reduce maintenance and energy consumption.

Thus, as reported by Borsenik in 1983, foodservice management is spending an average of 9 percent of sales for maintenance, energy, and new foodservice equipment (3 percent for maintenance, 3 percent for energy, and 3 percent of new equipment-all average percentages) Isolated foodservice corporation data indicate that these percentages have not changed significantly since 1983. When these percentage-of-sales figures are related to percentage of initial investment, the meaning of energy and maintenance costs can be fully realized.

Figure 5 shows the average breakdown of energy expenses for various types of foodservice units by energy use areas: food preparation, sanitation, food refrigeration, lighting, and HVAC (heating, ventilation, and air conditioning).

Percentage energy consumption

Foodservice type	*preperation*	*sanitation*	*refregeration*	*HVAC*	*total*
Cafeteria	40.5	28.5	3.5	20.3	100.0
Coffee shop	35.0	18.6	3.8	26.9	100.0
Dinner house	33.6	21.7	7.1	26.4	100.0
Dinner house	24.9	19.5	10.7	26.3	100.0
Fast food	35.8	6.8	6.6	37.9	100.0
Fast food	45.0	8.1	4.4	23.3	100.0
Pizza	32.3	17.2	8.4	30.3	100.0
Average	35.8	20.4	5.9	12.5	100.0

Fig 5: Foodservice percentage energy consumption by function area

6-Month energy consumption

Foodservice type	*Btu(millions)*	*Watts (thousands)*	*% of average*
Cafeteria	3,128	916,504	194
Coffee shop	1,100	322,700	68
Dinner house	2,500	732,500	155
Dinner house	1,600	468,800	100
Fast food	1,200	351,600	75
Fast food	1,150	336,950	70
Pizza	583	170,819	36
Average	1,600	468,800	100

Fig 6: Average energy consumption for different types of foodservice establishments for a 6-month period

There has been minimal change in recent years from the statistics reported in 1984. Minimal change has occurred from the statistics reported in 1984 concerning average energy consumption by foodservice establishments. Of all the units listed, a limited-menu dinner house has the average total energy consumption, whereas a cafeteria consumes twice the average energy, and a pizza unit uses only about one-third of the average.

Health-care units

Construction costs in health-care centers follow lodging cost trends. The American Hospital Association reports that the physical-plant investment per patient bed was equivalent to about 50 percent of the cost of a new lodging room. This is a first cost, not a replacement cost. Assuming a typical health-care patient room to have two beds, the patient-room value is equivalent to the investment in a new lodging guest room. Approximately 80 percent of the investment is for the structure and its related equipment, including medical equipment and special furnishings.

Expense item	*Hospital*	*Nursing home*
Depreciation of physical plant	3.0%	NA
Plant operation	4.0	5.0%
Maintenance payroll	2.5	3.0
Laundry	2.5	2.0
Subtotal	12.0%	10.0%
Housekeeping	4.0	3.5
Total	16.0%	13.5%

Fig 7: Comparison of typical hospital and nursing home plant-maintenance expenses

A new health-care unit, or a unit's replacement cost, may range from $75,000 to $250,000 or more per two-bed room for intensive-care units. The costs of health-care services have risen more than 10 percent per year during the past 10 to 20 years. This means that costs double every 6 to 8 years. Maintenance, engineering, and energy expenses have increased at even higher rates.Normal plant maintenance cost is close to 10 percent of total expenses. If housekeeping and laundry expenses are included, the cost could reach 16 percent of total income. Several housekeeping functions are performed by the nursing staff and that many units of equipment are leased or may have contract maintenance. The percentage figures just cited vary with the type of health-care property. They are frequently slightly lower for new health-care facilities, high occupancy units, high census counts, and extended-care facilities.

The activities and related costs of maintenance, engineering, and energy are generally considered as fixed, or set-dollar, amounts. The percentage figure may increase to 20 or 25 percent of the total expenses for older health-care buildings.

Clubs

Clubs may be classified as country or city clubs. The primary differences are facility services and the setting, or site, of the facility. The presence of a golf course may distinguish a country club from a city club.

Clubs can be further divided into tennis, athletic, or social clubs, to mention only some classifications. It is not the intent of this text to discuss all the possible variations or associated problems of such clubs. Emphasis is placed on the operation of the physical plant. Because the services and purposes of clubs vary with their membership, there can be large differences in operating data among clubs. It is almost impossible to develop construction cost data for clubs, as each is built for a slightly different purpose. Most have food and beverage service; hence, they have typical foodservice expenses. Some have guest rooms; hence, they are similar to hotels. Some provide special services such as a swimming pool, a golf course, tennis courts, and other facilities and thus are similar to resort hotels. Therefore, average construction costs are generally meaningless. Decor and furnishings can vary significantly between two similar properties. The services demanded by two different memberships can vary.

The amount and degree of renovation vary from one year to the next. Unlike hotels and foodservice units, the income structure can be adjusted each year through membership dues. These variables make it difficult to compare cost figures and percentages between clubs and other hospitality industry operations.

*Country club expenses.*The two primary expense categories in engineering, maintenance, and energy are: (1) energy-heat, light, and power; and (2) repairs and maintenance. In addition, there are two other maintenance-related categories for country clubs: (3) grounds and maintenance, excluding golf course greens; and (4) golf course maintenance.

Golf course maintenance is normally expressed as a cost per hole. The latest data indicate that this could average over $34,000 per hole per year. For example, golf course maintenance for an 18-hole golf course would be 18 x $34,000 = $612,000 per year. The average cost per hole increased 4.1 percent from 1991 to 1992.

Institutions

Maintenance, engineering, and energy costs are more difficult to analyse in the institutional area of the hospitality industry. Costs are frequently expressed as a percentage of the building budget or as dollars per square foot (or square meter) of space. In the case of rental or leased space, the basic charge per square foot (or square meter) may include normal repair and maintenance, while extraordinary repair and maintenance may be charged back to the renter as an assessment.

In addition, many rental or lease contracts may specify an energy surcharge that increases if energy costs increase. Often the utility company (electric, gas, or steam) bills renters or leased-space users directly. Energy and repairs and maintenance generally represent 10 to 20 percent of the budget for an institutional building. This excludes replacements, rehabilitation, or major changes in the building. Another method of allocation is to charge $6 to $20 per square foot ($65 to $215 per square meter) of space per year for normal energy and maintenance charges. Since some areas of the building have more volume than others, as measured in cubic feet per square foot (or cubic meters per square meter) of floor area, some property managers use a cubic foot (or cubic meter) space charge for energy, repairs, and maintenance. This technique appears to be superior to other methods for fair energy and cost allocations.

In institutional buildings that have limited hours of operation, it is easy to reduce energy consumption significantly during unoccupied hours by shutting off energy-consuming systems. Public utilities have developed excellent guidelines for buildings with limited hours of operation, and these rules should be followed. Guidelines vary with geographic area.

Safety and security

Safety and security are primary concerns of management. Crime and accidents cannot always be prevented, but risks can be reduced by taking certain precautions. Correcting and preventing safety hazards should be primary maintenance concerns. The safety of customers and employees is a high priority. Safety programs for employees should comply with the Occupational Safety and Health Act (OSHA), which imposes comprehensive, detailed safety and health standards and record-keeping requirements for employers.

The act states that each employer shall furnish to each of his or her employees a place of employment that is free from recognized hazards that can cause death or serious physical harm. Employees are also required to comply with OSHA standards and all rules, regulations, and orders issued pursuant to this act that are applicable to their own actions and conduct. A copy of the act can be obtained from the U.S. Department of Labour. In 1990, President George Bush signed the Americans with Disabilities Act (ADA) into law. This act entitled disabled people to the same rights and access as other U.S. citizens. The ADA required that facilities be modified to make them accessible to disabled people. Particular attention was focused on parking spaces, entrances, level changes, elevators, lifts, rest rooms, meeting rooms, foodservice, controls and equipment, signage, and hotel guest rooms.

The ADA required employers to identify the requirements that are bonafide occupational qualifications of a job, such as the physical or mental requirements. The activities of maintenance department include: routine maintenance and minor repairs; preventive maintenance, which is normally scheduled at weekly, monthly, quarterly, and annual intervals; ordering, inventorying, and issuing department supplies and replacement parts; maintaining energy records and administering energy-management programs; minor rehabilitation, such as painting and repairing guest rooms and public spaces; and administration and management of the department.

While these are the major activities for an on premises staff, some of these functions are handled through service contracts for properties with smaller staffs. This list is not meant to be all-inclusive, as groundskeeping and swimming pool maintenance, for instance, may be an activity of the department. Some departments are also required to handle convention, exhibit, meeting room, and special activity space setups. To manage the maintenance-and-engineering department effectively and direct its future performance, the manager should analyse current and past department activities. Activities must be designed to fulfill departmental responsibilities.

The primary responsibility of the department is to keep the property in mechanical readiness, so that the building can provide the services for which it is intended. Actually, the department regulates, controls, and operates the physical aspects of the property according to the policies established by management. The department should have some input regarding these guidelines, because its personnel know the limitations of the systems under their control.

A reporting system is essential for communication and eventual control by the building manager. Recommended reporting procedures will be detailed in the next section. There is normally a very high inverse correlation between energy consumption and maintenance: For electromechanical systems, as maintenance increases, energy consumption generally decreases. Therefore, the consumption of water, electricity, fuel, and other energy resources should be recorded. These records not only assist in measuring the impact of an energy-management program but, because they reveal characteristics of the property, they also provide valuable insights for future building design and renovation. If possible, utility requirements should be measured for each major energy consumption area of a building.

Total Quality Management (TQM) concepts were introduced and accepted in several hospitality maintenance-and-engineering departments in the early 1990s. While the definition of TQM is very basic and comprehensive (TQM has been defined as the systematic method of developing products and services that meet the needs and expectations of customers), its application to hospitality maintenance and engineering is very specific. TQM is action oriented.

The essentials of a TQM program include, but may not be limited to: The *customer is first*; teamwork and cooperation are essential; the internal customer (other employees) is important; the emphasis is on long-term improvement; *facts and data count*; the objective is a *final solution*, and not in finding fault; everyone is involved; TQM is not a separate program; TQM is people intensive. An objective of TQM is to empower workers to make spot decisions with the goal of fixing something once. This objective is best reached with good employee training and cross-training programs. When the employee is not required for maintenance activities, he or she is being trained or is being exposed to refresher training, or is being educated about related department activities. TQM programs are guided by *benchmarks*. A benchmark is a changing goal.

The department compares itself to recognized "world-class" departments and attempts to become "world class." The department must first establish where it is, or how close it is to a "world-class maintenance-and-engineering department." These world-class departments have similar characteristics and these become benchmarks for departments to follow or achieve. The common cost and productivity measures follow. Maintenance cost is expressed as a percentage of asset replacement value.

Labourer-to-supervisor ratios are determined. Maintenance labour and supplies costs are determined. Maintenance labour hours per unit of product output are determined. The common quality-related measures follow. Planned and scheduled worker hours are determined as a percentage of all maintenance hours. The percentage of jobs (work orders) requiring rework is determined. The average time for a repair is measured. The time between equipment failures is another measurement factor. The preceding ratios and ratio ranges are used to develop various "status" levels. The levels are *novice, journeyman, and master* The master level is world class.

Novice status. The novice characteristics follow. Business return on assets (ROA) is less than 2 percent. Value added per employee (VAE) is less than $47,000. There is some employee involvement, there is some employee training, there is limited teamwork, and the employee is empowered to resolve some customer complaints.

Journeyman status. Journeyman status characteristics follow. ROA increases from less than 2 percent to 2 to 6.9 percent. VAE increases to between $47,000 and $73,999. Employees are continuously finding ways to do their jobs better. Some departments even establish quality-assurance committees. New benchmarks are established; the department attempts to upgrade to market leader ratios and selected world-class ratios.

A market research program is used for new product adoption. Supplies are purchased with quality certification being foremost; price is secondary. Department head and employee evaluations are based on teamwork and quality contributions and improvement. Gains are documented and work practices are redefined to improve the value added per employee. The percentage of hospitality maintenance-and-engineering departments in the journeyman status can only be estimated at this time. Most estimates place the percentage at 15 percent or less.

Master status. The master status only includes the world-class departments, or 2 percent of the total number of maintenance-and-engineering departments. The common characteristics follow. ROA is greater than 7 percent.

VAE is greater than $74,000. Employees are generally self-managed, multiskilled, and are used to train new hires. New products are researched to determine if the latest acceptable technology is used and product quality is a major purchasing specification. Department evaluation is based on quality standards. All gains are documented and practices are redefined to improve VAE. The records, logs (forms), and department procedures that follow are all designed so TQM can be implemented in a hospitality maintenance-and-engineering department.

TQM programs and standards have been implemented by some larger hospitality establishments and corporations. TQM can be applied to foodservice corporations but generally not to individual smaller foodservice outlets. If TQM is to be implemented by a department, there is an apparent minimum maintenance department size level such as three or more employees. However, this is not meant to limit or restrict TQM to medium or larger properties.

Records, logs, and department procedures

Work-order systems

A work order reports that something is wrong and has to be corrected. It is used as a request for work to be done, usually maintenance or repair.

The least effective work-order system is an oral request between a supervisor from another department and the chief engineer (e.g., the lodging manager and the head maintenance person). Normally, records are not maintained with this system.

Emergency work orders. These work requests must be handled immediately and, if necessary, by all available staff, including the chief engineer. Human safety or the prevention of a major maintenance expense indicate the need for emergency work.

Routine work orders. Most work done by the maintenance-and-engineering department falls into this category, and there may even be subpriorities developed for routine work orders. A routine work order is handled as quickly and efficiently as is feasible.

Backlogging work. In some cases, requested work cannot be completed because replacement items have not yet been received. Hence, the work request is backlogged, to be completed when replacement parts are received. The work request can then be completed as regular building maintenance.

Dispatching maintenance workers

After the work priority is established, a dispatcher or supervisor must send a worker to do the job. In some cases, the decision is automatic. In the case of a water leak, the plumber may be sent. If the leak is within a wall partition, a carpenter is sent to the open wall before the plumber can deal with the leak. In some cases, a maintenance supervisor is sent to inspect what is wrong.

Requiring that a supervisor decide what is wrong and what personnel are necessary to repair the system can be a slow and cumbersome procedure, but it is often required to minimize labour costs. Some large buildings may have as many as 8 to 12 separate trade unions in the maintenance-and-engineering department. This is another reason why a supervisor frequently inspects the work that must be done, estimating what parts are needed and the approximate labour requirements to make the repair. Often, several work requests are given to one worker, who goes to one section of the building and completes a series of tasks.

A worker may also be sent to a specific location and asked to report back when the job is finished or to give a time estimate of when the required work will be completed. When the task is completed, the worker calls the departmental dispatcher for another assignment. The worker then completes the bottom half of the work-order form, indicating what was done, the time required to complete the project, and the materials used. The work-order request can also be used as a storeroom requisition to get replacement items when they are needed.

Analysing work orders

Work-order forms should be tabulated and analysed. The analysis can provide data that can be used for projections of future labour and material. They also form the basis for the management report. Table 1 shows the distribution of work orders for three different hotels by hotel function areas (guest rooms, food and beverage, and public/other hotel areas). The work orders are normalized to a common base, work orders per day per 100 rooms, so relative comparisons between properties can be made. Hotel C was the oldest property of the three. Hotel C also had an excellent preventive-maintenance program. Hotel B was built in 1989, and Hotel A was built in the mid-1970s and is in need of a major renovation.

Table 1: Work requests/day/ 100 rooms

Hotel area	*Hotel*		
	A	B	C
Guest rooms	6.8	4.8	2.1
Food and beverage	4.5	2.3	1.0
Public and other	4.0	2.1	1.1
Total	15.3	9.2	4.2

Table 2 shows the types of work orders and the workload

percentages for type of work order for the three hotels shown in Table 1 for the guest room function category. There are three types of work orders with large or unusual workload percentages that should be explained.

Table 2

Types of work requests and percentage of total work requests for three hotels for guest rooms

Types and percentage of work orders for three hotels

Type of repair	*Hotel A*	*Hotel B*	*Hotel C*
Heat/cooling	14.1%	7.7%	11.6%
Doors/locks	5.7	5.5	14.6
Windows/drapes	2.3	7.1	3.0
Lighting	34.1	32.6	8.3
Other electric	1.4	2.4	2.8
Plumbing	21.1	30.0	31.9
Smoke alarm	1.4	1.9	0.6
Television	10.8	4.3	7.0
Other	9.1	8.5	20.2
Total	100.0%	100.0%	100.0%

First, Hotel C's "doors/locks" percentage is much higher than Hotel A or B's. Hotel C had non-fire-rated doors that were easily damaged and it also had the key-lock system. Hotel guests frequently walked off with the guest room key after checking out of the hotel and the lock had to be rekeyed. Second, Hotels A and B had a significantly higher number of lighting work requests than Hotel C. Hotel C assigned one maintenance person the task of checking all hotel electric light bulbs each day (five days per week) and replacing all burnt-out bulbs.

The percentage of lighting work orders for Hotels A and B is very "normal" for most lodging establishments. Third, the number of plumbing work requests appears to be very high for all hotels. Once again, the percentage is very "normal" for hotels, regardless of their age. Clogged drains are very common and appear to be a never-ending problem in hotel guest room bathrooms.

Equipment inventory and maintenance logs

The accounting department usually issues an equipment inventory form (e.g., a separate card, a component of a property management computer software program, or created by the accounting department and kept on a spreadsheet, such as Lotus or Excel). Each piece of equipment of a prescribed value (say, $100 or more) should be inventoried on a form. Frequently, all guest room furnishings and equipment will be placed on one inventory form. The form must contain the location of the unit and all information concerning a warranty. If an installation manual is available, its location may be included on the form. When the unit is discarded, the form is removed from the current equipment file in the maintenance-and-engineering department and returned to the accounting department with the reason the equipment was discarded. All repairs and maintenance are indicated on the equipment inventory form.

Table 3
Work orders per 100 guest rooms per day by function areas for a casino hotel by day of week with weekly average and variance.

Day	*Rooms*	*Food/beverage*	*Casino/public*
Monday	5.96	2.23	4.66
Tuesday	5.96	4.65	4.46
Wednesday	6.15	6.70	4.10
Thursday	9.31	3.17	5.02
Friday	5.77	3.17	2.98
Saturday	5.24	3.91	4.66
Sunday	7.26	5.02	5.02
Average	6.52	4.12	4.42
Variance	±1.37	±1.49	±0.71

Equipment inventory form data are generally used to

develop preventive-maintenance schedules for equipment. If the inventory system is computerized, a simple computer program (or a property management software program) can be developed that groups together all equipment requiring monthly maintenance.

The equipment list is printed each month and, if the system is properly programmed, a computer printout can also indicate exactly what maintenance is required. All the chief engineer has to do is to assign preventive maintenance work to one or more workers. In addition, computer printouts and maintenance procedures can be made for bimonthly, quarterly, semiannual, and annual requirements. Once the chief engineer receives such a printout, it serves as a work-order request and authorization to complete these tasks.

Many properties (50 guest rooms or less) use a colour-coded, noncomputerized system. For example, equipment that requires monthly preventive maintenance would be inventoried on white index cards; bimonthly preventive maintenance on yellow cards; quarterly maintenance on orange cards; and semiannual and annual maintenance requirements on different colours. The colour coding can correspond to a yearly calendar that is similarly colour coded. Hence, a white-orange month would require preventive maintenance for all units of equipment having white and orange cards. The system simplifies scheduling preventive maintenance.

Energy records

All energy consumption figures from utility companies must be verified. This may be done by the chief engineer, who then authorizes payment of the various utility bills. Since payments are usually monthly, this procedure implies that energy consumption meters are read at least once a month. In most operations, utility meters are read more frequently in an initial effort to control energy consumption. More frequent meter reading also serves as a check on any energy conservation program being used for the property. Several electric utilities may retrieve energy consumption readings daily. This can be done with minicomputer electric meters and electromagnetic tape, with radio-transmitting minicomputer electric meters, or with a combination device. The lodging establishment may request a daily readout of its energy consumption if the electric utility makes daily readings. These readouts provide a 24-hour energy consumption record by 15-minute periods for each electric meter. In some cases, the lodging establishment, office building, or hospital is given direct access to the minicomputer electric meter readout. Energy consumption by selected units of equipment should be measured and monitored for various time periods in order to determine operating efficiency.

The results should be indicated on the equipment log. The equipment log can be analysed to determine if equipment should be overhauled or replaced. Energy use in various sections of a building can also be measured; hence, large energy consumers can initially be isolated within a section of the building.

Work plan and estimated expenses

The preparation of a department work plan enables the chief engineer to develop an employee work schedule, set department goals and benchmarks for a specific time period, estimate expenditures for a given time period, and communicate with management. The manager should require such a work plan for two reasons: (1) to be informed of the department's activities and (2) for management control, when necessary.

Management may not be properly trained in the specific areas of engineering, maintenance, and energy management and that chief engineers may not be trained in necessary management concepts. The use of a work plan helps to minimize these potential problem areas. If a work plan is properly used, management will approve a proposed work activity plan or provide input. Management will be kept informed regarding the status of special project work, such as guest room renovation, as well as the cost of the work. The form has also resulted in breaking down communication barriers between managers and chief engineers.

Management inspections

Management must schedule frequent inspections of the physical property. It is highly recommended that these inspections be done with the chief engineer. Management is also encouraged to spot-check the department randomly. Inspections are required for management control. Rental spaces and public areas must be frequently checked by an inspection team. For larger properties, the team should include the manager (or manager's representative) and the chief engineer.

At least 10 percent of lodging guest rooms should be inspected each year for very large properties, which amounts to about 1 percent of the guest rooms per month. At least 30 percent of the guest rooms should be inspected per year for medium-sized properties, which is about 2.5 percent of the guest rooms per month. All of the guest rooms should be inspected at least once per year for smaller properties, or almost 10 percent of the guest rooms per month. An inspection program has several purposes.

First, it serves as an evaluation device for various departments; the manager can determine how well each department is doing its work. Second, it allows the manager to assess the physical plant. Third, and probably most important, it is a communication device between the manager and a department head. Fourth, and related to purpose 3, it sets standards. Something may look entirely satisfactory to the chief engineer and entirely unsatisfactory to the manager. Two standards of evaluation are being used.

The manager's standard and the chief engineer's standard should coincide. This agreement can occur only when both serve on the same inspection team. The manager can tell the chief engineer what he or she considers acceptable and, if need be, the chief engineer can tell the manager what that standard compliance would cost in man-hours and materials. This alone can reduce management's standard. Actually, when inspection reveals no problems, the frequency of inspections is reduced. The opposite is also true; if numerous corrections have to be made after a detailed inspection, then the inspection frequency should be increased.

Management reports

There are two basic types of management reports: (1) the budget comparison report and (2) the work activity report.

Budget comparison report

The budget is an estimate and, as such, is not perfect. A good budget has an acceptable variance. A variance is an acceptable deviation from the expected expense.

For example, if the maintenance-and-engineering department has a budget of 20,000 annual man-hours, the acceptable variance could be 1000 man-hours (5 percent). If the work actually required 20,499 man-hours, this would cause no major problem because the actual figure is within the acceptable variance. Any variances larger than acceptable would require an explanation in the budget comparison report. If, however, the chief engineer used only 15,000 of the 20,000 man-hours estimated, he would have to supply a reason for this unacceptable variance.

The work activity report is a summary of the activities of the maintenance-and-engineering department for a defined period, usually a month. The report should include the following: work orders, shown by numbers and man-hours in priority order; special projects by room numbers and man-hours; preventive maintenance by man-hours; and other activities by man-hours. In addition, employees may be listed, with total man-hours worked by each one. There should also be space provided for any comments or recommendations. In this space the chief engineer can justify excessive or overestimated man-hours and explain any significant deviations from the budget.

The form becomes a primary source of information for department and chief engineer evaluations. Some managers may require from the chief engineer a bimonthly report or a report that coincides with a payroll period.Unless the budget included a business activity index, there could be large deviations between actual and budgeted activities and expenses. A property management computer software program normally includes business activity with its generated reports. The preceding forms are adequate if the budget is correct. It is recommended that the budget comparisons should be adjusted by a business activity index (lodging occupancy, meals served, meetings, and banquets), and the energy consumption data should also be adjusted by both business activity and environment changes (colder or warmer than normal weather).

Worker productivity

Several techniques for measuring worker productivity are available. The correct measurement technique depends on the department's objectives, the property's characteristics, to some extent customer requirements, and whether a TQM program has been implemented by the property.

Work-order production

One measure of worker and department productivity is based on the number of work orders. The total number of completed work orders is compared to the number of available workers. However, some work requests require much more time than others, and the manager must recognize this. A new building, or one that has been recently renovated, will probably have a high work-order requirement. After a period of time, work requests should decrease, increasing again as the age and use of the building increase.

Budget comparison

Another productivity measurement standard is the department budget. Unfortunately, it may not show the real picture because budgets generally depend on sales. This technique results in a major preventive-maintenance scheduling problem for the chief engineer. For example, when sales are high, the engineer's budget is high, so that preventive-maintenance procedures can be completed. However, some preventive-maintenance jobs require shutting down electromechanical systems that are needed when the property is fully occupied. Ideally, preventive-maintenance procedures should be undertaken when the building is at partial occupancy; at such times, however, the budget is frequently too low to permit preventive maintenance. Again, TQM measures such as ROA and VAE are generally better monetary productivity measures. For example, preventive maintenance keeps guest rooms in service, which increases both ROA and VAE, whereas, a high work-order level reduces both ROA and VAE because breakdowns are more costly than preventive maintenance.

Manpower forecast

Productivity should be based on manpower forecasts that depend on preventive maintenance, backlog work, special projects, and limited emergency repairs (work orders). Past records can be used to estimate emergency, routine, and backlog work requests at various levels of building occupancy. Preventive-maintenance routines are determined by the equipment in use and its maintenance schedule.

Man-hours and building use, or occupancy, correlation

Another productivity measure is the correlation between man-hour data and building use, or occupancy. Such a correlation may be developed with an acceptable management variance. The chief engineer can make estimates based on forecasts of building use and manpower availability, and schedule work in an effort to utilize the work force fully at a very high level of performance.

Chief engineering evaluation

It may be very difficult to state that any one item in a personnel evaluation list is most important when evaluating a chief engineer. Evaluation factors may be grouped as work environment factors, such as the physical plant and business function areas, and management environment factors, such as management organization, management style, and employee trade unions. It is possible that a "good" chief engineer (as viewed from outside of the organization) will be considered a poor one (as viewed from within the organization) because a poor management policy has been set for the department. It is critical to know the goals or purposes of the organization because they reflect the management style and the policies under which the department is operating. For example, it may be management's intent to operate at an absolute minimum cost to generate a very short-term maximum profit.

The chief engineer does not have an adequate working budget in this case and cannot keep the building in proper operation; 80 percent or more of the workload is emergency work orders. In this case, a "good" chief engineer stays within the budget and satisfies management's goals. The chief engineer (or equivalent) must be evaluated with respect to several factors, generally as follows: adherence to budget, work activity reports, TQM evaluators, guest reactions regarding the property, condition of the physical property as determined through management inspections, cooperation with other departments, and innovation and cost savings.

Budget

The chief engineer's ability to stay within a reasonable budget is of primary importance. For a fair evaluation, all items in a budget must be weighed. Budgeted man-hours, for example, reflect department productivity. Estimated materials and parts cost reflect the ability to anticipate expenses, since it is assumed that the chief engineer has budget input and can keep the physical plant in operation with adequate budgeted funds. Energy consumption data reflect on the efficiency and maintenance of the electromechanical equipment under the engineer's control.A good chief engineer controls costs and energy consumption.

Work activity reports

The work activity report indicates the activities of the department. This report and the engineer's budget must be evaluated together, as they both indicate how funds are being spent. Not only work orders but also special projects indicate general building improvements being done by the department. It is assumed that necessary preventive maintenance is being performed. If preventive-maintenance activities are light or inadequate, this will result in higher than normal work orders, and even special project work, usually within one to four months. The chief engineer's recommendations in these reports are valuable indicators of his or her management capability.

TQM evaluators

TQM evaluators could be used to replace many of the chief engineer's evaluators. TQM stresses the following: increasing ROA and VAE ratios, which should be improving from one evaluation period to the next; a reduction in emergency work orders, which should eventually decrease to 5 percent of the department's workload; preventive maintenance, which should approach 70 percent of the department's workload; continuous improvement of property quality and employee quality, which should approach 25 percent of the department's workload; and increasing the time between equipment breakdowns.

General condition of the property

It is easy to see that a property is deteriorating. Generally, the initial clue is the guest reaction forms. The management inspection form is critical to the general condition of the property. The chief engineer has the ability to look at a piece of equipment, a roof surface, or a door frame and to point out to the manager during the inspection what is likely to go wrong if certain corrective actions are not taken in the near future.

Computer applications

Work-order systems, equipment inventory, maintenance logs, energy records, work plans, estimated expenses, budget comparisons, work activity reports, and productivity evaluations are items now included in property management computer software programs. There are numerous software packages for preventive-maintenance functions alone, ranging in cost from several hundred to several thousand dollars. Some hotel chief engineers have worked with the hotel's director of information systems in developing cross-department property management software systems.

Advanced management concepts

Data (maintenance history and energy consumption) recorded in equipment logs are generally valuable in determining an equipment replacement cycle. Generally, there are two types of equipment operating patterns. Equipment may fail, apparently without warning. A common example is an electric lamp. If adequate numbers of units are available and in use within the property, data can be generated and accumulated on failure rates for that property. In some cases, manufacturers have accumulated extensive failure data for such units of equipment as sealed refrigeration units, television sets, small appliances, and electric lamps. Another type of failure is the gradual wearing out of a unit. As a unit wears, it generally becomes less efficient and its maintenance requirements increase. This is one reason for periodic energy measurements of selected pieces of equipment.

The equipment log can be analysed to uncover valuable data on wear that help to anticipate replacement needs. Both types of failure can be computer programmed to determine a cycle of replacement. If a computer is currently being used for inventory purposes and work-order-request record keeping, it can also be used to determine cycles of replacement for any unit or group of units. If manual data record-keeping systems are maintained, the following analyses can be made. The only certain fact regarding equipment is that someday it will fail. The exact time can only be estimated from probability theory.

A classic example is the incandescent lamp, which has an average life of 1000 hours for normal-life lamps of certain wattage ranges. All this means is that the probability that a particular lamp will operate for 1000 hours is 50 percent. If 1000 lamps were installed at one time and if all were operated for an equal length of time, only 500 would still be in operation after 1000 hours of use. If a simple adjustment by a maintenance person does not provide a satisfactory picture, the television set is removed and replaced with another.

The unit is repaired—on or off the premises—and placed back in inventory, to be used in another room at some future date. This type of exchange represents an item that fails; it is replaced with another item, and service is quickly reinstated, much as with a replaced electric lamp. The replacement procedure becomes economically feasible when labour costs are high in relation to the cost of the item being replaced.

The cost of labour includes the preparation, removal, installation, and cleanup man-hours for replacing items. It also assumes that if items fail prematurely, they will be replaced on a routine basis. This is called spot replacement. Or, it may be better to replace all the lamps in the room while a maintenance person is in the room (group replacement). This lowers the average replacement cost per lamp. Cost data are required to complete the analysis. Unit or equipment cost of, for example, incandescent lamps, fluorescent lamps, carpets, and television sets is considered.

Two equipment cost figures are required. One cost is for the purchase price of a single item, which is called the base unit cost. If a large number of items are replaced at one time, quantity purchasing discounts may be available, so that each unit has a lower unit cost. Furthermore, replacing a large number of items at one time implies that some units being replaced still work.

The best of these are retained for future spot replacement. The second set of cost data is the labour requirement for the replacement. Replacing a single incandescent lamp in a guest room usually has a high labour cost. (A study of a New York City hotel revealed that it required an average of 45 minutes of an electrician's time to replace a lamp in a guest room.)

The labour cost per unit for group replacement is generally lower. (The same study revealed that if all the lamps were replaced in the same guest room, the total time requirement was 52 minutes for 12 lamps, or an average time of 4.33 minutes per lamp.) Many items become less efficient with use, for example, air conditioners. This occurs even if the units are overhauled on a regular schedule. Repairs may also become excessive with equipment use and age. So, what should one do? Purchase a new unit? Continue to invest money in the present unit? The answers to these questions depend on accurate records that can be found in the maintenance log. The log should contain all repair costs and energy consumption data.

Life-cycle costing

Life-cycle costing considers all costs (present and future) for a unit of equipment, building section, or an entire building. The concept of life-cycle costing is not new. It was recognized as a useful concept in the hospitality industry in the early 1970s when energy costs were increasing. Its application became more widespread in the late 1970s when interest rates in the United States, as well as other countries, reached double digits (10 percent or higher on borrowed money).

Life-cycle costing is very useful in analysing or determining which alternative from a list of two or more is most economical, when each alternative has a different initial cost and different operating costs. The technique considers all costs, including future cost estimates, as present costs. It assumes, for example, that if you were to place $20,000 in an interest-earning account at the present time, you could purchase the equipment and pay for all its repairs, maintenance, and energy costs in the future from this account without adding any more money to the account. The initial purchase price is a present cost. If repair and maintenance costs are estimated at $500 per year over the life of the unit, the present cost of repairs and maintenance can be determined by applying an appropriate factor that represents the time value of money (current interest rates when borrowing money).

Future energy consumption can be estimated. Suppose that the cost of energy has been increasing. Another factor can be applied to future energy costs that represents both rates of increasing costs and the time value of money. Future taxes, insurance, and other costs can also be treated as a present cost. All these future costs are added together and represent a single present cost. This cost is calculated for each alternative, and the alternative with the lowest present cost is frequently selected as the most feasible.

7
Life Safety Systems

In November 1980, 85 lives were lost in the MGM Grand Hotel fire in Las Vegas, Nevada. The considerable media attention, with actual "on-the-scene" coverage via television, elicited an unfortunate response among arsonists as they began to see the lodging industry as a target industry for their criminal activities. The response of the lodging industry has been outstanding as all new construction has been fully covered by sprinklers and most high-rise properties have been retrofitted with sprinklers.

The success of that response was measured in the spring of 1995 when the National Fire Protection Association determined that the fire statistic relating to hotels and motels was so minimal that it should no longer appear as a separate indicator in the residential category of its annual fire statistical report. The 1990s have seen a significant increase in crimes against persons on the premises of lodging establishments. Tragically, this represents a crime war against all residents of the United States. In 1994, the crime statistics were a national disgrace. Among U.S. residents 12 years and older, there were 10.9 million incidents of victimization through violence or personal theft. In addition, there were 32 million property crimes. Sting operations by major television channels and considerable coverage in the daily newspapers and national journals pointed to hotels and motels as an industry with major crime problems. While there has been no national legislation to regulate this problem, the industry through its association, the American Hotel & Motel Association, in cooperation with the American Automobile Association, the American Association of Retired Persons, the American Society of Travel Agents, and the National Council for Crime Prevention, introduced an extremely effective "Traveler Safety Campaign." The amusement and theme park, foodservice, and lodging segments within the hospitality industry have installed many security systems and have expanded training so as to provide maximum security to the patron, the employee, and the visiting public.

Fire

In spite of considerable advances in fire protection technology and training, not a day passes in which there is not a fire in several hospitality establishments. Usually, such fires are in lodging or foodservice units. A report in 1981, which still holds true today, indicated that about 20 percent of those establishments will recover fully from the fire, and the remainder may suffer a loss of revenue that will never be recovered and may ultimately result in business failure. In order to understand fire protection, the hospitality manager should ask the following questions:

1. Does the building comply with the appropriate codes and standards?
2. Are fire suppression systems adequate?
3. Does the building design isolate toxic gas and smoke?

4. Are fire alert systems adequate?
5. Does the exiting system facilitate safe evacuation?
6. Is hazardous equipment in the building properly managed?
7. Does the staff training program include responding to a fire emergency?
8. Does the establishment comply with the Egress and Fire Protection sections of the Occupational Safety and Health Act (OSHA) Standards?

Codes and standards

In considering applicable, fire standards for the hospitality industry, one must be aware of the impact of the Williams-Steiger Act of 1970, better known as the Occupational Safety and Health Act (OSHA). Since it focuses on the employee, there is a tendency to overlook it as also pertaining to the patron, guest, customer, or the general public. However, in the hospitality setting, the employee and public will be in common areas where the law applies to the employee and consequently will directly affect any nonemployee.

The applicable OSHA Standards include Subpart E-Means of Egress and Subpart L-Fire Protection. The Means of Egress requirements are comprehensive and compatible with the stipulations under the National Fire Protection Association (NFPA) Life Safety Code 10 1. Under Subpart L, mandates refer to a portable fire extinguisher, fire detection systems, and employee alarm systems. Where specific installations are in place, OSHA will mandate certain maintenance and training procedures but generally does not require installation of the systems. These include standpipe/hose systems, automatic sprinkler systems, and fixed fire-extinguishing systems (general, dry chemical, gaseous agent, water spray, and foam). The Hotel and Motel Fire Safety Act of 1990 applies only to those establishments that provide lodging and meeting space for federal employees. This law requires that as of October 26, 1996, 90 percent of federal government travel stays must be in facilities complying with the act.

The law requires that all installations over three stories in height must be fully protected by sprinklers and must have single-station, hard-wired smoke detectors in each guest room. Properties of three stories or less may qualify by having only the single-station, hard-wired smoke detectors in each guest room. Applicable codes are developed by state and local government units, and considerable differences can be found between one government agency and another with respect to fire code requirements. A state or local government unit may adopt the entire model fire code, adopt it in part, or modify it to fit state and local concerns. For example, in 1981, after several hotel fires, Clark County, Nevada, adopted the Retroactive Life and Fire Safety Standards for Existing Buildings. This ordinance modified existing and prior codes to require hospitality buildings, as well as other buildings in the county, to follow tough new standards concerning emergency lighting, door closers, stairways, corridors, shaft and stairway enclosures, automatic sprinklers, elevator fire emergency control, HVAC (heating, ventilating, and air-conditioning) smoke control, evacuation route diagrams, and voice communication/paging alarm systems.

A periodic review of current research on the effectiveness of various protection methods is also very important. For example, the Factory Mutual Research Corporation, one of the independent firms involved in testing fire protection products and equipment, has corroborated over the years that in-room fire safety equipment is more effective than other approaches, such as corridor-only protection. In their tests, all in-room smoke detectors responded early enough to allow safe escape by room occupants. In-room sprinklers activated in time to suppress the fire and avoid appreciable damage.

However, no corridor detector ever went off during the simulated fire test, which in some cases lasted up to 13 minutes (0.2167 hours). The hospitality manager must ensure compliance with appropriate state and local codes. However, in the absence of such legal requirements, the manager should review model fire codes to determine what should be considered "reasonable care" for the protection of guests and employees. In addition, since code compliance means investing in products and equipment, care must be taken when considering such technology.

The manager should also be concerned with how the products and equipment will perform in an emergency. A number of independent firms are involved in testing fire protection products and equipment. Testing is done to ensure that products such as smoke detectors and fire extinguishers perform as they are supposed to in an emergency. Some of the larger testing firms are Underwriters Laboratories (UL), Factory Mutual Research Corporation (FM), Southwest Research Institute (SwRi), and the Center for Fire Research of the National Institute of Standards and Technology (NIST).

The hospitality executive can look to these organizations for their listings of fire protection products and equipment that have been submitted for analysis and testing. Technology that performs favourably according to a standard, for example, a simulated fire condition, against which it was tested is listed as having performed satisfactorily in a simulated emergency. A "stamp," or insignia of the firm conducting the test, is affixed to the product. An example is the familiar "UL" label.

Redundancy

A critical issue to be considered by senior management within the hospitality industry is the degree and level of redundancy to be installed in any and all of the systems reviewed in this chapter. In recent years, there have been spectacular examples of what happens when redundancy is not provided or when it becomes compromised. A "state-of-the-art" system was provided in a new hotel, including all the "bells and whistles"—auxiliary power, detection and alarm systems, full sprinkler suppression plus full water supply and pump capacity, emergency lighting, smoke exhaust and pressurization of stairwell capabilities, and so on. Within five months of opening, a transformer exploded and took the *adjoining* auxiliary power unit with it. Nothing worked!

Water-based fire suppression systems

Water-based fire suppression systems typically used on Class A (wood, paper) fires include a combination of automatic sprinklers and standpipe/hose lines. Of particular concern to the hospitality manager should be whether the system is wet or dry pipe and whether the sprinkler heads have been properly selected and installed.

Wet-Pipe Sprinkler System. A wet-pipe sprinkler system is one that is filled with water at all times. In essence, behind each sprinkler head is water that is readily available to flow onto a fire. Many local codes require this system. However, it is also important to note that during months when the temperature drops below freezing for any extended period of time, portions of the system exposed to these temperatures may freeze.

Frozen water can rupture pipes and create serious damage to the system and the property it is protecting. Thus, wet-pipe systems may require an antifreeze solution fill during freezing periods. Dry-Pipe Sprinkler System. In some locations where freezing conditions are a regular problem, dry-pipe systems are sometimes substituted if the code permits. Behind each sprinkler head in a dry-pipe system is a charge of air. If any sprinkler head should activate, the air in the sprinkler pipe is discharged, releasing a water control valve, which causes water to flow into the sprinkler pipe and out through the activated sprinkler heads.

Deluge Sprinkler System. Dry-pipe sprinkler systems should not be confused with deluge systems. The deluge system could result in excessive water damage in a fire. Although the piping in a deluge system does not contain water, each sprinkler head in the system is open at all times. Thus, if water flows out of one of the sprinkler heads in an emergency, it will now out of all the heads.

Since serious water damage can result from the activation of sprinkler heads, managerial personnel should be familiar with the location of all valves that control water flow to sprinklers throughout the building. It is typical for a standard sprinkler head at a pressure of 15 pounds per square inch (103.5 kilopascals) to distribute approximately 22 gallons per minute (1.4 liters per second), or at 30 pounds per square inch (207 kilopascals) to discharge 33 gallons per minute (2.1 liters per second)-for example, 0. 17 gallons per square foot per minute (0.12 liters per square meter per second) on an area of 130 square feet (12.1 square meters).

A deluge system would have little, if any, use in a lodging establishment. Its only possible use might be in a heavy storage area where conventional sprinkler suppression would be overcome by the high concentration of flammable or combustible materials. This system is presented for the information of a future hospitality industry executive so there is an awareness of the availability of such an intensive and extensive water source. Usually, it is advantageous within the lodging situation, in particular, to focus the water in a limited area to rapidly extinguish a fire before it can critically involve a large fuel mass. Such an action would help in minimizing water damage.

Preaction System. Preaction systems are often used in portions of a building containing equipment that is particularly vulnerable to damage by water from a sprinkler. These systems are similar to a dry-pipe system but contain a supplemental fire detection device designed to detect a fire before water flows through the sprinkler head. This detection alarm activates and allows water to enter the dry pipe; at the same time, it sounds an alarm to alert personnel that an emergency exists.

Sprinkler Heads. The hospitality executive should be aware that there are different types and installations of sprinkler heads. Sprinkler heads can be selected that activate at temperature levels ranging from 135 to 575°F (57.2 to 301.7°C). Careful consideration must be given to matching the head to the appropriate temperature condition. For instance, in an area where the ceiling temperature does not exceed 100°F (37.8°C), a head rated between 135 and 175°F (57.2 and 79.4°C) should be satisfactory. However, if the ceiling temperature in the area regularly exceeds 100°F (37.8°C) but does not exceed 150°F (65.6°C), a head rated between 175 and 225°F (79.4 and 107.2°C) would have to be utilized. In addition to the heat rating of the sprinkler heads, consideration must be given to their spacing and position.

The National Fire Protection Association has

developed sprinkler standards that show the maximum water coverage area for a sprinkler head. Generally, a standard sprinkler discharging 15 gallons per minute (0.95 liter per second) will cover a radius of 16 feet (4.9 meters) with a uniform flow of water measured approximately 4 feet (1.2 meters) below the deflector of the sprinkler. Sprinklers are also designed to be installed in set positions on the pipe to which they are attached. The positions are either pendant or sidewall, respectively. In some instances, upright models are used if piping is exposed.

The primary difference between the three positions is in the design of the deflector that determines the water discharge distribution pattern. Once the system is designed for a certain head position, it cannot be interchanged without modifications. For example, a pendant-designed head, which is to be installed below the sprinkler pipe, if installed in an upright position, would direct water upward toward the ceiling rather than downward onto a fire. For special applications, flush-mount, ornamental, cycling (on/off), and fast-response heads might be considered. If aesthetics are a concern, a flush-type or ornamental sprinkler can be used.

The flush design minimizes the protrusion of the working parts of the sprinkler below the ceiling. Ornamental heads are decorated with special coloured finishes that can blend with the decor of the area. Cycling heads, although relatively expensive ($20 to $40 for cycling heads and $3 per standard head), appear to offer great potential for lodging applications. This type of sprinkler is designed to cycle on and off automatically in response to changes in fire temperature. This type of head will minimize water damage while controlling and extinguishing a fire.

A fast-response sprinkler head should be considered for guest rooms where it is essential that water be distributed on a fire at the earliest possible moment, before any significant heat or smoke buildup is evident. This type of head has a high level of thermal sensitivity and is designed to reach the activation temperature rapidly in response to an early stage of fire development. This classification includes:

— *Residential sprinklers,* which have a fast response and are particularly effective against dwelling unit fires.

— *Extended-coverage (EC) sprinklers,* which provide a spray sprinkler with maximum coverage capability.

— *Quick-response (QR) sprinklers,* which provide a quick response and maximize the spray available for the suppression of a fire. This is one of the preferred sprinkler heads in conventional guest rooms in a lodging establishment.

— The combination of the above two heads is available as a *quick-response extended-coverage (QREC) unit.*

— For specific fire hazards, a *quick-response early-suppression (QRES) sprinkler is* also available.

— *Large drop sprinklers and early-suppression fast-response (ESFR) sprinkler heads* are among the other units available to address special needs within the hospitality industry.

The final point to consider in evaluating sprinkler heads is reliability. Once a sprinkler head activates, it must be replaced, thus making it difficult to test an installed sprinkler head. However, the independent testing laboratories mentioned earlier regularly run tests on various types of sprinkler designs, listing those that perform according to the standard against which they were tested. Only those sprinkler heads that have been listed should be installed.

Misting (Fogging) Systems. The suppression of fire through misting is being carefully considered as an alternative to halon, which is to be phased out by the year 2000. For years the fogging or misting system has been incorporated in some cooking equipment exhaust hoods. In the mid-1990s, attention focused on the misting technology and its potential application in elevator penthouses, computer sites, electrical equipment rooms, libraries, museums, and even in the guest room.

The obvious reduction of water damage with the application of such a small quantity of water makes this a system worthy of investigation and review. As with any existing system that is being moved through research and development to a more extensive use, there are problems of water purity, possible clogging of the orifices in the tubing, and back-up capabilities, if required, to name but a few. Nevertheless, this is an alternative suppression system that should be considered for appropriate application within the hospitality industry.

Standpipe/Hose Systems. Most codes require standpipe/hose lines in addition to automatic sprinklers as a means of applying water. Such systems are classified according to the use for which they are intended. A Class I system is provided in a building for use by the fire department or persons trained in handling heavy streams of water—2.5-inch (63.5-millimeter) hose line. Class 2 systems—1.5-inch (38.1-millimeter) hose line—are provided for use by building occupants until the fire department arrives. All codes relating to fire protection establish the "authority having jurisdiction" as the final arbitrator of fire systems within a community. This is usually a fire commissioner or other individual of senior rank. It is judicious and just common sense to review plans for all systems with the authority that will ultimately provide or withhold approval of an installation. It should be noted that there are many jurisdictions where the authority having jurisdiction does not want employees to become involved in the use of standpipe/hose installations. Such authority may even require that there be no hose, but only the standpipe and connections for use by the fire service hose, only.

Where permitted, employee training is essential for using standpipe/hose fire protection systems. For example, 100 feet (30.5 meters) of 1.5-inch (38.1-millimeter) hose in a building corridor will generate a pressure of 65 pounds per square inch (448.5 kilopascals) at the outlet and 100 gallons per minute (6.3 liters per second) of water flow. For untrained personnel, this hose can be extremely difficult and dangerous to handle.

Local codes will usually dictate the location and number of standpipes. However, all portions of the building should be within 30 feet (9.2 meters) of a nozzle attached to 100 feet (30.5 meters) of hose. Outlets for larger-diameter hoses are reserved for use by the fire department and are located in stairwells, whereas smaller-diameter outlets and hose for use by building occupants are located in corridors.

OSHA mandates that every 1.5-inch (38.1-millimeter) or smaller hose outlet used to meet the standard be equipped with hose connected and ready for use. Care must be taken to ensure that hose stored in corridor locations is properly protected. Lightweight, woven-jacket, rubber-lined hose must be used for interior standpipe locations. The alternative, unlined linen hose, does not meet OSHA Standards and is unacceptable. The presence of such a hose during an OSHA compliance inspection could result in a citation and fine.

Other system factors. If a water-based suppression system is in place in a building, regular inspections are essential. A fire water pump is essential to provide required water pressure for an automatic sprinkler system. A manually activated fire water pump should be used only in locations where sufficient water is already available to sprinklers and standpipes. It is desirable to use an automatically activated fire water pump in a fire emergency. An auxiliary power source is mandatory. Sprinkler and standpipe valves should be readily accessible, numbered, identified with labels indicating what they control, and there must be assurance that there is no leaking present within the system. (A flow alarm will provide that assurance-see the following discussion.)

Dry standpipe/hose connections that might be used by the fire department to pump external water to the upper floors of a building should be inspected to ensure that they are not blocked with stones or other debris. Hose lines stored within the building should be inspected to determine whether they have been damaged by moisture or vandals. A sprinkler system is usually required to be equipped with an approved alarm (electronic bell, horn, or siren). This alarm should be tested to ensure that it operates if any of the following occurs: any water flow from a sprinkler, electric power supply failure to the fire water pump, or significant water pressure fluctuations in the lines. Sprinkler heads should be inspected for any accumulation of mineral deposits, dust, paint, or other debris that could seriously hamper their activation.

For example, if the sprinkler heads in a guest room that was recently repainted were not covered, they could be permanently damaged and require immediate replacement. The piping carrying the sprinkler heads should be inspected to determine if its pitch is correct, if there are loose pipe hangers, and if there is a proper antifreeze charge, where appropriate. Finally, a critical component for the successful operation of a water-based suppression system is water.

A careful assessment of the reliability of the system supply, capacity, and pressure during normal periods and unusual occurrences should be made. Connection to public water mains that feed on a grid pattern, or from two or more sources of water, is more desirable than from a single water main. In addition, the diameter of the main should be considered. Building mains less than 6 inches (152.4 millimeters) in diameter are usually unreliable unless serving a small lodging unit or a small freestanding restaurant. Special reference should be made to NFPA 25, Standard for the Inspection, Testing, and Maintenance of Water-Based Fire Protection Systems. This places full responsibility upon the owner for all the functions noted in the standard's title.

Portable extinguishers

Water, carbon dioxide, halon replacement, and dry chemical can also be applied from portable extinguishers. However, when considering portable extinguishers, attention should be directed toward their installation and testing. Portable fire extinguishers must contain suppression agents that are properly rated for the class of fire that might occur in the area. The manager should also be aware that certain types of extinguisher designs are considered obsolete by most authorities and could cause potential injury to the users. Any type of extinguisher that must be turned upside down before the suppression agent can be applied to a fire should be removed from service. It has been determined that these extinguishers can explode if the discharge mechanism becomes blocked. In addition, these extinguishers, once activated, cannot be turned off.

Additional considerations should focus on who will use the extinguisher and where it will be used. For instance, a 2.5-gallon (9.5-liter) water- filled extinguisher weighs approximately 30 pounds (13.6 kilograms). This extinguisher would not be an appropriate selection for a housekeeper's cart. When fire extinguishers are installed, locations should be chosen that facilitate easy access, are near exits, and are safe from damage generated by other activities in the area (e.g., carts being carelessly pushed down corridors and into extinguishers). It is also recommended that an extinguisher weighing over 40 pounds (18.2 kilograms) be no more than 3.5 feet (1.1 meters) from the floor and that those weighing less than 40 pounds (18.2 kilograms) be no more than 5 feet (1.5 meters) from the floor. Following these height guidelines makes it easy to use the extinguisher and reduces the chance of its being dropped as it is removed from its mounting. Inspection and maintenance of portable fire extinguishers are essential. Each extinguisher should be weighed monthly to determine whether any chemical has been lost. Every 5 years, a hydrostatic test should be run on each unit to check for internal corrosion and damage that might not be visible.

Smoke/gas containment

The effects of heated air and fire gases are deadly. At a minimum, they result in obstruction of vision, disorientation, and loss of motor control. And, if inhaled, they contribute to immobility and respiratory failure. One of the most serious problems in many buildings is the inability to isolate or contain toxic gas and smoke produced by a fire. During a fire, the temperature and pressure of the air near the fire are increased. This causes the air near the fire to flow away from the fire area, resulting in the movement of smoke and gas to other parts of the building. Figure 1 indicates construction and remodelling practices that can lead to the spread of smoke and gas, a serious problem for lodging and institutional buildings. In a lodging or health-care facility fire, particular concerns are building exits and protection from smoke contamination of rooms not involved in the actual fire. Under the mandates of the Americans with Disabilities Act (ADA), a separate area of refuge is required. An exception was permitted in properties fully protected by sprinklers, but this comes under challenge from time to

---

Walls don't extend to underside of rated ceilings.

Holes or unrepaired damage in fire-rated walls.

Smokeproof enclosures not provided with adequate ventilation.

Non-fire-rated access panels on linen/trash chutes and electrical/plumbing chases.

No fire dampers in ducts penetrating fire walls.

No fusible links or self-closing devices on corridor or exit doors.

Plumbing and electrical chases extending from basement to root without fire stops or seals.

Linen and trash chutes not properly rated.

Seismic joints.

No separation of elevator lobbies from corridors.

Absence of smoke detectors or similar detection in HVAC ductwork.

Using corridor make-up air for HVAC in guest rooms.

Fig. 1. Problems contributing to smoke spread.

time. (The responsible hospitality executive will review this requirement to determine its current status.) These locations then become "safe areas" for guests or patients remaining in their rooms or for those attempting to use emergency exits and stairways to evacuate the building.

Unfortunately, smoke-resistant passageways are compromised during renovations or modifications when piping, wiring, or openings for telecommunication equipment are made through enclosed walls and are not properly resealed. Potential smoke contamination problems are increased when doors on utility access panels, guest rooms, stairways, and trash or linen chutes are not checked to determine whether they seal properly or whether they have been blocked open by employees working in the area, thereby increasing the chance of smoke seepage to "safe areas." In addition, it is critical to the survival of the guests, customers, patients, clients, and employees in a fire emergency that the HVAC system stop automatically when smoke is detected. This prevents the system from circulating smoke into areas of the building not affected by the fire.

Heat detectors

Heat detectors are the oldest form of automatic fire detection, dating back to the earliest use of automatic sprinklers in the 1860s. The automatic sprinkler, as previously discussed, includes heat detection and suppression capabilities. Heat detectors that provide only an alarm and no suppression are also available. A fixed-temperature detector activates when the heat-sensing element reaches a specified level. Management personnel must determine, as with automatic sprinklers, the normal temperature conditions in the area where the detectors are to be installed. Generally, the detector should be rated at least 25°F (13.9°C) above the maximum anticipated temperature.

The fixed-temperature detector located near the ceiling level will not initiate an alarm until the air temperature near the ceiling exceeds the design operation point. Therefore, in some instances, it is more desirable to utilize rate-of-temperature (heat)-rise detectors. Rate-of-temperature-rise detectors will activate when the rate of temperature increase exceeds a particular value. For example, a rise in temperature exceeding 12 to 15°F per minute (0.1 to 0.2°C per second) could activate the alarm. A thermoelectric detector contains a sensing element (thermocouple) that produces an increase in electric voltage as the temperature increases. The electric voltage is monitored and any abnormal increase activates the alarm.

Flame detectors

Flame detectors respond to radiant energy or flame. The flame detector responds very rapidly but only to energy that is visible. An object placed between a flame and the detector reduces its effectiveness.

When selecting automatic detectors, the manager must be aware of the types of fires that could be expected in the area to be protected. For example, heat detectors should be located in an enclosed space where a rapid buildup of heat could be expected from a fire. Photoelectric smoke detectors should be installed in areas where there is a strong possibility of a smouldering fire, for example, where there is a concentration of PVC-clad electric wiring. An ionization unit should be used if there could be a fire with little smoke, the type of fire that occurs with certain flammable liquids used in cleaning operations.

Detection control

The function of the control is to monitor and evaluate all components of the fire detection system, as well as the automatic sprinkler system and the public address and evacuation systems for the building. The control unit must be equipped with an emergency power supply since it has to operate in the event of a building power failure. The operator/indicator terminal is that point in the fire detection system where an alarm anywhere in the system can be accurately located and identified by those responsible for monitoring the system.

In a modern hotel, such terminals are located in more than one area of the building (engineering, security, front desk). The manager should ensure that the terminal is monitored 24 hours a day, 7 days a week. Fire codes may require that terminals be located in the main lobby or in areas easily accessible to fire fighters. In these locations, the terminals or panels may have limited operating capabilities, possibly identifying only the general location of the alarm. In such cases, the terminal is called an *annunciator.* Annunciators are particularly useful in properties with multiple buildings, where annunciator panels are located at the entrance to each building, or in buildings with multiple floors and rooms per floor, where annunciator panels are placed at the entrance to each floor.

The primary operation/indicator terminal should be equipped with a printer that records: time, day, and type of alarm; time and date of alarm acknowledgment; time and date of system reset; time, day, and type of fault signals (mistaken alarms or problems with the system); and time and date of fault corrections. With the continuing advances in microelectronics, fire alarm system manufacturers found that they can give each device connected to the system a unique identity by putting in a local transponder. These systems are called *addressable systems.*

With the use of transponders, the need for a local panel is eliminated; each device reports directly to the central fire alarm panel. When a device alarms, it gives the panel its specific address and status. This style of system reduces the wiring requirement to a single pair of wires, connected to each device in either a daisy-chain or a T-tap style. The central panel polls each device in sequence and, if the device does not answer, it will annunciate a trouble condition.

Many modern fire detection systems are also equipped with a special alarm transmission device that can automatically link the building with the fire department. These communications are superior to the telephone message that can often be misunderstood or incorrectly transmitted because of the stress the caller may experience in a fire emergency. Added intelligence in the central panel also allows for English language messages for each alarm and a graphic floor plan showing the building structure and the alarm location. Advances in microelectronics technology have further introduced English language interfaces to allow for simple commands in a question-and-answer format.

Graphic interfaces display information concerning point status (alarm, trouble), type of alarm (smoke detector, fire alarm [pull] station), number of alarms in the system, location of reporting unit (node), and a custom location label. Alarm, supervisory, and trouble conditions have dedicated knowledge push-button switches.

Exiting

In a building there are three essential components that must be reviewed by the manager. The components are the way of exit access, the exit, and the way of exit discharge. A *means of egress* comprises the vertical and horizontal ways of travel throughout a structure from any location within that structure. *Exit access* is that portion of the means of egress that leads to an entrance to an exit. *Exit is* that portion of the means of egress that is constructed in such a manner as to provide a protected way of travel to the exit discharge. *Exit discharge* is that portion of the means of egress between the termination of the exit and a public way. Adequate exit access further includes: number of exits, capacity of exit access, travel distance to an exit, protection of the exit access, and ease of determining the direction to an exit.

The discharge is the exit passageway, which must be protected by special construction and equipment to provide a safe means of travelling to the exterior of the building. Adequate exit discharge includes: capacity or number of persons that can utilize the exit, marking or identification of the most direct route to the outside, security, and lighting.

Elevator equipments and food service facilities

The manager must also ensure that certain essential building systems are designed and maintained for fire safety. Of particular concern are the elevator system and the kitchen exhaust system.

Foodservice facilities

Food preparation facilities are considered to have a high risk of fire. One common source of kitchen fires is an improperly designed and maintained kitchen exhaust system, as reported by the National Fire Protection Association.

Employee training

In the hospitality industry, fire prevention should be the responsibility of every employee. The first step in fire management is to provide the means to reduce fire damage through alarms and suppression. The second critical step is employee training. These fire problem areas should be brought to the attention of all employees, particularly those who are responsible for the operation and servicing of various building equipment. Fire training includes fire prevention, operation of fire suppression equipment, and alarm response. Each of these topics must be discussed with every employee.

Additionally, there is currently considerable interest in the hospitality industry in the concept of an in-house fire response team. Generally, the fire response team includes at least two employees from every shift, with the duties of the fire response team chief being handled by the chief engineer and/or the director of security. It is essential that members of the fire response team have hands-on familiarity with fire-fighting equipment, know all the exit locations in the building, and understand current evacuation procedures, as well as the operation of the building's evacuation alarm system.

However, it should also be noted that the actions of the fire response team during an emergency are essentially limited to the time between the fire alert and the arrival of the local fire department. OSHA has stipulated special training for employees who serve on a fire brigade, as this group of employees will essentially be called upon to fight structural fires.

Location and distance from a municipal or volunteer fire department may necessitate the development of trained fire fighters, who will train at an approved fire fighter school, have access to approved protective equipment, and, in some instances, have fire trucks on the premises, as in a large resort complex. In most hospitality facilities, the fire response team will be preferred to the fire brigade.

Security systems

The cost of crime in the United States is estimated to be averaging $140 billion per year during the 1990s, with anticipated costs of $200 billion annually by the year 2000. because guests and customers in the hospitality industry might be vulnerable to robbery, assault, rape, and larceny, the manager should seriously consider the effectiveness of security personnel, procedures, and equipment. In view of the tremendous cost of crime to the nation, it is critical that the hospitality executive consider the amount and nature of investment to protect the guest, employee, general public, and assets of the individuals and the property. The following information will focus on desirable design practices and equipment that decrease the likelihood of crime.

Lighting

Adequate lighting is a psychological deterrent to criminal activity. On the other hand, a dimly lit area creates a situation that may actually encourage criminal acts against guests and customers or the property. The only way to assess the adequacy of exterior building lighting is to inspect the facility during the evening hours.

Parking

Parking facilities need to be monitored in order to minimize such risks as hit-and-run accidents, vandalism, auto theft, and burglaries from automobiles. The security of a parking area is increased if the property utilizes uniformed security patrols, provides adequate lighting, and monitors the parking areas with CCTV (closed-circuit television).

Key control

Locks are useless without adequate key control. The manager evaluating the security of a building should ensure that keys to guest rooms are: unmarked and do not identify the property or room location in the property; stamped "Do not duplicate"; changed whenever a key loss is detected, or at least every eight months, regardless of key loss; and available to employees only on a carefully controlled basis (logs should be kept on who receives which keys and when they are returned, and a sign-out and sign-in procedure should be strictly adhered to).

However, even with the most stringent key controls, it may take a professional thief only a matter of seconds to record the impression of a room key in a bar of soap for later duplication or memorize the "cuts" on a key for future duplication. Questions must be raised as to who has access to the key codes and how frequently the codes are changed for particular rooms. Coded or computerized locks seem to provide greater protection and key control. Such technology is usually divided into three categories: those systems that rely on what the person desiring access knows; those systems that respond to who the person is; and those systems that rely on what the person possesses.

Valuables

Because problems can occur with key control or because of codes and ordinances, the manager may have to provide a safe or some other type of secure area at the front desk or in the guest room for the protection of expensive property such as cameras and jewellery. It is desirable for a safe to have:

1. A fire resistance rating established by an independent testing facility. The ratings in the case of fire specify the maximum temperature at which the safe will protect its contents and how long such protection can be provided at that temperature. Generally, the standard safe deposit box at or near the front desk does not provide this level of protection. If the needs of the guests dictate, consideration should be given to installing a vault or secured area that would have these fire-and burglar-proof ratings. The continuing movement of the lodging industry to properties fully protected by sprinklers supports the fire protection aspects of this requirement.
2. A burglary resistance rating established by an independent testing facility. This rating establishes the type of forcible entry the safe can withstand (hammer/bars, torch, explosives) and for how long. This matter requires special review by senior management.

8
FOOD AND BEVERAGE MANAGEMENT

In an earlier era food played a significant role in the organizational structure and product/service mix of hotels. It has been speculated that the preeminent role played by hotel food service in society became significantly diminished with the onset of Prohibition and during the 1920s. People stopped going to food service establishments in which they couldn't get a drink. Prohibition gave rise to competition from street restaurants that operated sub rosa as "speakeasies." These free-standing restaurants were not constricted by the very visible public nature of hotel dining rooms.

This trend appears to be reversing in recent years. Of the many factors mentioned earlier that mandated organizational change, return on investment seems to have played a dominant role in this turnaround. The "double whammy" issues of high construction cost and return-on-investment expectations by people from outside the hospitality world strongly suggest that space devoted to food service should contribute at least its share to the profit structure of modern hotel service.

Food

While operational management of food and beverage functions is well treated by many authors, the literature on food and beverage managers is fairly sparse. Unpublished research by the editor suggests a demographic picture of the hotel food and beverage manager, who can be characterized as a white male, between 30 and 39 years of age, married, a U.S. citizen, with a bachelor's degree in hotel administration making more than $35,000 a year. Most of the 49 people responding to this survey had not held a job outside of the hospitality industry, and had held about four different managerial jobs in their five-to ten-year hotel careers. These people tended to be very happy with their financial and managerial positions and uniformly looked forward to continuing their career in the hotel and restaurant business.

Data such as these strongly suggest a true element of professionalism among the managers of the hotel food and beverage function. While more research in this area is definitely needed, it should be noted that some major hotel firms now recruit specifically for people who seek to start their careers in the food and beverage area of hotel service operations. We are still waiting for a comprehensive study of hotel food and beverage directors. In 1966 Allen Hubsch suggested a number of prescriptions to revitalize hotel food and beverage service. Among the suggestions by Hubsch over 25 years ago were:

- — Hotel food and beverage facilities must become profit centers—no longer a necessary evil.
- — New and increased professionalism of food and beverage management—less reliance on the old chef-maitre d' model.

— Food and beverage outlets need to become amenities that produce room-nights.

— Hotel food and beverage units need to adopt street restaurant philosophies—merchandising, advertising, decor/ambience, menu, and service need to compete with local competition.

— Use food and beverage to fill marginally profitable space in rentals, storage, or production areas.

— New food and beverage outlets can leverage existing facilities like storage and kitchens by spreading fixed costs over a wider sales base.

At many hotels, room service has been treated like the proverbial illegitimate child. In many cases, it has been neither planned for nor designed for in new hotel construction. In recent years, providing close to full-service, in-room food and beverage delivery 24 hours a day became a competitive point, and hotels had to scramble for ways to effectively implement it. Few would argue that having a first-class executive chef should be anything but the norm at a hotel since it allows a hotel organization to compete effectively for food and beverage business in today's market. It is, however, fairly clear that the chef today does not have the dominant role that chefs had at the turn of the century. With the increased national attention on the importance of conferences, conventions, and meetings of all kinds, these food service professionals whose speciality is to plan and serve meals and beverages to large groups of people become increasingly important. These affairs represent a significant contribution to the profits of hotel food and beverage service.

The efficacy of a hotel's efforts in selling and servicing the group business market may very well be the difference between profitability of the food and beverage function and some less desirable outcome.

Beverage

In any hotel that has more than one formal bar, there is usually a separate function within the food and beverage department called bar or beverage management. Ideally, all matters that concern spiritous liquors, wines, and beers will be coordinated by that office. The beverage manager will have responsibility for purchasing, receiving, storing, and issuing liquor as well as for controlling wine and beer inventory.

Additionally, the beverage manager:

— Hires, trains, schedules, and controls all beverage and bar personnel

— Promotes the various beverage department services

— Coordinates the requests of other departments that require beverage services, for instance, banquet and catering, room service, chefs, management

— Assures that the beverage department is in compliance with federal, state, and local laws and regulations

The beverage manager administers or manages up to four different types of bars.

The *front or public bar* is the one in which the guest can, if he or she so desires, interact with the bartender and other service personnel. There are provisions for guest seating at the bar itself, which may be part of a restaurant or a separate room or area. There may also be separate tables and stand-up areas available for beverage service. A front bar may or may not include provision for entertainment.

A *service bar* is a "hidden" bar that's designed to be used by the hotel's food and beverage service staff only. It may serve one or more food service areas and/or room service, and it is designed specifically for efficiency and economy of service. In most cases speed is considered to be more essential in service bars than decorative ambience. Service bars are typically centrally located in the back of the house, out of guest view.

Portable bars are those that are designed for maximum flexibility and can be used in conjunction with beverage sales associated with guest activities anywhere in the hotel or on its grounds. This may be extended in resort areas to include recreational areas.

A new facility popular among many hotels is that of the *in-room bar, minibar, or honour bar.* While sometimes the responsibility for inventory of these bars rests with room service, the beverage manager in most cases is also deeply involved in their design, marketing, and control. In many ways the beverage manager's job can be seen in terms of historical stereotype of the housekeeper.

Often the beverage manager has worked his or her way up through the ranks of beverage server and preparer and through experience, longevity, and interest becomes the beverage or bar manager. There is reason to believe that in many ways this may be changing.

Like many other areas of management within the hotel, the beverage management function now faces a range of issues that are more sophisticated and complicated than the traditional beverage management problems of the past. Beverage managers of the future may very well have to be able to bring to their job a managerial, organizational, and administrative level of sophistication that heretofore has been unnecessary.

Hotel food and beverage organization and management

Similar to the overall lodging industry in general, food service in the hotel market has suffered in recent years. A general characteristic would be that the market will come back but with less significant growth and with an emphasis on cost containment. As lodging food service competes with the multitude of commercial food service operations for the consumer dollar, the focus of both operators and consumers will be of value. Most lodging executives would identify food and beverage operations as one of the more difficult areas to manage in the entire lodging arena. Lodging food service not only involves the traditional difficulties associated with both producing and serving food and beverages, but also must perform these functions every day, often 24 hours a day.

The resulting labour costs and operational expenses can prove burdensome for many lodging establishments. In order for these food and beverage operations to survive and thrive, they must draw not only guests of the lodging facility but also consumers from the external market of the property. In fact, the more profitable lodging food and beverage operations obtain more than 50 percent of their business from nonguests of the property.

The hotel or hotel guest is not a captive diner; today there exist too many other opportunities for dining. Yet, in order to have a profitable hotel property, a significant percentage of sales must be produced by the food and beverage operation. To accomplish this, lodging facilities must successfully compete with the numerous chains and independent restaurants that offer a variety of services. Many hoteliers are choosing not to compete in this environment. Instead, their strategy has been to eliminate food and beverage operations altogether, or to lease food and beverage operations to outside companies, either chain-operated or independent. While the reader may start to think that hotel food services are not major players in the overall food service market, 1993 projected sales were estimated at $16 billion (1993 Forecast). There are, according to information on hotel chains, six major chains whose food service sales per hotel average more than $2.3 million. At the top lies Westin, whose properties average well over $9 million each in food service sales. Clearly food service professionals in hotels have as much or more opportunity for success than in other segments of the food service industry. With potential sales like those noted, lodging food service remains a critical partner of both the revenue and profit of the property. A smart, resourceful manager will make the food service operation unique, thus attracting additional patrons to the lodging establishment. Thus, food service can be looked on as a means of gaining competitive advantage over other lodging operations. The field of lodging has had a long history of serving people during their travels.

From the earliest days of the Roman Empire, when people travelled on foot, on animal, or in vehicles drawn by animals, to the modern age of air, rail, and car transportation, hotels and inns provided for their needs. In fact, these early hotels were the center of community activity and often the only place one could eat away from home. The glamour years of the late nineteenth and early twentieth centuries produced grander hotel properties, the so-designated "palaces of the people," which solidified this perception of hotels as centers of public entertainment and as sources of food and drink for guests.

This reputation continued well into this century, as hotels became the logical place to meet for entertainment and business discussion. Food service operations independent of hotels were rare even in the larger urban centers. It was not until the post-World War II era that independent restaurants and restaurant chains grew both in number and in their influence over the market. As we approach the twenty-first century, lodging food service accounts for approximately 6 percent of the total food service market. From total domination of the market to its role as a minor player today, lodging food service has undergone dramatic change. As properties struggle with the decision of food service or not, number of food service units, and the level of service offered, future managers need to consider the goals and mission of the food service operation:

1. To provide the appropriate level and degree of food and beverage service to the property's guests.
2. To support the overall goal(s) of the property.
3. To assist the property in gaining a competitive advantage over other lodging establishments.
4. To function efficiently and effectively in order to produce a profit.

Organizational considerations

The organization of food service departments within lodging establishments varies depending on type of facility and, in the case of chain operations, corporate policies. Since this degree of variety exists, categorizing lodging properties can be difficult. For example, a property located in a resort environment may also have extensive convention space. A resort property provides all the amenities that focus on guest entertainment and relaxation. There will be a greater emphasis on speciality restaurant(s) as well as on room service. Unique problems may face resort managers with respect to seasonality of operations, location, and layout.

The last points are important since the property itself, as well as individual food and beverage outlets, may be located in hard-to-access areas, thus impacting on operational expenses. Airport properties have grown with the increase in air travel. Quite often travellers will choose these properties based on the convenience factor.

While occupancy rates are high during weekdays, weekend business tends to drag. Economy properties are currently the segment of the lodging area with the most growth. This segment often rejects the role of food service operations in the property. One example of how a hotel food and beverage operation can be organized was demonstrated by Four Seasons Hotel in Boston. The food and beverage division has four departments: food preparation, catering sales, stewarding, and sales outlets.

The last has five operations: private bars, room service, a full-service lounge, a fine dining restaurant, and banquet facilities. Each department has line employees who report to assistant managers, who, in turn, report to department heads, who then report to a director of restaurants and bars, who, in turn, reports to the director of food and beverages. Regardless of the size of the lodging facility, food and beverages need to be produced and served. However, the increased size and complexity of some operations make it critical that those managers communicate well with all levels of employees. There may be a trend toward flatter organizational structures, as well as to completely separating out certain functions of the food and beverage area.

Food service personnel

Who are the key people in the organization of lodging food service? Our attention here will focus on the operational players, those individuals most often responsible for the work of pleasing the guest and holding the line on costs. In most kitchen operations, an executive chef will be responsible for management related to production activities. Depending on the size and complexity of the operation, the executive chef may actually perform little in the line of food production. In a small operation, the chef may also be a part-owner and will perform most of the food-related functions.

With the trend toward downsizing operations, it would be the rare organization in lodging food service that employed numerous back-of-the-house employees engaged in a single function. Some examples of the past might include sous chef—the executive chef's assistant and often the staff supervisor; a saucier—a sauce cook; a garde-manger—cook in charge of all cold food preparation; a chef patissier—a pastry chef; and a banquet chef in charge of catering. There may be various assistants to each of these positions. In addition, there may be a steward, a purchasing manager, a storeroom clerk, and several janitorial staff. The dining room can have an equal degree of complexity, depending on the operation.

In today's cost-control environment, food and beverage operations are trimming payrolls and consolidating job responsibilities to cut operational expenses. This cross-training of staff allows an individual to take on multiple responsibilities. In the past, it was not uncommon for the food and beverage operation to employ workers around the clock, as most items were made from scratch.

With modem equipment and usage of more convenience food items, such as preportioned meats, it becomes rare to find such parts of the operation as the butcher shop or the pastry shop. Again, hotel operations are concentrating on quality, value, and cost. If the property can find a product rather than producing it, the trend then will be to purchase rather than make from scratch.

There has been increased attention to the education level of chefs in lodging operations. These individuals can command rewarding pay, but much will be expected of them as well. They must be able to produce quality products utilizing minimal resources. They must also direct all activities in the back of the house, including the training and supervision of employees. Their responsibility becomes the means by which a food and beverage unit produces profit for its parent institution, the lodging facility.

Operational interaction

Hotels are complex institutions that are divided into separate operational areas, among them rooms, engineering, administrative, accounting, human resources, and sales, in addition to food and beverage. These divisions interact in every imaginable way 24 hours a day to produce a quality experience for the guest(s). Roger Simon, executive steward of the New York Hilton and Towers, offers the following example.

An area often overlooked in food and beverage operations is the importance of the sales staff, as they book banquets and meetings rooms as well as guest rooms. The revenue-generation potential of a food and beverage operation can be facilitated or hampered by the type of client sleeping in your guest rooms.

Since a large portion of your food and beverage customers may be hotel guests, it is important you book the right type of people in the hotel. What is the utilization rate of the food and beverage outlets for the various market segments? Do business travellers eat more/drink more than the leisure/pleasure market? Which convention is going to use the food and beverage outlets more than others? Your convention sales staff has to know the answers to these types of questions. Your banquet sales staff has to know what is more profitable—a reception for 1,500 or a dinner for 900? Sales personnel cannot just be concerned with achieving room-night quotas or generating revenue; they must know the impact of their decisions throughout the rest of the hotel and how it affects the profitability of the hotel.

At the New York Hilton, hotel guests account for about 85 percent of restaurant/bar covers. The food and beverage manager has to know who the customer is and how many patrons one may expect. The front office is instrumental in providing the information about the hotel guest. House counts, market mix reports, group commitment reports, and arrival/departure patterns assist the food and beverage team in making informed decisions. Forecasted house counts assist in scheduling, food ordering, and making decisions whether or not to close a particular outlet.

Actual market mixes assist food and beverage managers in preparing utilization rates and provide insight into why the restaurants and lounges fared as they did. As an example, if half of your room-nights for a month were in the leisure/pleasure segment when normally only 20 percent are in this segment, it may help to explain why your dinner covers are down and your average checks in the lounges were low. Comparing menu abstracts against different market mixes assists in allowing you to determine eating patterns for different segments that can later be used in menu engineering. Group commitment reports allow you to plan for the future.

For example, certain groups have particular food and beverage needs. Arrival/departure patterns assist in staffing if you know when certain conventions are checking in and out of the property. And finally, every hotel employee is a sales agent for the property's food and beverage outlets. The staff must be trained to always refer and recommend hotel services to the guest. The quality of food and beverage operations can have an impact on overall hotel operations and profitability. Quality would be particularly important for convention hotels and resort hotel properties.

Guests have come to such properties for specific purposes. Therefore, a reputation as a quality food and beverage operation will serve to attract customers. These operations will generate word-of-mouth advertising from travel agents, corporate meeting planners, cab drivers, airline companies, and tourism offices. While this reputation can attract guests, it becomes the responsibility of management to plan effectively for client needs.

Trends in lodging food service

In presenting trends, we must exercise caution, as what works in one food and beverage operation, may not in another. For example, contrast what George Tanzman of Four Seasons Hotel in Boston and Roger Simon of the New York Hilton and Towers say about their respective operations. In order for your lodging food and beverage operation to succeed, sound marketing and keen observation of what people want must accompany quality food and service.

While consumers may choose your hotel for specific reasons, such as price or service, they seek more creativity in a food and beverage operation. If you cannot attract the hotel guest, you will find that attracting clientele from the local area is also difficult. Quite likely, each hotel has its own character, which suggests a variation of food and beverage operations in different markets.

The concept of branding, currently popular in various food service segments, could be utilized in lodging food service. While some limited-service lodging operations have entered into cooperative relationships with food service companies, this concept holds significant potential for the appropriate market. One example would be where the hotel's food service operation was marginal at best. The lodging property can concentrate its resources on rooms and lease the food and beverage service to an identifiable brand. Hotels should be aware, though, that in certain situations such a restaurant company may not be familiar with room service or catering. In an extreme case of moving away from food service, some lodging properties limit services to in-room mini-bars and microwaves, with limited food items available for sale in the gift shop. In some cases, the gift shop is being transformed into a convenience store. We have seen that Four Seasons senses a rebirth of simplicity in food and beverage operations.

A good example of this would be a coffee shop. What has occurred over the last ten years has been the abandonment of this concept in favour of more high-priced dining. But in letting a coffee shop be a coffee shop, you tap into the consumer's consciousness of value as well as menu variety and fast service. While some find the concept boring, very often customers seek the comfort of knowing they can get a good meal at a good price day after day in your operation.

The area of room service is also seeing significant changes. In some properties, room service has been eliminated, while in others, it has been revised. For example, menus have been limited to particular concepts, such as pizza or Asian food. Food items are packaged to appear as though they came from a free-standing restaurant. The key, again, is to know your clientele. But the move to simpler menus, accompanied by lower prices, could bring room service back as a major contributor to overall operations. Some larger hotel operations are focusing on a tighter menu and faster service through room service.

Hotel food and beverage departments

Increased emphasis on operations and the bottom line by today's hotel industry is sure to focus more attention on the food and beverage (F&B) department. While considered an essential element of the "service" provided by many properties, hotel food and beverage departments, are burdened by high costs and have fallen behind their free-standing counterparts in the competition for revenue and patronage. Consequently, hotel restaurants have frequently been a cash drain on hotel operations.

The cost-constraining environment of the 1990s presents special challenges to the enhancement of hotel F&B departments. Hotels feel pressure to maintain prices while facing increasingly price- and value-sensitive customers. In addition, new upper-tier limited-service properties that do not carry the burden of full-service F&B departments are competing successfully with full-service facilities.

Stiff competition erodes hotel food service business

As of the first quarter of 1992, nearly 14,000 hotels in the U.S. (49.5 percent of all properties) had at least one restaurant (Smith Travel Research). Nationwide, there are more than 391,000 free-standing restaurants. We can infer from these numbers that most hotel guests have a wide selection of dining places from which to choose, especially in urban areas. These departments have differed from free-standing restaurants in both their objectives and their method of operation. The main purpose of hotel F&B departments is to serve hotel guests.

Consequently, hotel food service is available for more meal periods per day than most free-standing restaurants, and services provided include not only dining rooms, but also room service, a unique hotel feature, and banquet areas, which may or may not be present in other eating and drinking places. Since banquet catering also attracts guests who rent rooms, it is in the hotel's best interest to book events that will maximize occupancy. More attention is likely to be paid F&B departments in the 1990s, because relatively low room rates and decreased bar/lounge revenues, due to increased public sensitivity to drinking and stricter drunk-driving laws, give heightened importance to hotel restaurants and catering as revenue sources. As hotel F&B departments are increasingly viewed as profit centers, rather than as merely a necessary amenity for a full-service facility, they are more likely to be given the managerial and financial resources necessary to be truly successful.

Comparing hotel performance to free-standing restaurants

Hotel F&B departments bear enough similarities to free-standing restaurants to make a comparison of operating ratios instructive. However, this exercise is complicated by different accounting standards. According to the Uniform System of Accounts for hotels, overhead expenses, like administrative and general, advertising and marketing, repair and maintenance, utilities, occupancy costs, and fixed charges, are not allocated to departments.

One solution is to format the restaurant income statement to look like the hotel income statement. This approach allows us to compare operating profits but not bottom-line results, because occupancy costs, unallocated operating expenses, and fixed charges are excluded. To overcome this problem, we formatted the hotel F&B department income statement to look like the restaurant income statement, allocating most costs on a square footage basis based on our hotel sources, the National Restaurant Association (NRA) report, and our professional judgment.

Hotel data sources tapped for this analysis include *Trends in the Hotel Industry 1991*, a 1990 study prepared by Pannell Kerr Forster (PKF) and U.S. *Lodging Industry 1989,* reporting 1988 data tabulated by Laventhol & Horwath (L&H). Data on 1990 hotel restaurant operations published in the NRA's *Restaurant Industry Operations Report 1991,* were also used. All free-standing restaurant data originated from the NRA study as well. Each of these data sources is based on a different sample with its own unique characteristics.

The hotel data, for example, are likely to be biased toward better performers. Properties participating in PKF's survey had higher occupancy rates and higher average daily rates than hotels in the much larger Smith Travel Research monthly survey. The percentage change in each indicator from 1990 to 1991 was similar, however, suggesting that both samples are broadly representative of industry trends. The two key differences between the PKF and NRA studies are statistical tabulation methods and coverage.

The PKF study reports means, whereas the NRA study reports medians. Since the median is unaffected by extreme outlying values that are more likely to be skewed by especially high revenues than by unusually high expenses, the PKF report is likely to show greater profitability than the NRA study. The hotel figures represent total food and beverage operations, including room service and catering, unlike the NRA hotel data that include only restaurants. The large role that high-margin catering plays for most properties suggests that hotel F&B departments are probably more profitable than hotel restaurants alone. Within the NRA study, data on 87 full-menu table service hotel restaurants enable us to compare selected cost and revenue items with all restaurants, but bottom-line profits are not reported due to the relatively small sample size. Based on the limited data available on gross margins, food cost, payroll and benefits, utilities, and occupancy costs, these hotel restaurants are at a 4.6 percentage point disadvantage before direct operating expenses, administrative and general, advertising and marketing, repair and maintenance, occupancy costs, and fixed charges.

High costs, low covers mean few profits

Hotel F&B departments perform substantially worse than their freestanding restaurant counterparts. Direct operating expense incurred by hotel F&B departments (as a percentage of F&B sales) is more than double the restaurant industry median. Consequently, total operating expense as a percentage of total food and beverage sales exceeds the ratio for restaurants by 17 percentage points. Outside patronage may be discouraged by the hotel's location, limited access, and high prices. Most full-service hotels with multiple outlets have too many seats per room. Our consulting experience has shown a negative correlation between food and beverage seats per room and hotel profitability.

After subtracting all prorated expenses, the typical full-service hotel F&B department is clearly in the red, with losses before income taxes equal to 5 percent of total F&B revenue, compared with a gain of 3.2 percent for the sample of all full-menu table service restaurants. While these figures suggest that some hotel F&B departments are a cash drain for their properties, the gap between hotel F&B and restaurant profitability should be viewed with caution. Even the best-run hotel F&B department is unlikely to have the same profit potential as a free-standing restaurant due to the administrative and service constraints discussed above.

These in turn have implications for costs and revenues. For example, although hotel F&B departments have lower administrative and general, advertising, and management fees than full-menu table service restaurants, their round-the-clock schedule and guest services offset these advantages, resulting in higher payroll and benefits and direct operating expenses. Fixed charges, such as occupancy costs and interest payments, are also higher at hotels, due to physical differences in the two types of buildings and possible differences in financing techniques. For these reasons, it is not appropriate to measure hotel F&B and free-standing restaurant profit using the same yardstick.

Shift to casual dining challenges hotel restaurants

The need to provide room service, high overhead, and the capital expenditures associated with the fancy dining rooms built in many properties, plus menu demands linked to highmargin catering, have made it difficult for hotels to keep up with the shift to casual dining that began several years ago. Health- and value-conscious consumers have begun to favour pasta, salads, fish, and other lighter fare in bistro-type settings over traditional steakhouses and signature restaurants.

Many hotel dining rooms would benefit from repositioning or updating, but weak revenue, scarce capital, and questionable payoffs make complete renovation of hotel dining rooms rare. Instead, menu changes are being instituted to accommodate the latest customer preferences. Repositioning may be easier for midmarket properties than for the most upscale hotels.

Holiday Inn, for example, is in the process of repositioning 18 company-owned restaurants by introducing different food styles with an emphasis on lower food costs. A typical scenario would be a shift from a steakhouse or signature restaurant to a pasta bistro through implementing changes in restaurant design, menu, and atmosphere. One such conversion is cited as resulting in a 12 percentage point increase in the dinner capture rate to 46 percent. Repositioning is especially important for hotel restaurants, since even unprofitable outlets cannot generally be closed unless there are multiple restaurants on the premises.

Hotels stress increased value rather than decreased price

New emphasis is being placed on food quality, presentation, and consistency from location to location. While competitive pricing remains important, maintaining a high price-value relationship is key. Guests, especially those staying in upscale hotels, are generally willing to pay premium prices for a high-quality dining experience. For this reason, hotels seeking to increase patronage by lowering prices without enhancing quality are not likely to be successful, and their price reductions could merely result in lower revenues. While most interviewees defended even holding the line on prices, none suggested major price increases in the near future. Technology and centralization are receiving more attention than in the past to help ensure high quality and consistency.

Specifications for food items are being tightened. Many inputs into the food preparation process, like cut fruits and vegetables, are being purchased already prepared, and meat is bought in preportioned packages. Labour and food cost reductions, a need for fewer kitchen staff, and less waste have been byproducts of these efforts. Shifting to the purchase of prepared products has resulted in food cost savings of 2 percent and labour cost reductions of 20 percent at some hotels. To further ensure consistency, one hotel chain is considering the preparation of food at a single central commissary in each major city, for distribution to all properties in that market. Standardization to enhance quality control appears to be a high priority for hotel F&B departments in the 1990s.

In an attempt to disassociate from the negative

image of hotel restaurants, many properties are stressing the independent nature of the restaurant. This takes many forms, including the selection of restaurant names unrelated to the hotel, independent marketing efforts, street access to the dining room, the sale of brand-name products at hotel outlets, and the opening of restaurant chain outlets on hotel premises.

Manager Burnout

During the years we were involved in designing wellness programs for the hospitality industry, we spoke with many food service managers who described stressful working conditions and exhibited a wide range of physiological symptoms of stress, from headaches to heart attacks, from indigestion to stroke, from fatigue to high blood pressure, and from dermatitis to bleeding ulcers. What we were seeing and hearing about were symptoms of burnout. After many such contacts, we decided to go out into the industry to find out what characterizes burnout in food service and how pervasive this phenomenon is throughout the industry.

Measuring burnout

The following dialogue is typical of our informal interviews with food service managers:

Manager: Burnout? Sure I could tell you some stories about burnout. Everybody I work with in food service management probably could, too.

Author: So you have experienced some sort of feeling that you might describe as burnout. How does your job fit in?

Manager: Well, you just get so sick of dealing with all the egos in the food business—guests, suppliers, even employees. The only way you can keep going is to tune out. Sometimes I'd be working 80 hours a week, trying to make everybody happy, and what do I get for it? Zip. Zero. In fact, if you don't work those hours, they think you don't have what it takes and they don't move you up.

Author: It must be rough. Do you feel that the company recognizes the effort you put into your job?

Manager: Not really. At least the line workers have overtime pay—managers like me just get the glory of sticking around through all the rough times with no extra payback. I get two consecutive days off about once every three months. I never see my family or friends. I mean, what's at the end of the road for me? I'll give my all to this company, and they'll come back and say 100 percent isn't enough in this industry. It's like they've built up this big mystique about being able to go the distance as a manager, but when it comes right down to it, there's no finish line—no end in sight.

Author: Do you feel any sense of accomplishment?

Manager: Not much. It's the same drag, day in and day out—half your staff is sick in the winter and on the beach in the summer. Suppliers change the standards on you and forget to tell you. The ice machine breaks down and floods your kitchen, and you can't get service because it's a holiday. You can't get to first base with your customers because they want whatever you don't have and when you put it on the menu, they want something new again.

Author: It sounds like someone in the company should sit up and take notice of what managers like you are feeling.

Manager: Oh, they know all right, but that's the food service mentality. What's going to change it?

This conversation illustrates the three symptoms

that constitute a clinical diagnosis of burnout: (1) emotional exhaustion, (2) a tendency to depersonalize others and become unresponsive to their feelings and needs, and (3) a low sense of personal achievement.

Respondents included food and beverage directors and restaurant, banquet, and catering managers.

Exhibit 1
Levels of burnout exhibited by a sample of hotel food-servicemanagers
(n = 532)

	Percent of Respondents		
Burnout dimension	Low burnout	Average burnout	High burnout
Emotion exhaustion	39%	33%	28%
Deposition	44%	36%	20%
Personnel accomplishment	64%	24%	12%

Managerial profile

Among the respondents, 80 percent were Caucasian and 76 percent were male. The average age of these managers was 32, and most of them (89 percent) were under 40. Sixty percent reported completing at least four years of college. Nearly 80 percent said that they worked 60 or more hours per week.

The burnout factor

most of the respondents demonstrated some evidence of burnout, and between 20 and 25 percent of the 532 participating managers fell into the high-burnout range. Over 25 percent showed high levels of emotional exhaustion in the middle range. Twenty percent indicated that they depersonalized others regularly to cope with the demands of the people they encounter on the job, and 36 percent depersonalized fairly frequently.

Tip of the iceberg

The demographic profile of our sample suggests that studies of this type may not be providing the whole picture. The average age of the participating managers was 32, and 90 percent of the sample had been in food service for fewer than 15 years. The question that comes to mind is, Where are the older managers with many years of experience? The answer may be that the food service industry is losing its mature, experienced managers to burnout.

Dissecting the problem

Our initial statistics validated the common understanding that manager burnout is a problem in the food service industry. But identifying and documenting a problem does not, in itself, lead to solutions, so we reorganized the data to see whether we could isolate specific factors that appear to contribute to burnout.

Exhibit 2
Levels of burnout by hotel chain

	Percentage of Respondents		
Burnout Dimension	*Low Burnout*	*Average Burnout*	*High Burnout*
Emotional exhaustion			
Hotel chain 1 (n = 120)	33%	30%	37%
Hotel chain 2 (n = 122)	39	35	26
Hotel chain 3 (n = 134)	40	37	23
Hotel chain 4 (n = 67)	46	30	24
Hotel chain 5 (n = 89)	42	28	30
Depersonalization			
Hotel chain 1	36	34	30
Hotel chain 2	44	33	23
Hotel chain 3	48	34	18
Hotel chain 4	42	39	19
Hotel chain 5	49	30	21
Personal accomplishment			
Hotel chain 1	60	22	18
Hotel chain 2	68	25	7
Hotel chain 3	66	24	10
Hotel chain 4	63	24	13
Hotel chain 5	61	27	12

Variation between chains 1 and 3 was significant at the 95 percent level.

Occupational hazard

There is little top managers can do to alleviate burnout other than hire more managers for their food service outlets to reduce each individual manager's work hours. Moreover, it would seem that there is little food service managers can do to protect themselves from burnout but to advance as quickly as possible to a managerial level that allows them to delegate the bulk of ongoing people problems to others. However, when we examined the content of our respondents' jobs, we observed that there were conflicts inherent in the typical food service manager's role that contributed substantially to burnout. In some cases, these conflicts could be reduced by changes in company policies and practices. Top management would do well to consider the demands and expectations placed on its food service managers and weigh the extent to which the company's philosophies and attitudes are encouraging burnout.

Mystique or malaise

The long hours and emotional exhaustion connected with food service management apparently have been accepted as the "dues" individuals must pay to climb the managerial ladder; and burnout has come to be regarded as part of the "mystique" of food service management instead of the malaise it actually is. The average age of the food service managers in our study indicates that belief in the mystique wears off. Once managers reach middle age, most are unwilling or unable to cope with the burnout-inducing work conditions generally associated with food service. Coupled with the inequity between hours worked and pay relative to other occupations, the prevalence of burnout clearly affects managers' incentive to remain in the field.

Contemporary hotel catering

Although catering is generally the second largest source of income for most hotels, following guest rooms, it has been virtually ignored in the hotel school curriculum. The colleges that do offer a course in catering usually focus on how to plan, cook, and serve a meal, which is good background but does not inform students about the role of the hotel catering department. Catering often offers the highest visibility the hotel has on a local level. It can create an image for the hotel, both locally and nationally.

Department organization

In most hotels, the director of catering reports to the director of food and beverage, with banquet managers and banquet set-up managers reporting to catering. In other hotels you may find a director of catering and convention service reporting to the director of marketing, with the banquet positions reporting to food and beverage.

The sales and service process

Selling is a vital part of catering. To sell a catering event, potential markets must be identified and cultivated. Target markets must be established. Potential markets include association meetings; corporate meetings, including training sessions and incentive banquets; weddings and anniversaries; bar mitzvahs; proms; garden clubs; holiday parties; reunions, both school and military; and fraternal organizations, such as Rotary and Lions. The list is endless.

The initial contact for a function can initiate from the client or the catering department. In many cases, the potential client makes the first inquiry. He or she may contact you by phone, by letter, or in person. If the contact is by phone, be sure the person answering the phone can answer questions, or that someone knowledgeable is always available. Too often a low-paid, ill-trained person in the office answers the phone, and this can hamper the selling effort. The phone should always be answered within three rings. Always get the name and phone number of the caller. If the initial contact is by letter or fax, answer with a phone call. Copies of the letter were most likely sent to several caterers, and it is best to be the first to respond.

Satisfied majority

Regardless of pay differentials, there were no statistically significant differences in job satisfaction scores between the different college major groups. One possible explanation for this finding is the principle of self-selection. The theory is that people tend to gravitate toward work that is suitable for them and that they enjoy. If this is true, time and self-selection would act as a "leveller" of job satisfaction cores.

This study employed the Brayfield-Rothe Index of Job Satisfaction (BRI), which records job satisfaction on a five-point scale. This sample's BRI scores ranged from 40 to 89. Its mean BRI score was 71.0, a figure remarkably similar to scores of general managers, sales directors, and personnel directors. (These mean scores varied from 69.8 to 71.1. The BRI's maximum score is 90.) The authors considered the possibility that the BRI might not be a valid measure of job satisfaction for hotel executives, but supporting literature and statistical tests indicate its probable validity.

Utilizing live entertainment in hotels, restaurants, and clubs

The selection, hiring, and monitoring of live entertainment can be a perplexing task for the hospitality manager. Not only do matters of public taste and artistic style come into question, the manager is also confronted with the entertainment budget and a number of legal questions involving copyright laws. There is no substitute for a knowledgeable booking agent regarding choice of talent, nor is there a substitute for sound legal advice on matters of copyright. But every hotel, restaurant, or club manager dealing with live entertainment should become knowledgeable in the primary aspects of this activity.

The entertainment budget

Expenditures for entertainment are usually expressed as a percentage of food and beverage revenues, since entertainment is normally provided in the same spaces where food and drinks are served. It is then logical to consider such an expense allocatable to food and beverage sales. While there are no norms per se, there are available industry averages on a worldwide basis.

The basic CVP formula is as follows:

Total sales required =

$$\frac{\text{fixed costs + profit desired}}{100\% \text{ - variable costs}}$$

A modification of the formula is as follows:

Total sales required =

$$\frac{\text{fixed costs + M\& E expenditure + profit desired}}{100\% \text{ - variable costs}}$$

Expressed verbally, the formula is used to calculate the total sales required to produce the desired profit after having incurred certain fixed and variable costs. In the formula, M&E is considered a fixed cost, but is shown separately for illustration purposes.

After considering the fixed and variable costs associated with making a decision about the entertainment budget, the next step involves locating suitable entertainment for your establishment. In the past, some hotel chains centralized their talent-purchasing functions. Ramada Inns had a national entertainment director who directed procurement activities for franchise operations, and the chain also established regional bureaus with marketing and entertainment representatives.

9
EMPLOYEE COMPENSATION

A goal in nonunion organizations is also to have a compensation package attractive enough to keep out a union. Many factors affect how wages and salaries are set. These factors include what is currently being paid in the area, the labour market, the minimum wage and other governmental regulations, the worth of the job, the cost of living, the employer's ability to pay, and the presence of a collective bargaining agreement. Pay rates are often adjusted upward to help employees cope with inflation. Cost-of-living adjustments (COLA) are seen in union contracts and also in the policies of many nonunion organizations.

Usually COLA are based on the consumer price index (CPI), a governmental measure of the average change in prices over a certain period of time for goods and services that people buy for day-to-day living. A good wage system has several requirements, starting with an evaluation of the job, followed by a determination of a wage and salary structure. This process needs to be as accurate as possible to ensure pay equity, or equal pay for equal work, and also to ensure that pay rates are competitive for the area. Clearly written wage policies and procedures are also needed. Wage policies and procedures can include how pay rates and raises are made, how jobs are put into pay grades, and personnel responsibility for the various components of the program. Next, pertinent policies and procedures are communicated to the employees so they understand how the system works. Last, at least once a year the process of job evaluation and determination of wages and salaries needs to be reviewed.

Job evaluation

Job evaluation is the systematic process of determining the relative worth of jobs in an organization, then determining which jobs should pay more than others, Job evaluation also helps to establish which jobs have the same worth to the organization. Because job evaluation is used to set up a salary structure, it is crucial to job satisfaction and productivity. Job evaluation is fairly simple for foodservices, compared to other industries, because there are rarely more than twenty-five to thirty distinct job classifications.

There are more classifications at hotels and motels, but still not nearly the number as in many other industries,. One factor that does complicate job evaluation and wages in the hospitality industry is tips. Tips must be considered remuneration and therefore part of wages when setting wage rates. It is not possible to evaluate hotel and motel or foodservice jobs on a standardized basis, because each operation is unique to some extent.

Table 1 shows a possible job ranking for a small hotel's food and beverage department. The factor comparison *method also* compares jobs to others, but it is the component parts or factors-referred to as compensable factors-making up a given job that are compared, rather than the jobs as a whole. Compensable factors are job elements such as knowledge, skills, efforts (mental and physical), responsibilities, such as supervision, and working conditions, such as stress or hazards. These factors are compared to those of key jobs in the organization, resulting in a factor comparison scale. Table 2 shows the ranking of three key jobs as an example, but normally between twelve and twenty key jobs make up the factor comparison scale. Other methods of job evaluation compare a given job with a scale of

Table 1

Possible job ranking for a small hotel's food and beverage department

Position	Ranking
Manager, food and beverage	Highest
Chef	
Restaurant manager	
Dining room manager	
Cook	
Bartender	
Server	
Storeroom clerk	
Kitchen helper	
Pot/Dishwasher	Lowest

worth. The job grade *me*thod groups jobs into broader, predetermined wage classes or *grades* that require increasing levels of knowledge, skill, efforts, and responsibility. For example, one such class may include dishwashers, potwashers, and housekeepers. Each *job* class includes a description, against which specifications for the various jobs are compared. In this method, the job is evaluated as a whole.

In the *point method,* which is more objective and popular, the relative value of a job depends on how many points it "scores" when evaluated on the basis of compensable factors. This method is more refined than either the ranking or grade methods and produces more valid results. Although it is difficult to establish, it is simple to use. Because management jobs have a broader scope and more complex tasks than others in an organization, they are evaluated using a detailed factor comparison or point method, or some combination of the two.

Table 2

Ranking key jobs by compensable factors

Job	Working Knowledge	Skills	Efforts	Responsibilities	Conditions
Cook	1	1	1	2	2
Server	2	2	2	1	3
Dishwasher	3	3	3	3	1

Salary structure

In order to determine a certain salary or salary range for a given job, that job must be placed in the context of a salary structure, or companywide range of pay rates. The salary structure, in turn, results from conducting a survey of wages and salaries, establishing pay grades with rate ranges, and putting job titles into pay grades. *A wage and salary survey* covers the wages paid to workers for various employers in an organization's relevant labour market, the area from which employers obtain their workers. By obtaining wage and salary information from other organizations that compete for the same personnel, a company is able to offer its employees salaries that are equivalent to-or better than-those paid at the other establishments. It should be done every one to two years.

Incentives

Incentives include bonuses, merit raises, and gain-sharing plans, motivational tools used to encourage special work effort. Many employee benefits to be covered in a moment may act as incentives. Bonuses are onetime or periodic payments given in addition to the basic wage to reward employees for extra work done; they may be given for individual or group effort. Merit raises are given to an employee based upon level of performance. They are usually given at the time of the performance appraisal interview. In some organizations, raises are not directly tied to performance, but rather are automatic. This method is giving way to merit raises, which are the most popular pay-for-performance method.

Employees who believe that their efforts will be rewarded become productive and stay productive. Studies of both executives and employees show that when pay is tied to performance, employees' satisfaction, motivation, and productivity increase. For some people, increased pay uplifts their self-esteem, pride, and prestige. The use of merit raises will fail to serve its motivational purpose under certain conditions:

— If the performance evaluation system is not functioning effectively

— If employees don't trust the managers who make the decisions that will affect their merit raise

— If managers make their decisions based on favouritism, seniority, or pity

— If employees can successfully pressure their supervisor to give them a higher increase

Depending on the rating given the employee and his or her position in the wage range within a particular class, wages will increase by a certain percentage. In some cases, the raise is given in a single amount, called a lump sum payment; this is often used for employees who are red-circled, which means that their wage rate is at the maximum for their grade. Gain-sharing plans are programs designed to improve productivity through sharing the financial gains of the organization with employees.

The most popular such plan is called Profit sharing. This involves any method that distributes a portion of the company's profits among the employees. It is common for employees to become eligible after reaching twenty-one years of age and having worked 1,000 hours. In a cash plan, the profits are distributed annually. In a deferred plan, which is more common, there is no significant payment until termination, retirement, disability, or death. Some plans combine both cash and deferred concepts.

According to a 1985 study for the National Restaurant Association, 17 percent of restaurants had a form of profit sharing, a figure lower than was found in manufacturing (25 percent) and retail and wholesale (33 percent). Its advantage is that it can provide an incentive for employee recruitment and retention as well as high levels of performance and productivity; its motivational value may not be so great, however, because it rewards all workers equally, although their performance and efforts are certainly not close to being equal. Additionally, during years when there are no profits to share, it can be demoralizing. In order for profit sharing to be successful, employees must feel they can actively participate in making their organization successful.

Governmental regulation of compensation

The major federal law regarding wages is the *Fair Labour Standards Act* (FLSA), commonly called the Wage and Hour Act or the federal minimum wage law. The major parts of the act are concerned with the minimum wage, overtime payments, definitions of exempt and nonexempt employees, child labour protection, and equal rights as stated in the Equal Pay Act of 1963 and the Age

Discrimination in Employment Act of 1967. For the major requirements of the FLSA as related to the hospitality industry. The Equal Pay Act of 1963 requires that men and women be paid at the same rate for work that is substantially equal in skills, effort, responsibility, and working conditions. Related to this issue is the more complex one of comparable worth, which concerns certain occupations in which women predominate, such as secretarial work, that have lower pay rates than predominantly male occupations, such as construction, that are different but require similar skills and abilities.

As of January 1, 1990, both private and public employers in Ontario, Canada with more than ten workers are required by law to evaluate jobs in which 60 percent of the employees are women. Jobs must be evaluated on the basis of skill, effort, responsibility, and working conditions. Employers are given a certain period of time in which to start eliminating any pay inequities between women and men. In the United States, twenty-two states have similar legislation that applies only to public agencies. Under the Consolidated Omnibus Reconciliation Act (COBRA) of 1986, employers with twenty or more employees must offer them the option to continue health care insurance under the employer's plan if coverage should terminate, such as on resignation.

The employee must pay for this coverage plus a handling fee, and must be able to continue coverage of spouse and dependents as well. Other legislation affecting benefits includes the Tax Equity and Fiscal Responsibility Act of 1982 (TEFRA), the Deficit Reduction Act of 1984 (DEFRA), the Tax Reform Act of 1986, and Section 89 of the IRS Code.

Employee benefits

Benefits were originally referred to as fringe benefits

because they were quite meager and given in addition to the paycheck. Their scope and costs have expanded widely. Employee benefit costs have greatly affected business expenses and profits since enactment of the first state compensation law around 1900 and passage of the Social Security Act of 1935.

According to U.S. Chamber of Commerce surveys, costs of benefits have risen from 3 percent of total payroll expenses in 1929 to 36.6 percent in 1984. Of that 36.6 percent, approximately 10 percent goes to paying for legally required benefits, 11 percent for time not worked, and 8 percent to cover health and life insurance; the remaining 7.6 percent pays for other benefits and services. Passage of the Employee Retirement Income Security Act of 1974 (ERISA) and increased Social Security taxes, as well as other legislation and worker demands, have all greatly increased the cost of employee benefits.

A benefits program should meet objectives the organization sets, which are likely to include improving morale, meeting health and security needs, and attracting and motivating employees. An organization's objectives for a benefits program will of course vary by its size, sales volume and profitability, location, and local industry patterns. A good benefits program allows for employee input through committees, surveys, or other methods, and is communicated clearly to all employees. Under ERISA, employers are required to inform their workers about pensions and certain other benefits in such a way that the average employee truly understands them. Employers should also periodically review the benefits program to be sure that it is meeting employees' needs.

The traditional benefit program was designed for a man who was the sole support of his family, with a statistical average of 2.5 children. This situation is no longer true for the majority of working individuals.

Legally required benefits

Legally required benefits include Social Security, workers' compensation, and unemployment compensation. Congress passed the first phase of the Social Security program in 1935. The program is divided into four major parts: old-age benefits, disability benefits, survivors' benefits, and Medicare. The employee pays a fixed percentage of his or her income (in 1990, 7.65 percent of the first $57,000 earned) to the federal government, and the employer pays a similar amount. Old-age benefits start at age sixty-five, but this is being raised gradually to sixty-seven years of age. In order to receive old-age benefits, an individual must have worked for at least ten years.

Persons under seventy who are collecting Social Security payments and are also gainfully employed can earn only so much income before having to pay back some of it to Social Security. Employees who have been disabled for at least six months, will be disabled for at least twelve more months, and have worked and paid into Social Security for at least five years are also eligible to receive Social Security payments. It is computed similarly to retirement benefits. Dependents of retired, disabled, or deceased workers are entitled to receive Social Security payments if under eighteen years of age and not married. Other survivors may qualify for payments as well.

Medicare is an amendment to the Social Security Act and is usually treated as a totally separate program from Social Security. Medicare's primary purpose is to help people sixty-five and older pay for health care costs. The intent of workers' compensation laws is to provide the cost of medical expenses and income to individuals who become hurt on the job. The payment of workers' compensation insurance is compulsory in most states.

Depending on state laws, employers may insure with private companies, join a state insurance system, or become self-insured. The premiums, which the employer usually pays, depend to a large extent on the company's safety record. Unemployment compensation refers to benefits paid to employees who are laid off from a job for up to twenty-six weeks. These employees must register to receive the compensation and be willing to accept any suitable employment offered.

Health and life insurance

Health insurance is the most common benefit in the U.S. In 1983, the most expensive benefit for employers to pay was Social Security pay for retirement. In 1988, health insurance became the most expensive benefit, largely because health care costs have been increasing dramatically since 1965. One result of this has been that more organizations are shifting part of the cost of health insurance onto the employees. By far a majority of employers in the United States offer health insurance to their employees. The most common features of the health plans include ninety-day waiting periods, maximum coverage of $1 million, coverage of dependents, thirty to forty hours per week of work required to qualify, and payment by the plan of 80 percent of the benefits after the employee pays the deductible.

More and more employers are offering a health maintenance organization (HMO) or preferred provider organization (PPO) option. An HMO is an organization of physicians and other health care professionals who provide all services to employees enrolled voluntarily under a prepaid plan. Some HMOs may require a minimal copayment of, for example, two dollars when an enrollee uses services.

Plan members must use HMO-approved physicians and hospitals. Often the HMO has its own building in which its health services are provided. HMOs emphasize preventive care, in part to provide care early and keep costs down. PPOs came about, as did HMOs, due to the spiraling costs of health care; both have helped contain costs. PPOs may be either a hospital or a group of physicians offering a plan to provide all medical services for employees using those facilities. Employers usually encourage employees to use the PPO by covering much more of their expenses if they do.

Pensions

Most employers offer some type of retirement or pension plan. Most plans are noncontributory; in other words, only the employer contributes, not the employee. Most are categorized as either defined benefit or *defined contribution* pension plans. In defined benefit plans, the amount of the pension upon retirement and the conditions for its payment are known ahead of time. In defined contribution plans, what is preset is how the employer and possibly the employee will contribute to the pension fund, which may be through profit sharing, *Independent Retirement Accounts* (IRA), or other ways. An IRA is a tax shelter available under certain circumstances to individuals who normally use it as a source of retirement income.

However, the amount of the actual pension is not determined until retirement, when the value of the funds invested is determined. Among defined contribution plans, salary reduction or 401(k) plans, named after section 401(k) of the Internal Revenue Code, are the most popular. Employees, particularly in small businesses, can save for retirement through payroll deductions of one to six percent of their paychecks, with the employer possibly matching their savings. All money contributed into the plan is tax-deferred. In most 401(k) plans, full vesting occurs immediately or within five years; this means that an employee who leaves the company has a right to the pension.

Flexible benefit programs

Flexible benefit programs, also called *cafeteria programs* or employee choice plans, offer participants options in terms of which benefits they want and what type of coverage. Reasons for implementing flexible plans include to control the spiraling costs of benefits, better meet the different needs of employees, improve employee satisfaction and morale, and educate employees about actual benefit costs. Flexible benefit programs have been around since the early 1970s, they are not yet widely used; but their numbers are growing.

Most flexible benefit programs fit into one of three approaches: the core method, the participation option method, and the additional allowance method. Using the core method, a core plan is devised, with a minimal level of coverage of certain benefits. All employees must keep this core plan and cannot trade it away for other benefits. An employee can then use the dollar difference between a traditional plan and the core plan to purchase more coverage. In the participation option method, employees can choose among several option plans.

With the additional allowance approach, the employer maintains the existing benefit program but offers an allowance of credits that can be used to purchase more or new coverage; these credits are usually based on the employee's salary and years of service. In almost all programs, employees can make changes periodically, such as yearly. The three most common flexible benefits are health insurance, life insurance, and dental care. The Internal Revenue Service limits the choice of tradable benefits to medical care, group term life insurance, short- and long-term disability, group legal services, cash or deferred plans under section 401 (k), and vacation days. Flexible benefit plans also often have a feature called a *reimbursement or flexible spending account.* An employee can set aside pretax dollars to pay for goods or services the benefit plan does not cover. These might include contact lenses or dental work that is not part of a dental plan.